# ETHICS AND
# THE CATECHISM
# OF THE CATHOLIC
# CHURCH

# ETHICS AND THE CATECHISM OF THE CATHOLIC CHURCH

Edited by

## Michael E. Allsopp

Scranton: University of Scranton Press

**Library of Congress Cataloging-in-Publication Data**

Christian ethics and the new Catechism / edited by Michael E. Allsopp.
    p.   cm.
    Includes bibliographical references and index.
    ISBN 0-940866-79-X (hardcover). – ISBN 0-940866-80-3 (pbk.)
    1.  Christian ethics–Catholic authors.  2.  Catholic Church.
Catechismus Ecclesiae Catholicae.  Pt. 3.  3.  Catholic Church-
-Catechisms.  I. Allsopp, Michael E.
BJ1249.C357   1999
241'.042–dc21                              99-27302
                                        CIP

Distribution:

**University of Scranton Press**
**Chicago Distribution Center**
**11030 S. Langley**
**Chicago  IL  60628**

For

**Rev. Fr. H.G. (Harry) Davis, O.A.M., Ph.D., L.S.S.**

**MENTOR & FRIEND**

# TABLE OF CONTENTS

# CONTRIBUTORS

**Michael E. Allsopp** (Ph.D., Gregorian University) has taught moral theology in Australia and the United States. As well as studies in *Irish Theological Quarterly, Explorations, Linacre Quarterly, Chicago Studies, Hopkins Quarterly,* and *Month,* he has co-edited with Ronald R. Burke, *John Henry Newman: Theology and Reform* (1992); co-edited with David A. Downes, *Saving Beauty: Further Studies on G.M. Hopkins* (1994); and co-edited with John J. O'Keefe, *Veritatis Splendor: American Responses* (1995).

**Mary Jo Iozzio** (Ph.D., Fordham) is the author of *Self-Determination and the Moral Act: A Study of the Contributions of Odon Lottin, O.S.B.* (1995), as well as reviews and articles on health care ethics in *Heythrop Journal,* and *Linacre Quarterly.* A specialist on virtue ethics, and decision making in health care, she is Assistant Professor, Department of Theology & Philosophy, Barry University, Miami Shores.

**B. Andrew Lustig** (Ph.D., Virginia), Academic Director and Research Fellow in Theological Ethics, Institute of Religion, Texas Medical Center, Houston, is the co-author or editor of eight books on medical ethics, including *Duties to Others* (1994). He also co-edits *Christian Bioethics,* and edits *Bioethics Yearbook* (Kluwer Academic Press).

**Gerard Magill** (Ph.D., Edinburgh), Chair of the Department of Health Care Ethics and Director of the Inter-Disciplinary Ph.D. Program in Health Care Ethics at the Center for Health Care Ethics, St. Louis University, has edited *Discourse and Context: An Interdisciplinary Study* (1993), *Personality and Belief: Interdisciplinary Essays* (1994), co-edited with M. Hoff, *Values and Public Life: An Interdisciplinary Investigation* (1995), and co-edited with R. Randall Rainey, *Abortion and Public Policy: An Interdisciplinary Investigation* (1996), as well as essays in *Theological Studies, Heythrop Journal,* and *Journal of Business Ethics.*

**Edward van Merrienboer,** O.P. (D.Min., Eden), was an Assistant General of the Dominican Order from 1983 to 1992. An educational consultant for NCEA, he chairs the Department of Theology & Philosophy at Barry University. He has lectured and written extensively on Catholic social teaching, sexual education, and pedagogy.

**Robert Nugent** is a priest of the Society of the Divine Savior. Since 1971 he has been engaged in ministry with gay and lesbian Catholics and their families. With Jeannine Gramick, he has co-edited *The Vatican and Homosexuality* (1988), *Building Bridges: Gay and Lesbian Reality and the Catholic Church* (1993), and *Voices of Hope: A Collection of Positive Catholic Writings on Gay and Lesbian Issues* (1995).

**John T. Pawlikowski**, O.S.M. (Ph.D., Chicago), is Professor of Social Ethics, Catholic Theological Union, Chicago. A senior editor of *New Theology Review,* he is a recognized authority on social ethics and Jewish-Christian relations. His books and studies include *Jesus and the Theology of Israel* (1989), "The Vatican and the Holocaust: Unresolved Issues," in Marvin Perry and Frederick M. Schweitzer, *Jewish-Christian Encounters Over the Centuries* (1994), and "Judaism and Catholic Morality: The View of the Encyclical," in Michael E. Allsopp and John J. O'Keefe, *Veritatis Splendor: American Responses* (1995).

**Todd A. Salzman** (Ph.D., Louvain) has taught at the University of San Diego and Creighton University. Besides reviews and essays in *Louvain Studies,* and *Heythrop Journal,* he is the author of *Deontology and Teleology: An Investigation of the Normative Ethical Debate in Roman Catholic Moral Theology* (1995).

**Edward R. Sunshine** (Ph.D., G.T.U.) specializes in religion, rhetoric, and social ethics. Chair of the interest group on the Church in Latin America within the Society of Christian Ethics, he is currently working on a critical edition and translation of two seventeenth century religious abolitionist texts from Cuba. His essays include "Catholicism in America: A Moral-Theological Perspective," *Chicago Studies* (1991); and *"Veritatis Splendor et Rhetorica Morum,"* in Michael E. Allsopp and John J. O'Keefe, *Veritatis Splendor: American Responses* (1995).

**Ann S.F. Swaner** (Ph.D., Iowa) is a specialist in the history of Christianity, sexuality, and marriage in the Roman Catholic tradition. An expert on the Marriage Encounter Movement, she coordinates the philosophy and theology courses at the South Florida satellite campuses of Barr University's School of Adult and Continuing Education.

# INTRODUCTION

Pope John XXIII gave the Second Vatican Council an explicit goal. In his memorable opening address on October 11, 1962, Pope John told his audience in St. Peter's Basilica that the Council's task was a pastoral one: to renew the Church by proclaiming Christ's message of salvation in ways more in keeping with the life and thought of contemporary Christians and all people of goodwill. The *Catechism of the Catholic Church,* an initiative of the Extraordinary Synod of Bishops held in 1985, is a significant result of the post-Conciliar renewal effort.

As the Church's first new catechism in more than 400 years, this *Catechism* has a precise aim: to present an organic synthesis of the essential and fundamental contents of Catholic doctrine as regards both faith and morals, in the light of the Second Vatican Council and the whole of the Church's Tradition (11). Based upon Scripture, the Fathers of the Church, the Liturgy, and the Church's Magisterium, it is intended for a specific readership: those responsible for catechesis ("the totality of the Church's efforts to make disciples"), i.e., bishops, as teachers of the faith and pastors of the Church, and through them to "redactors of catechisms, to priests, and to catechists, and to other Christian faithful" (12).

The essays in this volume focus on the *Catechism*'s Part Three: Life in Christ (1691-2557). They have been written to make the *Catechism*'s moral teaching more available by providing background, analysis, explanation, critique. The essays have been undertaken by scholars committed to the Council's purpose, women and men invited to contribute to this collection because of their ministry of Catholic education, and their ability to throw light upon the *Catechism*'s tightly organized and frequently complex text. All this, so that, as Pope John Paul II said in his Apostolic Constitution *Fidei Depositum* (1992), the *Catechism* will be "a sure norm for teaching the faith," and an important teaching instrument for renewing the whole life of the Church.

\* \* \*

These essays differ in style, length, and focus. However, on the basis of their approach and subject matter, they fall into several distinct groups. The first essay, Edward van Merrienboer's "The Political Culture of the *Catechism*," examines the cultural images surrounding the *Catechism,* the origin and development of its text, and some of the problems involved in its interpretation. The study closes with a discussion of the *Catechism*'s authority within the teaching mission of the Church. The second essay, Edward R. Sunshine's "Catechisms in the Americas," explores the *Catechism*'s links with two earlier catechisms that were vital resources for Roman Catholic educators in the northern Americas during the past two centuries: one written for black slaves in Cuba, the other, the *Baltimore Catechism* (1885). The author looks at the structure of these works, and at how each speaks about the sacraments, the commandments, prayer, and spirituality. The third essay, Mary Jo Iozzio's "Old Wine, New Skins," argues that the *Catechism* challenges the traditional understanding of holiness while moving it forward. The study compares this catechism and the Roman Catechism produced by the Council of Trent (1545–1563); it looks at what is unique in the new catechism, and at how this teaching instrument deals with the Commandments. While the author is disappointed with the *Catechism*'s use of non-inclusive language, she shows that the work rightly recognizes that "moral existence is a response to the Lord's loving initiative," and that God's invitations have been sent to all.

During the past twenty years, both religious and philosophical ethics have focused great energy on debates about moral norms, teleology and deontology, the distinction between directly and indirectly voluntary, on ontic and moral evil, the primacy of conscience, and the transcendence of the person to nature. The second group of essays takes up these metaethical issues. In "Conscience in the *Catechism:* Reading It Right," Michael E. Allsopp examines the literary sources of the *Catechism*'s terminology and emphases; he analyzes the way the text builds a new (if traditional) "mosaic" by selectively incorporating themes and images about conscience from the writings of Paul, Augustine, Aquinas, Ligouri, Newman, and contemporary ethicists (Joseph Ratzinger, Carol Gilligan, Sidney Callahan).

Todd Salzman's essay develops some of the topics considered in passing by Allsopp. He offers a lucid, tightly connected analysis of the *Catechism*'s description of the human act and its moral evaluation, and argues that "While Pope John Paul II promises that his specially appointed commission has created a text 'whose unity and coherence are assured'(*Fidei Depositum*), this coherence is far from evident. . . . In fact, upon close reading, one is left with a muddled presentation of the human act and its moral evaluation which is likely to cause more confusion than clarification amongst the *Catechism*'s intended audience."

The third group of essays deals with holiness, the body, marriage, and sexuality. Ann Farmer Swaner's essay "Marriage in the *Catechism: Pastoral Observations*," looks at human dignity, sacramentality, covenant, and sexuality; it argues that, although the *Catechism* repeats much of the language of Vatican II, its treatment of marriage mutes the personal emphases of the Council, and that its governing understanding of marriage is a juridical one focused on an indivisible bond rather than an interpersonal covenant. In "Homosexuality and the *Catechism* of the Catholic Church," Robert Nugent provides a detailed analysis of the *Catechism*'s language about homosexuality and its definition; he explores the *Catechism*'s biblical sources and its grasp of contemporary psychological research. "The treatment of homosexuality in the *Catechism* represents significant developments both in concepts and terminology over previous statements," Nugent writes. However, he sees a number of non-doctrinal assertions which are "difficult to sustain or defend without further explanations or justifications."

The final essays focus on the Church's social teaching, on biomedical ethics and the Church's health care ministry. John T. Pawlikowski's "Catholic Social Teaching in the Catechism" provides a detailed examination of the place of the Church's social encyclicals in the *Catechism;* it looks at the way the *Catechism* uses Leo XIII's *Rerum Novarum,* Pius XI's *Quadragesimo Anno,* John XXIII's *Pacem in Terris,* and John Paul II's three major social encyclicals. In his final pages, the author examines what is missing or underplayed in the *Catechism;* he concludes that the most glaring omission is "the failure of the *Catechism* to present the quest for justice as absolutely central to the authentic proclamation of the Gospel."

B. Andrew Lustig's "Assisted Suicide in Light of the *Catechism*" considers recent Roman Catholic discussions about assistance in suicide in the light of the Church's method of moral discourse and the core arguments against suicide developed in the Catholic tradition. The study closes with comments on the relevance of the *Catechism*'s appeals to the larger public. Finally, Gerard Magill's challenging essay provides an overview of the themes in the *Catechism* that can assist Catholic ministers in health care and can contribute to the transformation of health care in the United States. The *Catechism* does not discuss health care as such, the author reminds us. However, Magill believes that its doctrinal foundations can guide Catholic ministers through the current crisis in American health care. Thus, he examines the doctrinal themes in the *Catechism* (and in the revised directives for Catholic health care approved by the U.S. bishops in 1994) that touch upon escalating costs, the lack of universal coverage and access, and "the widespread disregard for human life at all stages of its development."

\* \* \*

In a recent interview, Milan's Cardinal Martini drew attention to one of the major problems faced by catechists in their use of the *Catechism*. "There is a contrast in attitude between northern countries and Latin countries on moral questions," Cardinal Martini said. "In Italy we believe the ideal is set high so as to attain something. In other countries they think they must actually achieve the ideal, and they are anxious if they fail." It is our hope that this volume will make it possible for readers to become more aware of this, and other major considerations when using this educational work, in presenting the *Catechism*'s contents, in constructing high school curricula or local catechetical materials which take into account "various situations and cultures."

I wish to thank the contributors to this volume for their trust and cooperation. I hope they are pleased with the editorial decisions. For their suggestions and support, I must thank colleagues at Barry University, as well as friends at Gonzaga, Creighton, Fordham, Santa Clara, and the Gregorian University in Rome. Special thanks must go, as well, to Stella Carroll and Jennifer Draper at Barry University, for their computer and secretarial support.

To Richard Rousseau, S.J., who directs The University of Scranton Press, I owe a special debt of thanks for his interest in this project, his support, and professional skills that have brought the book to readers.

Finally, let us pray in the words of Pope John Paul II that "the light of the true faith [will] free humanity from the ignorance and slavery of sin in order to lead it to the only freedom worthy of the name—that of life in Jesus Christ under the guidance of the Holy Spirit, here below and in the Kingdom of heaven, in the fullness of the blessed vision of God face to face" *(Fidei Depositum)*.

Michael E. Allsopp
Feast of Thomas Aquinas, 1998

# The Political Culture of the *Catechism*

## Edward van Merrienboer

The purpose of this chapter is to discuss cultural images that have evolved around the *Universal Catechism of the Catholic Church* in order to propose some guides for understanding and using the *Catechism* in ministry. Without addressing these issues the fundamental value of the document could be lost through misuse. As well, as other authors in this collection also emphasize, the writing style of the *Catechism* presents some challenges to the reader; therefore one must examine this feature carefully so that the meaning of some of its teachings can be fully appreciated. Confusion over the authority that the *Catechism* has for Catholics is another point that needs clarification. Last, I would like to propose some pastoral direction for its use in ministry.

## I. The *Catechism*'s Origins

The proposal that there be a new catechism to replace the *Roman Catechism* has its own political history which can help put the work in context. The notion of a new catechism had been proposed during the Second Vatican Council but it never gained a level of support to become a reality. After the Council, efforts would be made to give direction to programs of religious education through the *General Catechetical Directory* and the national editions of directories.

As the years passed, a number of Vatican officials proposed a new universal catechism on several occasions. Because of his high visibility in the international media, Joseph Cardinal Ratzinger's advocacy of a catechism stimulated discussion about the value of such a document and about the motives of those who proposed it. Because of his public image as a person who wanted to "restore" the Church's doctrine to its more solid foundations, most media discussion of a catechism was interpreted as an attempt by the Vatican to control and even stop theological discussion on some of the more debated issues facing the contemporary Church.[1]

In 1985, Boston's Bernard Cardinal Law made a proposal about a catechism during the Extraordinary Synod of Bishops celebrating the twenty-fifth anniversary of the Second Vatican Council. Cardinal Law argued that because the world today is a global village a new universal catechism is a necessity. Some of the delegates added their support to the proposed project because they saw it as an opportunity to give clarity to the teaching mission of the Church.

In the final report of the Synod, the following text appears:

> Very many have expressed the desire that a catechism or compendium of all Catholic doctrine regarding both faith and morals be composed. That it might be, as it were, a point of reference for the catechisms or compendiums that are prepared in various regions. The presentation of doctrine must be biblical and liturgical. It must be sound doctrine suited to the present life of Christians.[2]

On July 10, 1996, Pope John Paul II appointed a papal commission of twelve prelates to write the catechism. The chair of the commission was Joseph Cardinal Ratzinger and the secretary was Christoph Schonborn, O.P., of the theology faculty at the University of Fribourg, both known for their strong fidelity to the magisterium. Schonborn is now the archbishop of Vienna, Austria, but during the drafting of the catechism he would maintain simple quarters with the Dominican sisters on Rome's Via Cassia. With the benefit of a computer, the chair and secretary were able to effectively incorporate commentary from the other members of the commission and the contributions of the forty (or so) selected experts. The *Catechism* may be the first major Church document to benefit so extensively from modern word processing technology.

Schonborn did most of his theological work in French. As a student he was known by his professors as intelligent, gifted in languages, and sensitive to beauty. The foundation of his theological training was the works of Saint Thomas Aquinas of which Schonborn was credited with a high degree of mastery. As a professor, he had a reputation of being approachable to his students but often hurt by harsh treatment of his peers. In the later years of his teaching at Fribourg, he was less sympathetic to new expressions of theology (e.g., feminist and liberation theologies).[3]

## II. The Challenge of Interpretation.

From my personal knowledge of the experts, they represented the various classic areas of theology; they were drawn mainly from Europe and North America; and they were noted for their loyalty to the magisterium. The variety of contributors, their different insights and emphases, are not always evident in the final edition of the *Catechism* because the chair and secretary were given the task of giving unity to the text. For this reason, I believe that the *Catechism* is shaped by Thomist expression of theology with an effort to incorporate other schools of thought, especially the thought of Saint Augustine.

The actual text is a strange blend of French and German conceptualization with the official text being French. The final edition has a dense poetic quality throughout, but the German influence is most evident in Part One: "The Profession of Faith," while the French influence is most felt in Part Four: "On Christian Prayer." Readers with backgrounds in these languages, and a knowledge of recent developments in French and German theology and spirituality, will appreciate these remarks. Those who are involved in the preparation of educational materials and are struggling to grasp the meaning of a particular section of the *Catechism* might find that they will benefit by making reference to the French edition. At times the English language is not able to express certain French conceptualizations with literal equivalents.

The authors assume a readership with a higher level of theological education because even some of the more forthright sections demand an appreciation of the rich tradition that they often summarize. For example, the presentation of the "joint mission of the Son and the Spirit" (689–690) states what the relationship is and quotes St. Gregory of Nyssa as the final word on this complex theological question. A novice in theology could easily conclude that the Church has not looked at this question since the period of the early Church, and that its theology has not changed since Gregory wrote.

In a sense, these dense texts are like freezed-dried coffee. The quality of the drink is subject to the ability of the person reconstituting the coffee to use just the right amount of coffee and water at the correct temperature. In the same way, the *Catechism* is subject to a great amount of misuse if it is handed to the faithful without some skilled training on how to work with such texts.

Another point of potential pastoral confusion is that on a number of occasions the teachings of the Church on a particular subject are combined with pastoral reflections or applications. At other times, these pastoral reflections are absent. Does this mean that only on certain issues does the Church's teaching have a pastoral application? For example, 2352 speaks of masturbation as "an intrinsically and gravely disordered action," but adds a second paragraph giving factors that must be considered when making a judgment about the subject's moral responsibility. However, fornication is described as "gravely contrary to the dignity of persons and of human sexuality" (2353), but there is no discussion of the conditions that determine subjective responsibility. Is the reader to conclude that in the case of masturbation there is grave and light matter but not in the case of fornication?

Another example of this imbalance in presentation can be seen in the treatment of homosexuality (2357–2359), the subject of a later essay in this volume. Here, the *Catechism* proposes a number of pastoral conclusions, but there are none in the discussion of birth control (2366–2372). These differences in treatment demand that anyone using the *Catechism* as a guide for moral education study the entire section on moral theology.

My point is that care must be taken to respect the *Catechism* for what it is and to acknowledge its limitations. I think it is imperative that anyone using the *Catechism* reflect upon the comments of Cardinal Ratzinger regarding the nature of the text:

> Certainly, no expression, formulation, cultural mediation, and therefore not even the best catechism, has succeeded, is succeeding, or will succeed in expressing adequately, thoroughly, exhaustively the richness, the depth, the breadth of the Christian mystery, considering the historical, social, cultural conditions of human understanding and expression of any age or place. For this reason we are well aware of the structural and contingent limits of this Catechism. . . . It is not and cannot be considered the only possible way or the best way of giving a re-expression of the Christian message.[4]

Nonetheless, despite such indisputable limits, the *Catechism,* insofar as it tries to express, truly and worthily, if always inadequately, the essential and basic contents of Catholic faith and morality, has what it needs to present itself as a model, a point of reference, as a beacon to illumine and to lead to new and safe harbors the unceasing and eager effort at inculturation of the faith and catechesis.

The question I am raising is, have these cautions been taken to heart by those who encourage use of the *Catechism*? Second, are the faithful aware that it is the opinion of the person charged with the promotion of the doctrine of the Catholic faith that the *Catechism* has its limits? In my pastoral experience, I have observed too often that the *Catechism* is being used simply as a "proof text" and I believe this is a great disservice to the faith development of the Church.

A more responsible approach, in my opinion, would be to adapt a method of critical evaluation of the text under study, to expose the richness that the brief text expresses by deeper research on the subject, and to have an honest discussion of its meaning within the context of the local church where it will find its application. To do less would be to distort the very purpose of the *Catechism,* that is, to serve "as a model, a point of reference" (11), as stated by Cardinal Ratzinger. It is a means to an end, not an end in itself.

### III. The Authority of the *Catechism*

Closely associated with the challenge of interpretation is the matter of the authority of the *Catechism* within the teaching mission of the Church. This issue is urgent because of the political culture that conditions the discussion of the role of the *Catechism*. There are some members of the Church who insist that the work as a whole enjoys even infallibility.

On October 11, 1992, Pope John Paul II ordered the publication of the *Catechism* by the Apostolic Constitution, *Fidei Depositum*. An apostolic constitution is the most solemn form by which popes promulgate official Church documents. The new Code of Canon Law, for example, was promulgated by the Apostolic Constitution, *Sacrae Disciplinae Leges*. The pope states that the purpose of his ordering the publication as:

> *The Catechism of the Catholic Church,* which I approved last June and the publication of which I today order by virtue of my apostolic authority, is a statement of the Church's faith and of Catholic doctrine, attested to or illumined by sacred Scripture, apostolic tradition and the Church's magisterium. I declare it to be a valid and legitimate instrument in the service

of the ecclesial communion and a sure norm for the teaching of the faith (3).

The key sentence is the last one quoted above, that is, it is "a valid and legitimate instrument" for the service of the Church.

A careful study of the *Catechism* will illustrate to the reader that it does contain doctrinal definitions of the popes and ecumenical councils; it also contains teachings which have not been communicated in these most solemn forms. It would seem then that, in and of itself, the *Catechism* cannot be classified among these supreme and most solemn forms of Church teaching.[5]

Some authors make the argument that because it was the product of worldwide consultation among the bishops, the *Catechism* is collegial in character and should be considered to be of the same doctrinal authority as the documents of the Second Vatican Council. It would seem to me, however, that the *Catechism* did not benefit from the complete exercise of collegiality that took place at Vatican II. What was most clearly lacking in the development of the *Catechism* as compared to an ecumenical council was public, and extensive disputation, as well as a final vote on the text by the Church's bishops. It is important to note that this position has never been proposed by the pope or any official of the Holy See.

The pope asks all the Church's pastors and the Christian faithful to receive the *Catechism* "in the spirit of communion" (3). This phrase and others that follow it indicate to me that it reflects and represents the Church's *ordinary* teaching authority. Building upon this conclusion, I would argue that the faithful have a right to know the faith and a duty to accept these teachings with "docility in charity" (2037). In other words, Catholics should take a positive attitude toward the teachings of the *Catechism* as their primary stance. Their response should be guided by the teaching of Vatican II: "religious submission of will and mind must be given to the teaching authority of the pope even when he is not speaking *ex cathedra,* in such a way that the supreme magisterium is acknowledged with reverence, the judgements made by him are sincerely adhered to, according to his manifest mind and will" (*Lumen Gentium,* 25).

In other words, Catholics are obliged to adopt an attitude of docility toward the papal teaching and avoid any attitude of obstinance. This attitude does not rule out any form of dissent, however, but any dissent must be done in an informed and responsible manner. In 1968, the National Conference of Catholic Bishops spoke of permissible dissent, and stated:

> There exist in the Church a lawful freedom of inquiry and of thought and also general norms of licit dissent. This is particularly true in the area of legitimate theological specu-lation and research. When conclusions reached by such professional theological work prompt a scholar to dissent from non-infallible received teaching the norms of licit dissent come into play. They require of him [her] careful respect for the consciences of those who lack his [her] special competence or opportunity for judicious investigation. These norms also require setting forth his [her] dissent with propriety and with regard for the gravity of the matter and the deference due the authority which has pronounced on it. *(female gender refer-ences added)* [6]

Here we see a clear statement that some of the formulations found in documents such as the *Catechism* allow some room for dissent, but it must be done in a responsible manner. It would seem to me that if religious educators find problems with some of the content of the *Catechism* there should be some effort on their part to communicate these problems to the local bishop, who in turn can communicate them to the proper authority. Too often, it is only the professional theologian who expresses reservations about such teachings and the faithful remain silent.

With this type of responsible exchange of religious insight, the Church, as a community of faith, can continue to search for the most profound meaning of the Gospel. The "people of God" will become impoverished if those who daily labor to communicate the message do not encourage those not in leadership to provide candid feedback. The message of Christ's church is dynamic because it is proclaimed by a living community committed to active listening, learning, and Spirit-filled conversation.

### IV. New Directions and Developments

Already, some of the teachings of the *Catechism* are in revision by Pope John Paul II. For example, in a press conference given on March

30, 1995, less than three years after the publication of the text, Joseph Cardinal Ratzinger said that, "the encyclical letter of the pope, *Evangelium* Vitae, expressed reservations about the death penalty that are even stronger than those already present in the catechism and are a real development" of Catholic teaching (56).[7] The pope affirmed the *Catechism*'s teaching that the death penalty is acceptable under some conditions (2266–2267), but in the encyclical he said such conditions are very rare or even nonexistent in the modern world. "The pope has made important doctrinal progress," Ratzinger said. And he added, "What is written in the *Catechism* will be reformulated." The cardinal went on to say that Catholic teaching develops by building on past affirmations rather than by overturning them.[8]

In the same encyclical letter, Pope John Paul II discusses abortion, euthanasia, and suicide at great length, wherein he develops the Church's teachings on the value of human life adding strong moral condemnation of the taking of innocent life. Yet, there is a development in the encyclical's treatment of these issues beyond that found in the *Catechism* (2270–2283). The development that I find in the *Catechism* on the question of abortion is the explicit concern for a woman who might face this tragic reality. The pope makes the point that the decision to have an abortion by the mother is painful and complex. There is a pastoral call to show compassion to those who might have had an abortion for whatever reason and for the Church's members to express their forgiveness. John Paul asks women who have had an abortion not to give up hope but to renew their commitment to life.

The encyclical's treatment of suicide is a clear discussion of the action in the context of objective and subjective morality (66). The pope is even more explicit as to how psychological, cultural, and social conditions might lessen or even remove subjective responsibility. In this instance, and the others, I believe that the pope is giving us a responsible model of using the *Catechism* in that ideals are taught with clarity and they are applied to actual pastoral situations with compassion. If religious educators limit themselves to simply pointing to the highest ideals without enabling their hearers to see that human life is an imperfect journey which requires growth through forgiveness, then the beauty of Christ's teachings gets lost in abstract dogmatism.

It is the task of the religious teacher to move into pastoral reality the Church's doctrinal tradition as found in the *Catechism* and the Church's other teachings. The purpose of evangelization is to transform people in the core of their being. First and foremost, the teachers must love their students to the degree that they are willing to tell them the truth. At its best, teaching is a context to experience the grace of God. The goal for teacher and student is not to master the *Catechism*'s content; rather it is to encounter Christ. Those who heard Jesus' message were impressed with his words because he spoke the truth with authority. The ultimate truth is that our faithfulness to the word of God will lead us to eternal salvation.

The modern world offers all people competing understandings of what it means to be human and what will bring humanity true happiness. The *Catechism* is a serious attempt to collect the wisdom of those who have known the truth of Jesus in their lives and have found happiness in that truth. As Aiden Nicols says in his Preamble to his comments on the *Catechism*'s ethics, "The *Catechism of the Catholic Church* is an authoritative instrument for ascertaining that life which can truly be called good. It needs, however, the complement of innumerable persuasive examples—both clerical and lay—if those seeking moral direction are to apprehend the intrinsic 'authority of goodness'."[9] It is an invitation to Catholics to study, ponder, and discuss all aspects of their faith life. Its purpose is not to end the search for the fullness of truth but rather to encourage the journey. Pope John Paul II has already moved forward and beyond the *Catechism* on a number of points. I believe that this document will continue to be a major point of reference in our teaching and discussion of the faith. It will require a serious academic discipline on our part to reveal the richness of the tradition and to move beyond its limitations.

## Notes

[1] For additional background on the development of the *Catechism,* I recommend the "Introduction" by Thomas J. Reese, S.J., in *The Universal Catechism Reader* (San Francisco: Harper, 1990), 1–12; also the *Commentary on the Catechism of the Catholic Church,* edited by Michael J. Walsh (Collegeville: Liturgical Press, 1994), 1–5.

[2] Synod of Bishops, "The Final Report," *Origins* (December 19, 1985), 448.

[3] For some useful remarks by Schonborn about central themes, and editing the Catechism: Christoph Schonborn, "The divine economy woven through new catechetical work," *L'Osservatore Romano* (March 17, 1993), 4, 9; "Les criteres de redaction du *Catechisme de l'Eglise Catholique*," *Nouvelle Revue Theologique* 115, 2 (1993), 161–168.

[4] Comments reported in *Catechism Update* (United States Catholic Conference), May 1993.

[5] For an extended discussion of the authority of various types of papal teachings, Francis Sullivan, *Magisterium: Teaching Authority in the Catholic Church* (Ramsey, NJ: Paulist Press, 1984).

[6] *Human Life in Our Day* (Washington, D.C.: National Conference of Catholic Bishops, 1968).

[7] Pope John Paul II, *The Gospel of Life* (Vatican City: Vatican Edition, 1995).

[8] *Origins*, 24, 42 (April 6, 1995), 690.

[9] Aiden Nichols, O.P., *The Service of Glory: The Catechism of the Catholic Church on Worship, Ethics, Spirituality* (Edinburgh: T & T Clark, 1997), 108.

# Catechisms in the Americas

## Edward R. Sunshine

Catechisms have been a vital part of Catholic Church life in the northern Americas for the past two hundred years. At the end of the eighteenth century, a catechism for black slaves appeared in Cuba.[1] Toward the end of the nineteenth century, the first and most famous American catechism appeared.[2] At the end of the twentieth century, the Vatican released a catechism for the whole Church.[3] Each of these works addressed the needs of their times, though they did so with varying methods and success. Even a cursory review of them reveals the different ways in which they present Christian teaching to their learners.

### I. A Catechism for Black Slaves in Cuba

The treatment of slaves from Africa was a problem from the time of their arrival in the Spanish colonies during the early 1500s. Physical abuse was obvious and widespread, and their spiritual preparation was almost non-existent. Instead of benefitting from the emancipation of indigenous slaves in the 1540s, they took the place of the newly freed natives. At various times the Spanish Crown attempted to control these problems, but with little success. Colonists simply disregarded edicts which were inconvenient, as occurred in 1789 when a Royal Order commanded slaveowners to "instruct (slaves) in the principles of the Catholic religion and in the truths necessary for them to be baptized within a year of their residence in my dominions."[4] Slaveowners protested and found excuses. Old slaves already had charge of the instruction, they said; they, the owners, could not be godfathers for the baptized because this "stimulated" the slaves; the different abilities of the slaves made a year's time too rigid.[5]

At the same time that the king was trying to improve religious instruction for black slaves, the Church in Cuba was passing a milestone of development. After twenty-three bishops and almost three hundred years of existence, the Diocese of Santiago (which included Florida as well as Cuba) was split to form the Diocese of Havana. In 1797, a priest from the new diocese, Oratorian Father Nicolas Duque de Estrada, published a catechism for black slaves to counter the prevalent stereo-types and the resistance of the owners. Many people presumed black slaves could not comprehend or even pronounce the lessons; they thought that baptizing them was something like branding cattle for shipment to the slaughterhouse. Such attitudes led to what Father Duque called "the cruel neglect of what there is to teach [the slaves] in the things which they should know and understand as a necessary means of salvation."[6]

Father Duque was confident that black slaves could benefit from the lessons, if catechists took the time and care to work with them. He told chaplains that they themselves should do this work, without delegating it to others who were not well informed or who instructed in haste, because "each black has a rational soul." He suggested that chaplains who pronounce the words of the lessons slowly and carefully, giving the slaves a chance to see the motion of the lips as they formed the words. He counseled the use of "homemade" examples taken from the slaves' life experience to illustrate the truths of the faith, and he made extensive use of such illustrations in his catechism.[7]

## II. A Catechism for American Immigrants and Their Children

At the same time that the Cuban Church was beginning to develop materials for the religious instruction of slaves, the American Church was just getting organized. In 1792, the first U.S. bishop, John Carroll, issued his first pastoral letter. Almost a hundred years later, in 1885, the Third Plenary Council of Baltimore ordered the publication of the famous catechism known by that name. For the American Church, the occasion for the publication of a catechism was not the neglect of black slaves but the needs of immigrants and young children.

The *Baltimore Catechism* was simple in style and language and brief in treatment. A theological summary more than anything else, it gave a list of key words, with accents for pronunciation and definitions at the start of each lesson. The explanations were direct and somewhat abstract, with none of the lively and everyday imagery found in the Cuban catechism. Though written for Americans, it was more like a universal catechism because it had no examples peculiar to American culture. Adaptations for school children did use everyday illustrations in their elaborations, however. The *Baltimore Catechism* was adequate for the times; it survived in Catholic schools and religious instruction programs for eighty years, until the Second Vatican Council.

## III. A Catechism for the Whole Church

The third catechism under consideration was written for the universal Church. Published in 1992 (although the English edition did not appear until 1994), the *Catechism of the Catholic Church* contrasts with the Cuban and American catechisms in a number of ways. Since it is intended to be a comprehensive statement of Catholic faith for all cultures, its audience is explicitly universal. Thus it stands in stark contrast with the Cuban catechism's very specific focus on rural black slaves in that country. On the other hand, it is much more developed in teaching and example than the American catechism, which implicitly shares its universal focus. If the *Catechism of the Catholic Church* is the whole work, the *Baltimore Catechism* is the table of contents in propositional form.

## IV. Structure of the Catechisms

All three catechisms follow the same general structure taken from the *Roman Catechism* of 1566, which was prompted by the Council of Trent: "faith and the Creed, the Sacraments, the Decalogue and the laws of God, prayer and its necessity, chiefly the Lord's Prayer."[8] These divisions, present but not clearly so in the Cuban and American catechisms, are well-defined and fully elaborated in the *Catechism of the Catholic Church,* which expands the final section on prayer into a presentation of spirituality.

## V. Various Treatments of Catechetical Themes

To explain the basic and initial catechetical concept of God, the Cuban catechism had an advantage: the Spanish word for Creator. Both the words *"Creador"* and *"Criador"* translate the concept, but Duque de Estrada's catechism appropriately uses *"Criador,"* which also means "breeder" and "nourisher," metaphors very familiar and meaningful to people who live in rural areas.[9] To convey the concept of God as Almighty, Father Duque contrasted God's simple action of willing creation to come into being with "what it costs the slave/masters to make sugar, the expenses they have, the men, and the animals they need to make it."[10] This use of the plantation owner/slavemaster metaphor to explain God is typical of this catechism, and gives it a tone of immanence. In contrast, the *Baltimore Catechism* simply calls God "Creator," while the *Catechism of the Catholic Church* emphasizes that "the verb 'create'—Hebrew *"bara"*—always has God for its subject.[11] These explanations, and their lack of development with concrete images, in effect give the text a tone of transcendence.

To explain the Trinity for the slaves, Father Duque used concrete examples: a finger (three distinct bones, but one finger); an egg (yolk, white, and shell, but one egg); an orange, avocado, or melon (peel or husk, seed, pulp, but one fruit).[12] The *Baltimore Catechism* presented the Trinity without illustration: "In God there are three Divine Persons, really distinct, and equal in all things—the Father, the Son, and the Holy Spirit. . . . By the Blessed Trinity I mean one God in three Divine Persons."[13] The *Catechism of the Catholic Church* employs a more theological image: "The Christian family is a communion of persons, a sign and image of the communion of the Father and the Son in the Holy Spirit" (2205).

To explain the Virgin Birth, Father Duque used the illustration of the lantern: "Our Lord Jesus Christ left the womb of his mother, the Virgin Mary, as light leaves a lantern; it does leave and light up the house, and it doesn't break the glass."[14] The *Baltimore Catechism* does not mention this teaching, while the *Catechism of the Catholic Church* says: "The meaning of this event is accessible only to faith, which understands in it the 'connection of these mysteries with one another' in the totality of Christ's mysteries, from his Incarnation to his Passover" (498).

Many of the illustrations which Father Duque used to elaborate Christian concepts in the Cuban catechism came from the sugar plantation, which was so familiar to the slaves. To explain Christ's descent into hell, Father Duque described the *"infernos"* as four dungeons in the middle of the earth. (Dungeons were used to punish and even house slaves on the plantations.) Hell, which was in the exact center of the earth, was for devils and those who died in mortal sin. Purgatory, which was above hell, was for those who needed to be purified from mortal sins which had been already forgiven or from venial sins. Limbo, which was above purgatory, was for children who had died without being baptized. Limbo of the Holy Ancestors, which was above Limbo, was for the good people who were awaiting the coming of Christ.[15] The *Baltimore Catechism* said the descent into hell "was not the hell of the damned but a place or state of rest called Limbo, where the souls of the just were waiting for Him" (#86, p. 16). Hell was "a state to which the wicked are condemned, and in which they are deprived of the sight of God for all eternity, and are in dreadful torments"; Purgatory was "the state in which those suffer for a time who die guilty of venial sins, or without having satisfied for the punishment due to their sins" (#413, #414, pp. 69–70). The *Catechism of the Catholic Church* does not mention Limbo, and it emphasizes the intention behind Jesus' descent into hell: "Jesus did not descend into hell to deliver the damned, nor to destroy the hell of damnation, but to free the just who had gone before him" (633). It describes hell in a personal rather than a graphic way: "To die in mortal sin without repenting and accepting God's merciful love means remaining separated from him for ever by our own free choice. This state of definitive self-exclusion from communion with God and the blessed is called 'hell'" (1033). Purgatory is simply a "final purification of the elect, which is entirely different from the punishment of the damned" (1031).

The Cuban catechism elaborated its explanation of Purgatory by using the refining process of sugar cane as an analogy. Slaves learned that this was a place where people settled their debts for the sins they had committed and where the stain from those sins had to be removed before they could enter heaven:

> It's like sugar: sugar which comes out burned goes to the troughs or to the molasses tank, because it's no good for making rum. Sugar which comes out in good condition goes to the purging house because it has to be made white, and it stays there until it becomes white, well purified. . . . Well, then, those who die in mortal sin are like burned sugar: they are good for nothing but cooking in the large pans of hell.[16]

This catechism compared heaven to the plantation house, with its different areas of restricted access: "To be saved is to go to Heaven, to be with God, to live in the very house of God, not in the kitchen, but in the living room, to eat at the very table of God with the Most Holy Virgin who is our mother, with the angels, and with the saints who are our brothers and sisters."[17]

The *Baltimore Catechism* refers to heaven in terms of relationships: "Heaven is the state of everlasting life in which we see God face to face, are made like unto Him in glory, and enjoy eternal happiness" (#420, p.

70). The *Catechism of the Catholic Church* emphasizes heaven as a network of interpersonal relationships in a communal setting without the down-to-earth imagery of the Cuban catechism: "This perfect life with the Most Holy Trinity—this communion of life and love with the Trinity, with the Virgin Mary, the angels and all the blessed—is called 'heaven' . . . the ultimate end and fulfillment of the deepest human longings, the state of supreme, definitive happiness" (1024).

When he had to explain the hierarchical structure of the Church, especially the papacy, Father Duque had a good example at hand in the organization of the sugar plantation: "The head of this sugar plantation is its master; but the one who governs the plantation (because his master has put him here to govern it) is the Boss. For that reason, he is called the Boss, and also is the head of the plantation. Likewise the Pope is the head of the church because Our Lord Jesus Christ put him there to govern it. The one who governs the plantation is called the Boss; the Pope, who governs the church is called the Vicar of Christ. When the Boss commands something, his master commands it; and when the Pope commands something, Jesus Christ commands it. And just as those who don't do what the Boss commands shirk their duty and are worthy of punishment, so also those who don't do what the Pope commands shirk their duty and are worthy of God's punishment."[18]

In their explanations, both the *Baltimore Catechism* and the *Catechism of the Catholic Church* are less graphic. The *Baltimore Catechism* says: "Jesus Christ is the invisible Head of the Church. . . . Our Holy Father the Pope, the Bishop of Rome, is the Vicar of Christ on earth and the visible Head of the Church" (#116, 117, p. 21). The *Catechism of the Catholic Church* simply quotes the Second Vatican Council's *Lumen Gentium*: "'For the Roman Pontiff, by reason of his office as Vicar of Christ, and as pastor of the entire Church has full, supreme, and universal power over the whole Church, a power which he can always exercise unhindered'" (882).

## VI. The Sacraments

The Cuban catechism described the Sacraments as "remedies which Jesus Christ made, from his very blood, to cure souls of their sicknesses, which are sins" (p. 95). It used the metaphor of a medical doctor to portray the action of Jesus Christ in the Sacrament of Penance: "so that they might be beneficial, so that the soul might cure itself of sins and be made well, it is necessary to use these remedies as Our Lord

Jesus Christ, who is the doctor, commands" (p. 98). It explained confession by way of contrast and comparison with practices on the sugar plantation:

> Look: there is a confession for punishment and one for forgiveness. When a slave has done something bad, they put him on the board, and there, with the bar, they make him tell by force all the evil he has done. They punish him first so that he confesses, and afterwards they punish him because he did wrong. That confession is for punishment, not for forgiveness. The other confession is for forgiveness, when he himself (without them getting a confession by force) comes with a sad face and says to his master or to his boss: Sir, I have done a bad thing in truth, may your mercy forgive me, for the love of God, I will never, never do it again. Then his master or his boss forgives him because neither the master nor the boss can have a hard enough heart to punish him since they think that he comes with a good heart, with the desire to serve his master always, without doing wrong.[19]

The *Baltimore Catechism* describes Confession sparsely ("the telling of our sins to a duly authorized priest, for the purpose of obtaining forgiveness"), and intricately ("Our Confession is entire, when we tell the number and kinds of our sins and the circumstances which change their nature").[20] The *Catechism of the Catholic Church* has an extensive discussion of the Sacrament of Penance and Reconciliation which refrains from concrete images (1422–1498).

## VII. The Commandments

In the Cuban catechism, Father Duque explained (with a bit of humor and a real-life example for the slaves) that we have to serve God by keeping the commandments:

> Q. What does it mean to keep the Commandments? How are they kept? Are they kept in a box or in a handbag?
> A. No. Keeping the commandments is doing what is commanded. Those who do what their Father orders them keep the commandments of their Father. Those who do something which their master orders them keep the commandment of their master. Those who do something which

God orders them, keep the commandment of God. And those who do something which the Church orders them keep the commandments of the Holy Church.[21]

He also explained that what he called the obligations of State were a part of keeping the commandments. Good masters give their slaves religious instruction, food, and clothing and care for them when they are sick. The good slave "is courteous toward the master, serves him because God wants him to serve him, loves him much because God wants him to love him much, and thus for all: the monk as monk, the nun as nun" (p. 103). The *Baltimore Catechism* specified different types of wrongdoing in each of the Ten Commandments, and briefly treated the obligations of one's state of life under the Fourth Commandment:

Q. Have parents and superiors any duties towards those who are under their charge?
A. It is the duty of parents and superiors to take good care of all under their charge and give them proper direction and example (#364, p. 62). The *Catechism of the Catholic Church* simply says that "God's fourth commandment also enjoins us to honor all who for our good have received authority in society from God. It clarifies the duties of those who exercise authority as well as those who benefit from it (2234).

## VIII. Spirituality

Father Duque ended the section on the Commandments with an exhortation on what would be called today the spirituality of work:

God acts like a master to whom a slave brings a bunch of bananas or a yam. His master does not need that; he has everything. He does not see the yam or the bananas but the good heart with which the slave brought the bananas or the yam, and he sees it kindly, thanks him, and gives him a gift also: he gives him money to buy tobacco.

Poor slaves! You always have work, and if you are hungry, if you are sleepy, if you are tired, you can't take a rest, you can't sleep, you can't eat until there is a break. If you have a headache, if you have a toothache, you have to work, don't lose your work, don't work like a mule. You have to work if you want to; if you don't want to, you are forced to work. So work like Christians, with the good desire that your work be in the service of God, and with that it will not be lost. . . . If you remember a time when you are working or are tired or are hungry and can't eat or rest, then speak with God, there inside your heart, and say: My God you already know the thing that I want. In doing this nothing, nothing is thus lost, everything is good for reaching heaven.[22]

The *Baltimore Catechism* does not end with a treatment of prayer or spirituality but rather with a lesson on the Last Judgment and the Resurrection, Hell, Purgatory, and Heaven (#408–421, pp. 69–70). The *Catechism of the Catholic Church* has a full section on "Christian Prayer." It speaks about what prayer is and contains a reflection on the Lord's Prayer (2558–2865).

## IX. Evaluation

The examples given from the three catechisms, typical of each of them, reveal very different ways of presenting Christian teaching. While the *Catechism of the Catholic Church* is more theologically accurate and fully developed than the other two, it does not have the concrete quality of the Cuban catechism because its audience is diverse. For its immediacy and vividness, the catechism for slaves is the most successful as a pedagogical tool. The *Baltimore Catechism* is barely a skeleton of theology, even in its classroom adaptation for children.

The very qualities which make the Cuban catechism stand out, however, are the ones which make it objectionable to us. People today are sensitive to the horrors of slavery in ways which would have been incomprehensible two hundred years ago. The use of images from those inhuman relationships to describe God and the teachings of faith sound blasphemous to the believer and certainly scandalous to the non-believer. What is worse, the Cuban catechism used the power of religion to support the slave system. Father Duque counseled chaplains to act "with much circumspection and prudence with the Boss. He [the Chaplain] shouldn't oppose the punishment of slaves even though he thinks it unjust, unless he does so by way of request; and even this is not convenient to do before the Boss has relieved his anger somewhat. Otherwise he runs the risk of losing twofold and being unsuccessful."

Father Duque did tell chaplains to "never stop interceding for [the slaves]" and

> Never agree with them when they complain about the Boss, even though you know that the complaint is just, so as not to give it currency (as they say); but try to excuse the Boss. You can tell them (without denying them justice). You yourselves are at fault because all of you don't fulfill your obligation. You are many, the Boss is no more than one. Today one person makes a mistake, tomorrow another one does. One day one person does some mischief, another day another person does. The Boss has to put up with this everyday, everyday, everyday. For all he might not want to, it's necessary; he gets angry.[23]

## X. Conclusion

Which is worse, however, the jarring images of the slave catechism or the bland abstractions of the *Baltimore Catechism*? Father Duque's catechism was a simple work written in simple language for simple people, based on the firm conviction that they could learn Christian doctrine. It was paternalistic in the way it addressed the slaves, but at the same time it accepted them as fully human, as people who could be taught the mysteries of the faith and be brought to understand and incorporate them into daily life. Its scandalous imagery was a practical way to communicate concepts which had no meaning for slaves in the abstract. Though necessarily a limited tool, it was a sincere attempt to further the pastoral work of the Church.

In a sense, the slave catechism was a forerunner of the *Catechism of the Catholic Church:* for the most part it presumed the intelligence of the learner and tried to give theological explanations in meaningful ways. In some ways it even went beyond the new catechism: despite its insensitivity to slavery, it was careful to include everyone among its learners. For instance, in answer to the question, "And the body of man, does the body of people die forever?" it says:

You should know that when we speak of man we also mean women, because women are female men and men are male men. Horses and mares both are horses, and the male is called a horse and the female a mare. In the same way that there is a male horse and a female horse, and the male is called a horse and the female a mare, there is a male man, a man, and a female man, a woman. Both are men, but one is called a man and the other a woman.[24]

The authors of the *Baltimore Catechism* did not think it necessary to make gender-inclusive meaning clear to those whom they were instructing; it was not a problem at the time. The translators of the *Catechism of the Catholic Church* refused to use gender-neutral expressions, even when these were easily available. In this respect, these two universal catechisms are as much a curiosity as the slave catechism. The Cuban catechism focused on a particular group so much that it identified God with an inhuman system of relationships. The universal catechisms transcend particular groups, especially women, so much that they divorce God from the realities of human relationships. All are sincere attempts to explain the Christian faith, but in doing so all evidence in part the human condition which fails to achieve full consciousness, adequate understanding, and appropriate expression.

## Notes

[1] Nicolas Duque de Estrada, *Explicacion de la doctrina christiana acomodada a la capacidad de los negros bozales,* in Javier Lavina, *Doctrina para negros* (Barcelona: Sendai Ediciones, n.d.).

[2] *A Catechism of Christian Doctrine* (Cleveland: Mastercraft Studio, n.d.). Hereafter, references to this catechism will be by page number.

[3] *Catechism of the Catholic Church* (Rome: Urbi et Orbi Communications, 1994).

[4] Quoted in Lavina, p. 47.

[5] Representation made by owners of sugar plantations, Havana, 1790. Referred to in Lavina, p. 48.

[6] Duque de Estrada, Prologo, p. 66.

[7] Duque de Estrada, p. 67.

[8] *New Catholic Encyclopedia* (1967), vol. III, p. 228.

[9] The Spanish edition of the new universal catechism uses the word *"Creador."* See: *Catecismo de la Iglesia Catolica* (Libreria Editrice Vaticana, 1992).

[10] Duque de Estrada, p. 78. When I was learning the school edition of the *Baltimore Catechism* in the mid-1940s, I recall a statement about God being supreme (perhaps #22, p. 8: "There can be but one God because God, being supreme and infinite, cannot have an equal"). Since the meaning was not clear to me, I asked about it. What I heard in response was: God is a Supreme Bean. Although my Jack and the Beanstalk image of God may have been theologically inaccurate, it seemed to satisfy me at the time, at least more than explanations based on Heidegger's concept of Being do now.

[11] *Catechism of the Catholic Church,* p. 290.

[12] Duque de Estrada, pp. 79–80.

[13] *A Catechism of Christian Doctrine,* #23, #27, p. 8. In the classroom explanation of

this sparse text, the three-leafed clover was the preferred image of how something could be three-in-one.

[14] Duque de Estrada, p. 83.
[15] Duque de Estrada, pp. 86–87.
[16] Duque de Estrada, p. 102.
[17] Duque de Estrada, pp. 92–93.
[18] Duque de Estrada, pp. 92–93.
[19] Duque de Estrada, p. 98.
[20] A Catechism of Christian Doctrine, #208, #213, p. 36.
[21] Duque de Estrada, pp. 90–91.
[22] Duque de Estrada, p. 110.
[23] Duque de Estrada, pp. 67–68, 69.
[24] Duque de Estrada, p. 90.

# Old Wine, New Skins

**May Jo Iozzio**

## I. Introduction

Since the widespread availability of the English translation through Paulist Press, I have used the *Catechism of the Catholic Church* in my graduate class on the Principles of Christian Morality and as a reference for my undergraduate classes in Moral Theology. This paper reflects my experience with the *Catechism* as a teaching text and as one of the sources which the Church provides "in the framework of the universal call to holiness and discipleship."[1] I am especially concerned with the invitation to holiness and how, through the teaching office of the Church presented in the *Catechism,* holiness is prescribed. The tenor of the Second Vatican Council witnesses the language of an invitation to holiness.[2] Does this teaching document, "prepared following the Second Vatican Ecumenical Council," witness likewise?[3] "Old Wine, New Skins" is a play on the Gospel story of the new wine that breaks old wineskins (Mt 9:17; Mk 2:22; and especially Lk 5:37–39), challenging the tenor and testing the teaching of the *Catechism.* The aging of new wine produces gases that require container flexibility and/or expansion room. Old wineskins, by definition, have met their expandable limit; new wineskins on the other hand are pliable, flexible, and have "room to grow" and accommodate fermentation. Thus, as the pericope indicates, when new wine is poured into old skins, the old skins do not meet the demands of the fermentation process and they burst, spilling the wine and wasting skins that could have been used for some other end. Traditions and teachings, like catechisms, just as wineskins, must accommodate growth and development or they will lose their power to engage the present and influence the future.[4]

I am aware of the post-conciliar intent of the *Catechism* as I read Part Three, the teaching devoted to considerations on the moral life, and I am concerned with how the teaching has met the challenges of Vatican II. I am not surprised by the linguistic move away from law to life; this move is accomplished swiftly in the title: "Life in Christ." Part Three of the *Roman Catechism* (1566), which forms the basis of the structure of the teaching in the *Catechism*, by contrast, is entitled simply "The Decalogue." Does this linguistic move engage sufficiently the growth and development of the Church faithful? In terms analogous to the gospel pericope, I am interested in finding the insights of the tradition, the old wine, secure in the spirit and renewal challenges of the Second Vatican Council, the new wineskins.

Apologetically, perhaps the nature of a catechism does not lend itself easily to the phenomenon of historical consciousness, the epistemological insight that our experience, understanding, and knowledge of the world are conditioned by historical reality. Historical consciousness recognizes the dynamic interplay of subjects, intentions, and development in time[5]—but objectivity necessarily stands outside time. After all, the nature of catechisms is to teach the truths of faith, and these truths must be object lessons. But these truths are matters of content (the metaphorical wine), not form (the metaphorical wineskins); now, form is at issue; the subject is the conception and presentation of the teaching according to a measure of the insights of historical consciousness.[6] Does the manner of teachings in this *Catechism* betray a preference for the old form or has a new form been embraced? What kind of wineskins have been used?

To return to the metaphor then, the biblical texts challenge stasis over change, complacence over engagement. The synoptic gospels each establish a parallel between the Pharisees and the disciples of the Baptizer (Mt 9:14; Mk 2:18; and Lk 5:33). Luke adds "and no one after drinking old wine desires new wine, but says, 'The old is good'" (Lk 5:39). The challenge is to those who, in matters of fasting and devotional practices, prefer (complacent) pious conservatism to liberating revelling (engagement) with the bridegroom.[7] In fact, those who cling to a proscribed manner of devotion jeopardize the authentic meaning of devotion they seek to maintain,[8] and they miss a celebrated new vintage. Moreover, within the larger context of the pericope, Jesus reminds us that we are not made for laws or traditions; rather, laws and traditions are made for us (Mt 12:1–14; Mk 2:23–3:6; Lk 6:1–11). Thus, to guard against traditionalism (the dead faith of the living), tradition (the living faith of the dead) must adapt the manner of teaching its insights, truth, rules, and formulas to meet the demands of our time.[9]

To superimpose the metaphor upon the *Catechism*, three questions arise. In the first place, have old wineskins been used for new wine, causing the skins to break apart?[10] That is, does the *Catechism* resort to the language and manner of teaching akin to the classicism of authoritarianism and non-historical orthodoxy[11] over (and against) the reforms and spirit of Vatican II? To answer briefly, at times (within the text) this seems to be the case. Second, has old wine been poured into new skins as my title suggests? That is, does the catechetical tradition witness the reform to accommodate the growth, development, and building up of the Kingdom that the insights of historical consciousness and the revolution of *aggiornamento*[12] require? Again briefly, I do not find this to be true. Third, do we find new wine and new wineskins? Despite what "traditionalists" charge, the *Catechism* neither invents nor offers a new faith. Continuity is maintained.

The first part of this paper presents a generally historical comparison of the *Roman Catechism* produced shortly after the Council of Trent (1545–1563) and the recently published *Catechism* composed at the request of the 1985 Episcopal Synod. The historical setting provides the context for catechetical material insofar as particular catechesis responds to particular historical needs. The second part considers material which is unique to catechesis in the *Catechism*, but not foreign to the Catholic moral tradition. This distinct material concerns the teachings familiar to the tradition of fundamental morals. The third part returns to material common to both catechisms—the exposition on the Ten Commandments. This common matter illustrates the accommodation of form and an extension or broadening of content to the times. The conclusions of the paper offer final reflections on the language and tone the *Catechism* employs.

## II. The Historical Setting

The *Roman Catechism* of 1566 was an innovation of the teaching office of the Church. The innovation was occasioned by the crisis of the Reformation and represents an early response of the Catholic Counter-Reformation attending the concerns of the Council of Trent: The *Roman Catechism* was a response to a hierarchical call. This catechism, also referred to as the *Catechism of Pius V,* the *Catechism of the Council of Trent,* and the *Catechism for Parish Priests,* assumes the general catechetical structure of the *Didache*.[13] Before this catechism, no such singular exposition[14] of the dogmas of the faith existed apart from the oral catechesis directed to converts. The Council itself was convened to address the abuses that had for long plagued the hierarchical/ administrative Church and to clarify the beliefs under attack by Luther and other Reformers. The *Roman Catechism* was completed three years after the close of the Council so that bishops and parish priests could more systematically and uniformly instruct the faithful in matters of dogma and Christian piety.[15]

The *Catechism*, like the *Roman Catechism*, is the result of a call from the Extraordinary Synod of Bishops in 1985, twenty years after the close of Vatican Council II. It responds to the episcopal concerns of the teaching of the faith, which, subsequent to Vatican II, has suffered media soundbites and misinterpretation, liturgical laxity and moral turpitude, and conceptual doubt. Vatican Council II itself was convened to address "no immediately obvious crisis"[16] but a new era. However, unlike the *Roman Catechism*, whose audience was singularly parochial ministers, this catechism is addressed to the hierarchical members of the church, the bishops, and to all the People of God who collaborate in the teaching ministry. Further, unlike the *Roman Catechism*, which distinguished the teachings of the Catholic faith from what the reformers subsequently articulated, the *Catechism of the Catholic Church* responds to concerns that have arisen within the Church that will clarify that faith. Additionally, for the *Roman Catechism*, uniformity of teaching was the rule to correct error and thwart defection. For this catechism, continuity with tradition seems key to demonstrate the very catholicity of the Church. While the Council of Trent and the *Roman Catechism* sought the security of the faith defined, the *aggiornamento* of Vatican II challenges that faith; the *Catechism* is but one response.

The matter at issue for the rest of the paper concerns specifically the teachings on morals and the manner in which the *Catechism* presents those teachings of the Christian way of life. Given that historical contexts color the exposition in both catechisms, however, we should not expect the teachings in the *Catechism of the Catholic Church* to be so contrary to the teachings of the *Roman Catechism* in content as to betray the continuity with tradition needed to mark it *as Catholic*. Nevertheless, if the teachings are to reflect the spirit and renewal challenges of Vatican II, a certain discontinuity with a tradition founded in a Counter-Reformation document (with all its polemic agenda) is to be expected.[17] Thus, while the content of the truths of faith would be fixed, the form of the teaching would be always accommodating.

Further, to return to the metaphor of wine and skins, with the insights to be gained from historical consciousness, even old wine may acquire dimensions not yet considered when placed into new wineskins.

## III. A Catechetical Morality

Section One of Part Three in the *Catechism* presents a teaching that distinguishes the subject matter of morals according to fundamental concerns, material not usually found in a specifically catechetical text.[18] Here, however, catechesis extends its consideration of the moral life beyond an exposition of the Commandments, first to the moral agent and then to the agent's acts. Unlike the *Roman Catechism,* this work provides a kind of preface to the "laws" by its address of our vocational calling and response through Christ-informed action. This material would be familiar to anyone who has studied the treatise on human acts either in Aquinas' *Summa theologiae, prima secundae 1–21* or any of the manuals of moral theology.[19] But the juxtaposition of this material with specific catechesis braves the tradition by its effort to heed the insights of historical consciousness.

"Man's (*sic*) Vocation: Life in the Spirit" models the exposition on human acts of the tradition-familiar neo-scholastic manuals of moral theology. These manuals were designed to prepare seminarians as judges in the administration of the Sacrament of Penance and to indicate from previously determined decisions of the "manualist" theologians the morally acceptable from the pulpit.[20] The manner of their teaching is technical and directed specifically to the pathological in consideration of properly human/moral activity.[21] The focus of the manual tradition and its adoption here is directed toward acts, not agents, despite the historical effort following the Second Vatican Council. This ahistorical attention to the act reinforces the artificial divide between moral theology and dogmatic and mystical theology.

Act-centered moral concerns more particularly indicate classicism as a style over the transcendental turn to the subject.[22] This classicist model defies both the insistence on the subject and experience as the starting places for moral reflection by the schools of contemporary historical consciousness. Like the manuals (and rather than finding adequate integration on people and their actions), the ideals of Christian perfection that would be embodied in the moral agent, though formally present, are relegated to the treatises on sacramental life and prayer. We find as a result that the language and form of historical consciousness and invitation, which will figure prominently in the teachings on the commandments, is lost to definitions and principles.[23] Thus, while the context-at-large suggests an invitation to holiness and a life of Christian perfection, the internal form/immediate context presents an abstract summons rather than a concrete call.

The life of Christian perfection requires certainly that we, as Christian, know of what perfection consists, and know it perhaps both abstractly as classicism would hold and concretely as historical consciousness holds. It is not without merit then that the *Catechism* should begin its teaching on fundamental moral matters with a consideration of a specifically Christian understanding of the human person. The anthropology that the *Catechism* presents establishes our being the image of God, in whom our dignity is rooted and our likeness is to become—consider the meaning of "Christ-like." Christ-likeness is a most important consideration that forces by its referent and with all its ramifications an extraordinary ideal. Thus, for me, a specifically Christian theological anthropology is the hermeneutics of moral theology. And, while anthropological hermeneutics may not always be explicit, these hermeneutic interpretations or presumptions always begin the investigative project. Thus, for example, we are either a *massa damnata* or we are little less than the gods; we are mischievous or inquisitive; we are depraved, and in need of explicit/authoritative instruction, or graced, conscience-bound, and prudence-directed. Anthropological considerations set the stage for all subsequent thought in morals, about whether or not we come close to being and doing, who Christian revelation, in the person of Jesus of Nazareth, says that we are and can do. Further, if we are to take seriously the transcendental turn to the subject, that anthropology must start from the particular and experienced life lived by Jesus and by ourselves.

Thus, revelation engages us (as invitations do) when, from creation through redemption, we are the subject of a relationship with God; the *Catechism* could engage likewise if its voice was personal and familiar. However, its form is discursive rather than dialogical, and so does little to engage the particular and experienced life. Compare the following, for example, where some third party is addressed. "[T]he human person is the only creature on earth that God has willed for its own sake. From his (*sic*) conception, he (*sic*) is destined for eternal beatitude. . . . The human person participates in the light and power of the divine Spirit. . . . [M]an (*sic*) is endowed with freedom."[24] Now, replace all those persons without faces or bodies with "you," who are enfaced and embodied. Thus, *you* are the only creature on earth whom God has willed for *your* own sake. From *your* conception (in *your* mother's womb), *you* are destined for eternal beatitude. . . . *you* participate in the Spirit. . . . *you* are endowed with freedom. With the particular, even the objective truths of origin and end found abstractly in the *CCC* challenge our concrete relationship and transcendent potential as adoptive children of God, as sisters and brothers of the enfleshed—enfaced/embodied—God, as conspirators of love.

Next the *Catechism of the Catholic Church* considers beatitude *as our perfection,* our anthropological potential, and founds that consideration in Jesus' own sermon on the mount. In fact, the Greek term the Gospel authors (both Mt 5:3–11 & Lk 6:20–22) use, μακάριοι, signifies the supremely blest, derivative of the term, μάκαρες, referred properly of the gods.[25] Surely these authors intend that those who hear, or who read, understand that they too will be so blessed if their conduct similarly reflects the conduct of the "already" blessed poor, mournful, meek, righteous, merciful, pure, peaceful, and persecuted. The implication appropriate to the *Catechism* then enjoins us to want this beatitude, this perfection, this life. The consideration of the beatitudes forms a bridge between a theological anthropology that finds our origin and end in the Creator and a moral theology (of acts) that indicates the way in which we can hope to attain (excluding Pelagian self-sufficiency) that end.

Now, consider freedom, the first step on the other side of the bridge of beatitudes. Here the *Catechism* conflates the contemporary distinction in moral theology of two degrees of freedom, fundamental and categorical freedom. This contemporary distinction recognizes the anthropological ground of freedom as a transcendental reality and the categorical this or that as ways of being and doing.[26] Sadly, the *Catechism* has missed the opportunity to speak of the freedom to love and the freedom to choose. Free loving and choosing, though distinct, are intimately intertwined realities that, when exercised, engender growth and maturity in goodness and truth.[27] Goodness concerns love; truth concerns choices. Thus, consider the yes-response, as a fundamental option, to the invitation of our vocation to holiness and relationship to God and others; then consider the many decisions we make that bring us closer to or take us farther away from the realization of that vocation. The ground of freedom is our self-determination to the absolute, which the Absolute inspires in us as origin/Creator; the categorical this or that of our choosing determines us toward particulars. This distinction permits an examination of how we may exercise freedom and how that exercise expresses lives lived more precisely than the generic treatment of freedom allows in the *Catechism.*

With the second step over the bridge of beatitudes, the *Catechism* considers the morality of human acts (without reference to the distinction of the categorical freedom of choice). This consideration implicitly devolves into the debate between deontology and proportionalism. The tradition that the *Catechism* presents which finds the sources of morality in the object chosen, intention, and circumstances, has enjoyed widespread acceptance. However, and at least since Peter Abelard (1079–1142) sparked the debate in the medieval schools over the locus of the morality of the human act, the determination of moral species is popularly accepted as intrinsic to the act.[28] The purpose of that debate and its resolution was to aid the growing profession of confessors[29] in the administration of the Penitential Sacrament, forgiveness by determination of number and kind of sins. Notwithstanding that debate and returning to the source or locus of morality, if the sin is in the (material) object chosen, it is in fact external to the agent who then ought (simply) to avoid that object in the future. However, if the object is (formal and) in the intention, it resides, or adheres, and very likely remains in the agent, who then ought to examine whether this or that object is fitting to the development of a rightly ordered life.

Rather than continue the development of the vocational theme, however, the *Catechism* returns to the act-centered moral theology of non-historical orthodoxy. Here it confuses the formal object of the intention that specifies the act of the will with the material object of choice that is external to the agent.[30] Further, with the conflation of the formal (internal) object into the material (external) object, the *Catechism* misses the transformative over the performative nature of moral action and the development of the rightly ordered life. When the teaching in moral matters emphasizes acts over agents, moral matters are distanced from personal life; that matter is objectively out there (and presumably, can be avoided easily). But when the teaching turns to the agent, moral matters are recognized rightly as the stuff of personal life, of the ends I intend for myself, and whether I accept the vocation to which I am called.

Moral acts arise from moral agents, human subjects, you and me. Therefore, what I do reveals something about me. What I do reveals, upon examination, an end for which I act and an object I have chosen in order to attain that end. What I do reveals likewise, upon evaluation, whether I intend and choose rightly. What I do reveals (lastly), upon review, me, that is, my life (in general) as rightly or wrongly ordered. The agent, not the act, figures prominently in these "revelations." How then does the agent secure the rightly ordered life except by prudently reasoning and choosing according to virtue?

The *Catechism* favors consideration of acts over agents and deductive reasoning and conformity to objective standards over an inductive and historically conditioned development of prudential reasoning. This bias again neglects the transformative nature of moral action and the possibility of a more virtuous and rightly ordered life. The remedy to this neglect rests in an expansion of the discussion on the growth and development of freedom and responsibility referred to in Articles One and Two. This developmental theme can carry over (and rightly should) with the vocational call to the discussion on the passions, moral conscience, virtues, and sin. Thus, let us turn to the responsibility for the self-determination, for the future, for the transformation of the historically conditioned agent.

Recall the implication appropriate to the *Catechism* that enjoins us to want the beatitude to which we are invited. If we consider the proper response to the invitation, it would be an unqualified "yes" (fundamental freedom); and the working out of that response would remain the task of a life of virtue, an intent to perfection (categorical freedom). Over the course of our development as moral agents we exercise these freedoms with more or less knowledge of how that exercise will influence our lives. The life of virtue strives toward ever more awareness of right-orderedness by the immanent power of moral acts to engage us. Further, their engagement inheres in us to the extent that, by force of immanent activity, we are the object of our own intentions (the ends that we intend are for ourselves). Thus engaged by virtue, we become always and more attentive to the exercise of the virtues and to the perfection of a rightly ordered life. While the beatitude to which we are invited is beyond the scope of acquired/moral virtue's power (attaining this beatitude depend on God), the power of virtue finds a dynamics for life.

## IV. The Commandments Interpreted in the Key of Virtue

A brief look at the *Catechism*'s exposition on "The Ten Commandments" suggests the agenda of the *Roman Catechism:* to confirm for the faithful the dogmas and beliefs of the Roman Catholic Church. An examination of the dogmatic passages of the *Catechism* (Parts One, Two, and Four)—on the matter of justification, the seven sacraments, the Real Presence of Jesus Christ in the Eucharist, and the proper sacrifice offered to God in the Mass[31]—likewise indicate this subtle apologetic. The order of teachings is significant for the agenda of the *Roman Catechism,* from the Creed through liturgical life and observance of the Law to Prayer. Error and confusion are lessened by heeding the catechetical instruction. "It shows the Catholic pastor and catechist how to transcend the Protestant despair of human ability to keep the Commandments."[32] In so doing the *Roman Catechism* provides a definitive motive for the observance of the Church's teaching on the commandments and counters the Reformers' insistence on faith alone— "obeying God's law is necessary for salvation."[33]

The *Roman Catechism* takes special care to direct the pastor in the teaching office. Three principles are promoted for the pastor in order to accomplish the purposes of catechesis: to know Jesus Christ, to zealously teach and observe the commandments, and to love God in whom is our happiness.[34] Hence, the exposition on "The Commandments, in General" requires of the pastor "the greatest vigilance and the most practiced acquaintance with the interpretation of the law, [. . .] to teach sound doctrine, free from error, and heal the diseases of the soul, which are sins, in order that the people may be acceptable to God."[35] These principles promote the pastor's attention to his own vocational love and ability to adjudicate correctly according to the interpretive teaching of the laws on the penitent's concerns. The pastor thereby gains an appreciation of the law and its application, which either from the pulpit or in the confessional is offered to the faithful for their edification. Thus, for example, contrary to the Reformers' distrust and suspicion of the cult of the saints,[36] the first commandment forbidding the worship of alien gods or the making of images does not prohibit the veneration and invocation of saints of Catholic piety. And, as a remedy to the Reformers' concerns about the buying of indulgences, the benefice system, and the simony of parochial offices,[37] the seventh commandment prohibiting theft implies the duty of almsgiving to those in need.

The exposition on "The Ten Commandments" in the *Catechism of the Catholic Church* (Part Three: Section Two), assumes a decidedly different guise than the parallel teachings in the *Roman Catechism*. The context of this teaching in the key of virtue explicitly commends the vocational teaching of Section One and the concrete demands of obedience that engender a life of virtue in response to the call.[38] This is not to say that the *Roman Catechism* neglected the vocational spirit of the Christian way of life, but the manner of teaching in the earlier catechism assumes an apodictic style. Further, the *Catechism of the Catholic Church* deliberately situates the commandments of the Exodus and Deuteronomic texts in the light of the two-fold commandment of Jesus to love God and neighbor as self.[39] The agenda here emphasizes a respect and dignity due individual human life and the leading of that life in a manner worthy of the Gospel.[40] Thus, instead of an emphasis on the cult of saints that in the earlier text covered 25 paragraphs, the *Catechism,* without dismissing superstition, idolatry, and magic,[41] addresses the contemporary post-Enlightenment concerns with irreligion, atheism, and agnosticism.[42] Additionally, the *Catechism* transfers the immediate focus from sins against the commandments to "What must I do to inherit eternal life?"[43] This shift in emphasis from prohibition to requisition suggests an interpretation of the commandments in the key of virtue. That interpretation moves away from the imperative voice of an authority to the inquisitive of the faithful.

Another significant difference is the placement of the instruction on the commandments. Again, the context indicates a change. Here the teachings on the commandments follow teachings on our vocation as Christian by our "Life in the Spirit." This first section of Part Three, which in both form and purpose is absent from the Third Part of the *Roman Catechism,* considers our vocation, the human community, and law and grace.[44] What surprises there (in the first section of Part III), as discussed earlier, is the return to the manualist non-historical/orthodox approach, which seems interested more, like the *Roman Catechism,* in the purpose of confession. This is not to say that that teaching lacks validity but it takes little note of the contemporary developments in moral theology, for example, on fundamental freedom, self-determination, and virtue.

Personally, I am encouraged in Section Two of Part Three by the presentation on the commandments and the demonstrated wealth of our tradition. Here the faithful are invited to do more than follow the prescriptions of the words of the commandments, perhaps because each "word" (i.e., *logos*) concerns the two-fold command to love God and neighbor.[45] Thus, faithful in content yet brave in context, the *Catechism of the Catholic Church* insists on the duties incumbent upon the faithful, be they duties of the virtue of religion,[46] duties of family members,[47] or duties of civil authorities and citizens.[48]

Consider the context of the first three commandments in the key of the virtue of religion. First, the *Catechism* identifies these commandments with the first part of the two-fold commandment of Jesus, "You shall love the Lord your God with all your heart, with all your soul, and with all your might" (Dt 6:5, *cf.* Mk 12:30, Mt 22:37, Lk 10:27). Then, it devotes 13 paragraphs to the little noted virtue of religion.[49] Inasmuch as "religion" is more often than not understood as a system of beliefs to which a community holds, the focus change to religion as virtue is both refreshing and invitatory. The judgment of religion as one of the virtues is not new although it does not receive the press that the list of either acquired moral virtues or theological virtues enjoy today. Whereas Thomas Aquinas attended explicitly to the virtue of religion in no less than 20 questions in the *Summa Theologiae* alone,[50] the manualist Thomas Slater devotes a single paragraph in his instruction on the precepts of the Decalogue.[51] In spite of the neglect from the manualists, the *Catechism of the Catholic Church* recognizes, as did the *Roman Catechism*, that this virtue belongs properly to the manner in which the faithful are to be disposed toward God. The virtue of religion disposes faith-filled persons to right action: genuine worship of God in common and in private, and respect for things sacred. What fails here is a lack of instruction concerning how to acquire and various ways to exercise this virtue. That instruction would serve as an antidote to the pitfalls and a guard from the sins against religion, such as the contemporary attraction to areligiosity or poly-pantheism, and disregard for those commandments pertaining directly to God.

I am edified when the teaching on the laws turns to the invitation to genuinely Christian living. Even though the content of seemingly prohibitive commandments requires the language of obligation and obedience, the spirit of challenge permeates the internal form of the instruction. Here, with both external linguistic and internal form that forces introspective examination of who I am and what I do, I am held in a tension between complacent obedience *to the laws* and the dynamic appeal of *charity*,[52] *justice*,[53] *solidarity*,[54] and *safeguarding peace*.[55] What little disappoints here is a lack of more exhortatory prose to accompany the catechist's lecture.[56] Nevertheless, I am moved by the implicit call to virtue that has informed the very generation of the laws.

The context of this second set of commandments could be read in the key of the virtue of solidarity. Again, the *Catechism* identifies these seven commandments with the second part of the two-fold command-ment of Jesus, "You shall love your neighbor as yourself" (Mk 12:31, Mt 22:39, Lk 10:27, *cf.* Lv 19:18). Then without devoting more than three specific paragraphs to the virtue of solidarity,[57] it begins to instruct the faithful of all God's people in the key of the justice that is required of family members toward one another—"solidarity is an eminently Christian virtue."[58] The instruction from the context of kinship/solidarity goes beyond the damage control characteristic of the *Roman Catechism* to considerations of the ways individuals, families, community groups, states, and nations can be toward and with one another. These are the concerns of a justice that recognizes the interdependence of all peoples and a justice in practice which could signal the realization of the Kingdom of God.

The *Catechism* recognizes that the virtue of solidarity belongs properly to the manner in which family members, both immediate kin and the kinship of all God's people, are disposed toward one another. Inasmuch as the virtue of solidarity belongs properly to the more widely encompassing virtue of justice, both solidarity and justice are concerned with the right orderedness that relationships require. The virtue of solidarity disposes members to right action: respect between parents and children and that which is due legitimate authorities (fourth commandment); respect and protection of human life and the maintenance of health (fifth commandment); sexual integrity and the fidelity due spouses (sixth commandment); moderation in respect to the acquisition of material goods (seventh commandment)—this teaching is not just about "not stealing" but about temperance over the sway possessions can hold and the poverty that unbalanced distribution effects in the wider community; truthfulness in word and deed and why offenses against truth harm both individuals and the human community (eighth commandment); detachment from things which confuse the pure of heart and poor in spirit who otherwise desire rightly the Kingdom of God (ninth and tenth commandments).

The instruction on the sixth commandment is deliberately and most explicitly interpreted in the key of virtue. While the virtue of solidarity remains an integral part of the discussion on sexual integrity, inasmuch as sexuality is expressed properly between persons, which requires the attention to others indicative of solidarity, the virtue of chastity is given appropriate priority. And chastity, like solidarity, belongs through this interpretation to the virtue of justice since chastity concerns affections, which are properly shared with others. As with all virtues by definition, chastity concerns right orderedness. The right orderedness that virtue accomplishes in matters of sexuality is chastity—the mean between the defect and excess of an absence of affectivity and of promiscuity. Since every virtue holds a mean between defect and excess that is appropriate for the individual both in context and content, the *Catechism*'s teaching on chastity aims at the contexts of persons who are single (hetero- or homosexual), engaged, and married.[59] Each of these contexts in turn presents compelling information for the determination of the content of chastity to be engaged. The mean of chastity for single persons rests between a handshake and a comforting embrace. The mean of chastity for engaged persons, inasmuch as the tradition applauds virginity in this context, rests between holding hands and a place (no doubt) just short of irrepressible genital stimulation and intimacy. The mean of chastity for married persons rests between embracing the beloved and spousal abuse. Perhaps it is not surprising that the *Catechism* should present the teaching on adultery in the contexts of the virtue of chastity. Minimally, adultery bears resemblance to the excess of promiscuity, but rather than cast the teaching singularly in the key of the punitive, it returns deliberately to its purposeful move from law to life.

It appears from the manner of exposition on "The Ten Commandments" that old wine has been put into new wineskins, subtly and without the catastrophe that new wine in old skins would occasion. All in all, little has changed between the two catechisms in terms of the content and extent of Catholic teaching on the commandments. With the exception of the deliberate explication of the "negative aspects,"[60] that is, the prohibitions under penalty of sin, that we find in the *Roman Catechism,* we have a rich tradition underlying the interpretation of the "positive" offered in the *Catechism.* The social teaching of the Church, unfortunately, still remains our best-kept secret. The objective truths of justice, by definition of objective, remain valid. It will always be right to give God thanks and praise whether or not we have an explicit instruction on the first three commandments. And it will always be right, according to the order of charity, to give our parents (and then our neighbor) honor and respect with or without an instruction on the fourth through tenth commandments. An examined look at the teachings concerning the moral life as occasioned by the commandments in the *Roman Catechism,* moreover, reveals the time-honored validity of this interpretation, however veiled or secreted or left to the missionary elite in the past. What the teaching on the commandments in the *Catechism of the Catholic Church* has accomplished is the adaptation and a greater interest in the positive of those lessons for our time; the commandments have been presented, however implicitly, in the key of religion and of solidarity . . . of virtue.

## V. Old Wine, New Skins—Concluding Remarks

I have been considering the nature of the teaching on morals in the *Catechism of the Catholic Church*. I have been primarily interested in whether the tenor of teaching assumes a legalistic and authoritarian or an invitatory tone, and whether the focus is directed toward the human act or the agent. If the *Catechism* is true to its intent to follow the Second Vatican Ecumenical Council, we will find in its teaching the form and content insights of *aggiornamento* and historical conscious-ness. The teaching must reflect the times in which we live: the context must address issues of contemporary concern; the content must speak to a faithful perhaps (but not necessarily) more sophisticated than any previous generation. I believe that the *Catechism* is generally successful to its preparatory intent. It challenges the tradition while moving it forward—old wine has been transferred to new wineskins with all its expendability, unpredictability, and future. But, the matter of language adopted demands remark.

I have never been known as an arithmetic whiz but I do know that numbers tell important tales in games, in elections, in weights and measures. I am disheartened by the tale of imbalance instanced in the male-gendered language. In an examination of the *Catechism*'s Part Three, I find 725 occasions of the words "man" (to indicate presumably men and women, human beings, people), "he" (to indicate he and she), and "him/his" (to indicate him/his and her/hers).[61] In sharp contrast to this figure, I find only 33 occasions of the words "she" and "her"—five of these instances refer to the biblical wisdom, twenty-eight refer to the Church. Even if these numbers are but approximate, the tale tells me that *Catechism* has not recognized the power of words to harm or heal, to insult or compliment, to exclude or include.

What do these words symbolize if not what they signify? The symbol of the word man must signify a human being of the masculine gender, and the masculine pronouns must refer to that same masculine gendered human being. Thus, man's vocation, his life in the Spirit, his dignity rooted in the image of God the Father, his deliberate actions directing himself freely to his true good,[62] means that this man or that man has as his origin and means and end some other Man (even if God). Why should we expect that women will understand that they as feminine gendered human beings are implied in these masculine gendered words? Why should we expect that anyone should accept an *implied* identity or calling? Consider reading that *we* are called, this is *our* vocation, bearing the image of the Creator or of a Lover, *we* can freely respond and direct *ourselves* to that happiness of beatitude as the lovers of Love. The symbols of these words more closely signify the teaching on revelation, the Trinity, and Christ that becomes the relationship we, women and men, are invited to cultivate.

My experience with the *Catechism of the Catholic Church* as a teaching text raises these questions of language, of the subject of moral theology, and of the invitation to holiness. Invariably, I have women students in my classes who ask about the Church's attitude toward them *qua* women; my response to them returns to the power and implied meaning of words so carefully chosen to teach. The official teachings fail to include the feminine pronouns, the first person plural, or gender inclusive language in reference to humankind. The implication of the teaching thus fails to acknowledge the presence, the contribution, and the shared potential of women as equal members of our Church. When my students (women and men) ask about the subject of moral theology presented, a nuanced response is required: I want to respond "YOU," so, we sift the text to find that "you" are centered in an act yet in the act "you" are the subject. And when the question turns to holiness and discipleship my response turns to the teaching on the relationships held for us to develop with God and neighbor. As disappointed as I may be over its shortcomings, the *Catechism* rightly recognizes "moral existence is a *response* to the Lord's loving initiative."[63] The invitations have been sent *to all*.

## Notes

[1] USCC, Guidelines for Doctrinally Sound Catechetical Materials, 1990, #59.

[2] "[The Council's] documents are redolent of wisdom rather than legislation. Generally speaking, they invite rather than prescribe. They are religious documents." John W. O'Malley, S.J. *Tradition and Transition: Historical Perspectives on Vatican II* (Wilmington: Michael Glazier, 1989), 179.

[3] See the Apostolic Constitution of Pope John Paul II dated October 11, 1992, *"Fidei Depositum,* On the Publication of the Catechism of the Catholic Church prepared following the Second Vatican Ecumenical Council."

[4] McCormick adds, "For surely Jaroslav Pelikan is correct when he notes that one of the marks of a living tradition is 'its capacity to develop while still maintaining its identity and continuity.' In a real sense, then, tradition is always in transition. To think otherwise is to confuse tradition (the living faith of the dead) with traditionalism (the dead faith of the living)." Richard McCormick, "Tradition in Transition" in William J. O'Brien, ed., *Riding Time Like a River* (Washington, D.C.: Georgetown University Press, 1993), 17.

[5] On the surprises of historical consciousness and the insights of its necessary context providing for theology, see Michael J. Himes, "The Human Person in Contemporary Theology: From Human Nature to Authentic Subjectivity" in Ronald P. Hamel and Kenneth R. Himes, *Introduction to Christian Ethics* (Mahwah: Paulist Press, 1989), 49–62.

[6] "Non-historical orthodoxy has given good service to the Church . . . it has brought the Church intact through the collapse of the Middle Ages, and leaves her (sic) hardy and eager at the threshold of the new era on which the world is now embarking. . . . Now it is time for a new form of life, not discontinuous with the old . . ." Michael Novak, *The Open Church: Vatican II, Act II* (New York: Macmillan Company, 1964), 348.

[7] Kelly cautions, "[t]he pastoral leaders of the Church will have to be vigilant lest the immense achievement of the CCC be undercut by the efforts of some in the 'catechetical establishment'" to go home to the old sureties of the old faith. "The Catechism of the Catholic Church: its literary form, authority and catechetical implications," 404–405.

[8] As O'Malley recognizes, "[c]hange does not, therefore, jeopardize a deeper identity; it is, rather, the precondition for maintaining the authenticity of that identity." *Tradition and Transition,* 83.

[9] Francis Kelly, Livio Melina, and Marc Ouellet reckon that the *Catechism* considers the challenge in form and content that Vatican II invokes—new wine has been transferred (?) to old skins. Thus, as Ouellet indicates (387): "[i]n North America, there was alarm over the principle of a hierarchy of truths, over the use that was made of Scripture, and over the tenor of the part dealing with morality. After sober reflection about form and content the editors made a clear choice: the CCC is meant to be a witness to the Catholic faith." Kelly, "The Catechism of the Catholic Church: Its literary form, authority and catechetical implications"; Melina, "The call to holiness in the Catechism of the Catholic Church: the morality and spirituality of 'Life in Christ'"; Ouellet, "The new Catechism: an event of the faith," *Communio* 21 (Fall 1994), 399–408, 437–449, 385–398.

[10] O'Malley uses this metaphor in a different vein but in reference to persons who believe that "[t]he Council tried to force new wine into old wineskins, and the skins are now spewing it forth." See O'Malley, *Tradition and Transition,* 181–182.

[11] For a general discussion on the non-historical orthodoxy of the pre-Vatican II Church and its distinction to the present, see Novak, *The Open Church,* 343–362.

[12] O'Malley suggests that the aggiornamento of Vatican II "was a revolution in the

history of the idea of reform." For a full discussion of his appreciation of this reform revolution and its impact, see his Tradition and Transition, especially "Reform, Historical Consciousness, and Vatican II's Aggiornamento" and "Developments, Reforms, and Two Great Reformations: Towards an Historical Assessment of Vatican II."

[13] "The four areas of the *Roman Catechism* reflect thus the basic structure or pattern of Trinitarian catechesis, as it came from the teaching of Jesus to His Twelve Apostles [i.e., the *Didache*] . . . Thus the original oral catechesis of the Church is maintained with its simple syllabus for oral teaching, . . . : the Twelve Articles of the Apostles' Creed; the Seven Sacraments; the Ten Commandments; and the Seven Petitions of the Our Father." Robert Bradley, S.J. and Eugene Kevane, trans., *The Roman Catechism* (Boston: St Paul editions, 1985), xii, xiv.

[14] Other catechisms had been in circulation at the time of the publication of the Roman Catechism; two of the more widely used in schools were authored by Peter Canisius, S.J. (1521–1597) and Robert Bellarmine, S.J. (1542–1621) for the instruction of children in particular (Canisius) and the Jesuit scholastics. On the development of catechetical materials in the early Church to the Tridentine Reform and the singularity of the Roman Catechism as it is directed to pastors for the instruction of the faithful, see Joseph Andreas Jungmann, *Handing On the Faith* (New York: Herder & Herder, 1959), 1–26.

[15] "The Fathers, therefore, of the General Council of Trent, anxious to apply some healing remedy to so great and pernicious an evil, were not satisfied with having decided the more important points of Catholic doctrine against the heresies of our times, but deemed it further necessary to issue, for the instruction of the faithful in the very rudiments of the faith, a form and method to be followed in all churches by those to whom are lawfully entrusted the duties of pastor and teacher." John A. McHugh, O.P. and Charles J. Callan, O.P., translators, *Catechism of the Council of Trent for Parish Priests*, "Introductory: The Necessity of Religious Instruction" (New York: Joseph F. Wagner, Inc., 1934), 4.

The call to compile a catechism based on the canons and decrees of the Council of Trent are only hinted in the fourth session (1546) of that Council concerning the canonical scriptures and Christian doctrine; the catechism is alluded to in the twenty-fourth session, "Decree Concerning Reform," chapter seven; and the work is referred to as finished, though waiting papal acceptance, in the twenty-fifth session, "Decree Concerning the Index of Books and the Catechism, Breviary and Missal." See H. J. Schroeder, O.P., trans., *The Canons and Decrees of the Council of Trent,* Fourth Session (Rockford: Tan Books and Publishers, Inc., 1978), 17–20, 197–198, 254–255.

[16] O'Malley, *Tradition and Transition,* "Vatican II: The Event," 11.

[17] "In other words, continuity and discontinuity are perhaps the most fundamental historiographical categories with which we must come to terms in interpreting Vatican II." O'Malley, *Tradition and Transition,* 174; in the same volume, see also "Aggiornamento and Historical Consciousness," 65–81.

These categories must be reconciled also with other official teachings, e.g., Episcopal letters and Papal encyclicals.

[18] The *Catechism* presents the treatise on morality in two distinct sections: Section One: "Man's (sic) Vocation: Life in the Spirit"; Chapter One: "The Dignity of the Human Person"; Chapter Two: "The Human Community"; Chapter Three: "God's Salvation: Law and Grace." The traditional catechesis begins in Section Two: "The Ten Commandments." The comments of this part of the paper are limited to a discussion of Chapter One, Article 1: "Man (sic): The Image of God," Article 2: "Our Vocation to Beatitude," and Article 3: "Man's (sic) Freedom."

[19] Examples of the manuals in English are: Henry Davis, *Moral and Pastoral Theology* (London: Sheed & Ward, 1935); John A. McHugh and Charles Callan, *Moral Theology: A Complete Course Based on St. Thomas Aquinas and the Best Modern Authorities*

(New York: B. Joseph Wagner, Inc., 1929); Thomas Slater, S.J., *A Manual of Moral Theology* (New York: Benziger Bros., 1908).

[20] The laxity or minimalism of this period was due to a variety of reasons, from a less-well-educated laity to a heavy emphasis in moral theology on what is sin. "Notice the overall demeanor of the parish priest and the laity. They simply wanted to know what the moral theologian permitted or prohibited. The attitude was not to read what the moral theologian wrote, but simply to find out his decision." James F. Keenan, S.J., "Learning to Reason Well: Moral Theology Since Vatican II" in Anthony Cernea, ed., *Vatican II: The Continuing Agenda* (Bridgeport: Sacred Heart University Press, 1996).

[21] "They [the manuals of moral theology] are as technical as the text-books of the lawyer and the doctor. They are not intended for edification, nor do they hold up a high ideal of Christian perfection for the imitation of the faithful. They deal with what is of obligation under pain of sin; they are books of moral pathology. They are necessary for the Catholic priest to enable him to administer the sacrament of Penance and to fulfill his other duties; they are intended to serve this purpose, and they should not be censured for not being what they were never intended to be. Ascetical and mystical literature which treats of the higher spiritual life is very abundant in the Catholic Church, and it should be consulted by those who desire to know the lofty ideals of life which the Catholic Church places before her children and encourages them to practice. Moral theology proposes to itself the humbler but still necessary task of defining what is right and what is wrong in all the practical relations of the Christian life." Thomas Slater, S.J. "Preface," *A Manual of Moral Theology*, vol. I, 3rd ed. (New York: Benziger Brothers, 1908), 6.

[22] Melina offers a different reading on the tenor of teaching and finds "the rediscovery of the classical perspective of the first person" precisely where I have not. See Melina, "The call to holiness in the Catechism," 441.

[23] With the exception of the pastoral principle (25), the fundamental principle of the interpretation of sacred scripture (111, 137), and the right to information (2494, 2512), all of the fundamental principles that the *Catechism* presents are found in Part Three, Section One, 1883–1885, 1886–1887, 1889, 1894, 1896, 1904, 1924–1925, 1931, 1948.

[24] 1703, 1704, 1705.

[25] Henry George Liddell and Robert Scott, *A Greek-English Lexicon* (Oxford: Clarendon Press, 1968), s.v. μάκαρ and μακαρία.

Further, Kittel's volume IV recognizes, in addition to usage in reference to the "godlike blessedness hereafter in the isles of the blessed" (362), "[t]he special feature of the group μακάριοσ, μακαρίζειν, μακαρισμόσ in the NT is that it refers overwhelmingly to the distinctively religious joy which accrues to man (sic) from his (sic) share in the salvation of the kingdom of God" (367). Gerhard Kittel, ed., *Theological Dictionary of the New Testament* (Grand Rapids: Wm. B. Eerdmans Publishing Company, 1967), 362–370.

[26] See, for example, Josef Fuchs, "Basic Freedom and Morality" in his *Human Values and Christian Morality* (Dublin: Gill and MacMillan Ltd., 1970), 92–111; and his *Christian Morality: The Word Becomes Flesh* (Washington, D.C.: Georgetown University Press, 1987); Klaus Riesenhuber, "The Bases and Meaning of Freedom in Thomas Aquinas," *American Catholic Philosophical Association* 48 (1974), 99–111; and my *Self-Determination and the Moral Act: A Study of the Contributions of Odon Lottin, O.S.B.* (Leuven: Peeters Press, 1995), chapter 1.

This distinction resembles also that between goodness and rightness, see James F. Keenan, "What is good and what is right, a new distinction in moral theology," *Church* (1989), 22–28; and his *Goodness and Rightness in Thomas Aquinas's Summa Theologiae* (Washington, D.C.: Georgetown University Press, 1992), 52–56; and Richard

McCormick, *Notes on Moral Theology 1981 Through 1984* (Lanham, MD: University Press of America, 1984), at many places.

[27] Per the *Catechism* (1731), "[f]reedom is the power, rooted in reason and will, to act or not to act [according to the Thomistic distinction, this refers to the exercitium of the will's movement], to do this or that [the Thomistic specification of the will's movement toward the object presented by reason], and so to perform deliberate actions on one's own responsibility. By free will one shapes one's own life. Human freedom is a force for growth and maturity in truth and goodness; it attains its perfection when directed toward God, our beatitude."

[28] In the high scholastic period of the twelfth and thirteenth centuries the debate over which end determines the morality of an act wavered between the end of the intention, which (for Thomas Aquinas) is the formal object of the act as an end abiding in the agent, and the end of the realized act, i.e., the material object of choice. On the development of this thought and the history of this debate, see Odon Lottin, *Psychologie et Morale aux XII et XIII siècles,* tomes 2 & 4 (Louvain: Abbaye du Mont César, 1948 & 1954); and my *Self-Determination and the Moral Act: A Study of the Contributions of Odon Lottin, O.S.B.,* chapter 2.

[29] Although the beginning of this debate precedes the Fourth Lateran Council's decree obliging annual confession, by almost 100 years, "from the eighth century [among the Celtic peoples], regular confession was becoming a general rule. . . . Elsewhere in Europe of around the same time, regular confessions were now becoming obligatory, sometimes as often as three times a year." Mahoney, *The Making of Moral Theology,* 15–16.

[30] This confusion does not surprise. The debate between the traditionalists and the proportionalists considers in part the influence of the object, the intention, and the circumstances for the determination of species, and so of the evaluation of the act, and has failed likewise to recognize the distinction between the immanent object in the will, i.e. the intention, and the transient object external to the agent. See Bernard Hoose, *Proportionalism: The American Debate and Its European Roots* (Washington, D.C.: Georgetown University Press, 1987), especially 41–47.

[31] For a synopsis of the Protestant theses on these matters which were condemned by the General Council, see Philip Hughes, *The Church in Crisis* (Garden City: Hanover House/Double Day, 1961), 325–328.

[32] Bradley and Kevane, *The Roman Catechism,* p.v. Further, "[i]t accomplishes this immense spiritual benefit by giving the catechumen first the teaching and formation in the Faith, then the teaching and formation regarding the Sacraments, and only after this, the teaching on the law of God. This enables the catechumen to take up the Christian way of life according to the Commandments of God, with the supernatural joy of authentic hope. First, the Faith; then the fruits of redemption coming from the Sacraments; and then the Commandments of God. Thus, without mentioning Protestantism, the taproot of the Protestant difficulty is surmounted."

[33] Bradley and Kevane, *The Roman Catechism,* 351.

[34] See Bradley and Kevane, *The Roman Catechism,* 7–8.

[35] McHugh and Callan, *Catechism of the Council of Trent,* 358.

[36] "Should it be said, as some say, that the patronage of the Saints is unnecessary, because God hears our prayers without the intervention of a mediator, this impious assertion is easily met by the observation of St. Augustine . . ." McHugh and Callan, *Catechism of the Council of Trent,* 371–372.

[37] On the relation of these abuses to "the Christian duty to give alms to pious causes," see Hughes, *The Church in Crisis,* 314–315.

[38] "The novelty of the prima tertia of the Catechism essentially consists in two aspects:

above all, in the very fact of its existence, and, then, in understanding Christian morality within the perspective of a 'vocation to holiness'." Melina, "The call to holiness in the Catechism," 438.

[39] As previously indicated, n. 20 above, "Part Three: Life in Christ" is divided into two sections. Section One, "Man's (sic) Vocation: Life in the Spirit," comprised of 3 chapters.

The new style-set of the teaching in Section Two, "The Ten Commandments," is comprised of 2 chapters. Chapter One, "You Shall Love the Lord Your God with All Your Heart, and with All Your Soul, and with All Your Mind," is further divided into 3 articles instructive of the first three commandments; and Chapter Two, "You Shall Love Your Neighbor as Yourself," is divided into 10 articles instructive of the fourth through tenth commandments.

The *Roman Catechism* does not reject the thematic use of the two-fold commandment of Jesus; however, its presence is less pronounced. For example, from the instruction on the connection between the fourth through tenth commandments and the first three, "[t]he former have as their direct object the End itself, which is God. The latter reach God only indirectly, i.e., through the neighbor, whom we are commanded to love because of God. That is why our Lord says that these two commandments—love of God and love of neighbor—although distinct are interrelated and similar." Bradley and Kevane, *The Roman Catechism,* 397.

[40] See the introductory text of "Part Three: Life in Christ," 1691–1698.

[41] See 2111–2117.

[42] 2118–2128. The earlier catechism devoted but one paragraph to these concerns; see McHugh and Callan, *Catechism of the Council of Trent,* 369.

[43] See the introductory remarks in "Section Two: The Ten Commandments," 2052–2055.

[44] These teachings are not entirely overlooked in the *Roman Catechism;* however, they differ significantly in form and purpose. The morality of human acts, in particular, is addressed in the instruction on the Sacrament of Penance in order to facilitate, for priest and penitent alike, administration of the graces of the Sacrament. Much of the other content matter can be found throughout exhortatory passages.

[45] See 2067–2069.

[46] See 2095–2096, 2102, 2104–2106.

[47] See 2214–2231.

[48] See 2235–2243.

[49] See 1807, 1840, 2095–2096, 2105, 2118–2122, 2142, 2143, 2149.

[50] Thomas Aquinas, *Summa Theologiae* 2.2. 81–100.

[51] "The acts of this worship, which natural reason thus prescribes, belong to the virtue which theologians call religion." Slater, *A Manual of Moral Theology,* vol. I, p. 208.

[52] See 2055, 2093–2094.

[53] Throughout Section Two, Chapter Two on the "Ten Commandments," where the subject concerns the love of neighbor, we are reminded of the definition of justice "to preserve our neighbor's rights and render him (*sic*) what is his (*sic*) due." 2407.

[54] See 2407–2442.

[55] See 2302–2317.

[56] An exception to this apparent lacuna is found within the teaching on the seventh commandment forbidding theft: "St. John Chrysostom vigorously recalls this: 'Not to enable the poor to share in our goods is to steal from them and deprive them of life. The goods we possess are not ours, but theirs.' 'The demands of justice must be satisfied first

of all;  that which is already due in justice *is not to be offered as a gift of charity.*' "
2446 (emphasis added).

[57]  See 1942, 1948, 2407.

[58]  1948.

[59]  See 2359, 2350, 2364–2365.

[60]  While providing some manner of the positive requirements of the commandments, the emphasis in the *Roman Catechism* was to illustrate those actions that were (always and everywhere) contrary to the commandments and so sinful. For example, in the teaching on the commandments we read: "What is commanded and forbidden by the first commandment" and "The negative aspect of this commandment"; "The positive and negative aspects of this (the second) commandment" and "The sanction of this commandment"; "The punishment accompanying its (the third commandment's) nonobservance"; "The punishment due to the violation of this (the fourth) commandment"; etc.

The *Catechism of the Catholic Church*, while not neglecting those things the tradition has considered sinful (e.g., irreligion, false oaths, abortion, sexual incon-tinence, etc.), presents a strikingly deliberate emphasis on the positive application of rather than the negative prohibitions inherent to the Commandments.

[61]  I deliberately acknowledge that 30 or 25 years ago the exclusivity of male-gendered language was common if not absolute in most if not all forms of intellectual enterprise. However, with the success of the feminist critique, we can no longer abide gender exclusivity in writing practice. Further, in the determination of 725 male-gendered refer-ences, I have not included instances from Scripture, from the Church's tradition pre-Vatican II, or the masculine referents for God.

[62]  1700, 1701, 1704.

[63]  2062.

# The *Catechism*'s Teaching on Conscience: Reading It Right

**Michael E. Allsopp**

"Moral conscience, present at the heart of the person, enjoins him at the appropriate moment to do good and to avoid evil. It also judges particular choices, approving those that are good and denouncing those that are evil. . . . When he listens to his conscience, the prudent man can hear God speaking" (1777). This is a key section of the *Catechism*'s statement on the nature and life-guiding authority of conscience in the Catholic's life. However, because the text, like Vatican II's, uses the term "conscience" in a variety of ways, and incorporates elements from separate (in some cases, conflicting) intellectual traditions, this study aims to assist catechists by undertaking two exercises: to relate what the *Catechism* says to its sources; and to look at the *Catechism*'s teaching in the light of its sources, that is, the writings of St. Paul, Aquinas, Ligouri, John Henry Newman, the Second Vatican Council's documents, and contemporary Catholic moral literature.

## I. Conscience in the *Catechism:* Introductory Observations

To better understand the *Catechism's* teaching about conscience, its features and authority, we should recall several key points. First, Pope John Paul II's words in his Apostolic Constitution *Fidei Depositum* (1992) about the *Catechism* containing both "the new and the old," its repeating the traditional order followed by the catechism of St. Pius V, and its efforts to present the Church's doctrines in a way that responds to the questions of our age. The *Catechism*'s Article 6: Moral Conscience (1776–1802) selectively reflects more than two thousand years of comment on this fundamental human experience: it contains glimpses of the insights of Sophocles, St. Paul, Cicero, Augustine, Aquinas, and Scotus; it bears the scars of the debates sparked by Martin Luther and deliberated upon by the Council of Trent. The *Catechism*'s text cannot be read right unless one is aware of more recent discussions as well: the clash between ancient and modern thought; the rise of new research disciplines, the discussions about conscience and its place in an individual's life involving Ligouri, Newman, Freud, and (more recently) Karl Rahner, Joseph Ratzinger, Germain Grisez, John Paul II, Charles Curran, and Sidney Callahan.

It is useful to note, second, that the *Catechism* provides simply a summary outline of the *Roman Catholic* doctrine of conscience. As we have come to see in recent years, all accounts of the moral life are narrative-dependent; Roman Catholic morality cannot be separated from the Catholic understanding of God's commands, the purpose of human life, the Church's past and present teaching about God's creating a people "to seek him, to know him, to love him with all his strength" (1). Like the Second Vatican Council's *Pastoral Constitution on the Church in the Modern World (Gaudium et Spes),* its *Declaration on Religious Liberty (Dignitatis Humanae)*, the pastoral statements following Pope Paul VI's *Humanae Vitae* (1968), and Pope John Paul II's encyclical on the foundations of morality *Veritatis Splendor* (1992), the *Catechism* presents a summary of the essentials of the Catholic Church's *official* teaching about the human person's "most secret core and his sanctuary" (1776).

This means that the *Catechism*'s statements distance themselves from: (i) positions seen to be in conflict with the Church's understanding of conscience, e.g., the Baptist; and (ii) opinions about which there is still unresolved debate within the Church, e.g., legitimate dissent by Catholics from papal teaching on birth control, abortion, capital punishment.

## II.  The Sources of the *Catechism*'s Teaching: I. Paul's Letters

The *Catechism*'s statements about the nature and authority of conscience in the Catholic's moral life aim to provide an up-to-date summary of the Church's thought. The highly condensed paragraphs embody both modern insights into this complex phenomenon, as well as the legacy of influential traditional sources that have been selectively used in the composition of the *Catechism*'s text. Like the documents of Vatican II, or the United States Declaration of Independence, Article 6: Moral Conscience is best seen as a contemporary narrative, an original work with its own voice, style, and point of view—in which it is not difficult to see earlier writers, unifying metaphors, significant academic debates. Looking at these sources, if briefly, allows us to better appreciate the *Catechism*'s teaching.

The first source is Paul's remarks about *"syneidesis"* and *"conscientia,"* as found in Rom. 2:15; 9:1; I Cor 8: 7, 10, 12, 10:28–9; II Cor. 1:12–13; Titus 1:15; I Tim 19. In these places, Paul expresses his belief in a God-given interior "law" that seems to play several distinct roles: it both guides future action, and pronounces judgment after action; it is presented as a sovereign moral authority that has as much force for the Gentiles as the Mosaic law does for the Jews. According to Delhaye, Gaffney, and Mahoney, Paul sees this phenomenon as the center of the soul where individual moral decisions are made and personal ethical responsibilities are undertaken; where acting according to one's conscience means acting according to one's inner convictions, one's subjective (sometimes erroneous and flawed) perceptions of morality.[1] "In Pauline usage, conscience is viewed as a possession of all men by which they evaluate the moral worth of their behavior in the light of their beliefs, appearing sometimes as witness for the prosecution and at other times as witness for the defense," John Mahoney writes (185).

While, first, we need to be aware of the implications of the scholarly debates about what we find in Paul's letters (C.A. Pierce in his masterful study *Conscience in the New Testament* maintains that Paul did not see conscience as a prospective, action-guiding authority), and, second, we must to be careful not to select from Paul only those phrases that fit our own modern or postmodern worldviews, the case can be made that Paul was aware of discussions about the origin and role of this experience in Hebrew and Roman thought. And, from his usage, he seems to be attempting to reconcile (as best he can) several diverse sources: (i) the prophetic tradition's emphasis on personal moral responsibility and fidelity to God's law written on the heart, and (ii) the rabbinic tradition's emphasis on corporate duty and code morality; also the Greek and Roman efforts (Seneca, Cicero) to construct moral theories in which *"conscientia"* is a valid source of guidance, as well as a sanction and warning to those who have sinned. Educators who focus on Paul's teaching, and invite students to research and explore his letters, will see rewards.

From its beginnings, the Christian Church has built its understanding of conscience on Paul's appeals to *"syneidesis."* It has seen truth in his words about the pagans being able to "point to the substance of the Law engraved on their hearts—they can call a witness, that is, their own conscience—they have an accusation and defense, that is their own mental dialogue" (Rom. 2:12–15). Since the Protestant Reformation, Baptists, Lutherans, Anglicans, and Roman Catholics have used themes and phrases of Paul's teaching (taken directly, as well as through Ambrose, Augustine, Jerome), to defend their own developing traditions about the moral authority of the individual vis-à-vis the pope, councils, the Bible—in particular about the baptized individual's freedom to follow the dictates of his or her conscience in the face other acknowledged moral authorities.[2]

### III. The Sources of the *Catechism*'s Teaching: II. Aquinas

There are definite signs of Paul's thought in the *Catechism*. However, some of the technical terms, e.g., "synderesis" (1780), and specific details about conscience's role in the Catholic's moral life, are drawn not from Paul, but from Aquinas's writings, his *Summa Theologiae, de Veritate,* and *In I Ethicorum Aristotelis ad Nicomachum Expositio,* where Aquinas looks not only at Paul (as well as Augustine, and Jerome, both of whom contributed to the discussion), but also at the lively debates involving his thirteenth century contemporaries about ethics and moral decision making.

Because the *Catechism* uses Aquinas' scholastic thought and terminology selectively, and incorporates his terms and ideas into its own moral vision, it is important to grasp the outlines of Aquinas' highly structured psychology, as well as the basics of his meta-ethics. This is in keeping with the fact that the catechist does not simply enable students to go through the hoops, but assists them to understand why the hoops are placed where they are.

First, like Dante's and Shakespeare's, Aquinas's medieval worldview is different from that found in current science textbooks that emphasize evolution, improbability, individuality, and the implications of chaos theory. Scholars disagree about the originality of Aquinas' philosophy. There is evidence, however, that he supported Aristotle's basic belief in an ordered yet dynamic universe; that he saw the moral life as living according to and progressing toward a specific and rationally knowable goal; and that he viewed the role of human reason (practical) as directing the voluntary acts of the will ("rational appetite") as it pursues its God-given end ("telos"). Further, Aquinas' moral theory is based upon Aristotle's analysis of *"ergon,"* i.e., the particular form of life or activity which makes sense of a thing's structure; and the optimistic belief that "All things, not only those which have knowledge but also those things which are without it tend to good." This last insight means: (i) that nothing is naturally evil in itself (*de Malo*, 16, 2 corp.); (ii) there is no ontological evil opposed to ontological good in the act of existing; and (iii) evil is the privation or lack of a particular good that should be present, e.g., sight in humans, or flight in birds. (Aquinas was well aware of pre-Christian and later dualistic theories of good and evil, but he did not support them.)

Now what is morality all about for Aquinas? What is it that makes a human act moral?[3] For the majority of contemporary ethicists, morality means weighing consequences (Utilitarians), or assessing *prima facie* duties (W.D. Ross). Aquinas' answers to moral questions are embodied in such gnomic statements as, "good and evil in human acts are considered insofar as the act is in accord with reason informed by divine law, either naturally, by instruction, or by infusion"(*de Malo*, 2, 4 corp). Or "As man's mind is subordinated to God, so is the body subordinated to the soul, and the lower powers to reason. But it pertains to divine providence, of which the divine law is but a rational plan proposed by God to man, to see that individual things keep their proper order. Therefore, man must be so ordered by divine law that his lower powers are subject to reason; his body to his soul; and external things subserve his needs" (*Summa Contra Gentiles*, III, 121, n. 2943).

To explain. For Aquinas, the human person like the medieval cathedral is a complex (if much smaller) structure in which form follows function; the laws of morality like the laws of physics embodied in the stone foundations that support the cathedral's windows are based upon God's eternal decrees. Consequently, morally correct human behavior means action in accord with these divine laws, i.e., the orders and dynamisms either believed by faith or known by reason. Now, as stated in Genesis, we have been made in God's image, which means, for Aquinas, that we possess intellect and will; we have been given power over our own works unlike some creatures (rocks) that act instinctively without thought or freedom. To be moral, therefore, means two things: (i) to act in such a way that our action is in accord with reason informed by divine law; (ii) to act in such a way that what we do perfects the powers of our soul, since such actions strengthen our humanity. Morality lies, therefore, in acting in accord with our God-given gifts, especially the best that is in us, i.e., the element that is responsible for our linguistic, social, deliberative capacities; and to make a unity of life, since (as Aristotle implies) the true nature of humanity is seen in those individuals who actualize their potential most clearly. "It is the Aristotelian saint who is most especially human," Stephen R. L. Clark writes. "In that it is his life which gives sense to human structure and society."[4]

Again Aquinas's moral theory like Aristotle's contains a complex analysis of the interactivity between intellect and will in making moral decisions; it also deals with motives and intentions. Aquinas' distinctions, while excessive (for some), are in fact crucial for understanding the Church's discussions about "right" and "wrong," and the ways that pastors (as well as judges in criminal and civil courts) assess praise and blame, guilt and innocence. In summary, Aquinas sees reason constantly presenting the will ("rational appetite"), with particular "goods," i.e., objects of desire; the intellect and will as judging and weighing, making shared decisions and shared choices in specific circumstances. Where an adult's reason possesses adequate knowledge, and his will is well-integrated, the decision to act or not act is both reasonable and moral, since the decision is based upon sound data, and the will does not incline toward some unsuitable ("indebitum") means or end. However, where there is ignorance (culpable or inculpable) that results in error (due to immaturity or complexity); or where a will is highly excited by some pleasure (due to compulsion or appeal), and unsuitable means and ends are chosen for which the individual will or will not be held accountable—this leads us to Aquinas' teaching about "conscientia."

As seen above, the basis of morality, for Aquinas, is God's eternal law. In the case of humans, this divine law (revealed in the Ten Commandments) is identical with the primary principles of morality as known by reason, for instance, "Thou shalt not commit murder, steal, or commit adultery." These broad, rationally defensible precepts are known to all, according to Aquinas, and cannot be completely removed from the human heart (*Summa Theol.* I,II, q.100, a.8. ad 3). Moral judgments are the result of decisions and choices; they are essentially rational deductions resulting from the application of principles to particulars. Now Aquinas uses the term *"synderesis"* in a compound sense to stand for the familiar natural habit that prompts humans both toward what is good, and away from what is evil; and that also enables them both to make these deductions from first principles and to judge their individual decisions. He writes, "synderesis dicitur instigare ad bonum, et murmurare de malo, inquantum per prima principia procedimus ad inveniendum, et iudicamus inventa. Pater ergo quod synderesis non est potentia, sed habitus naturalis" (*Summa Theol.* I, q. 79 a. 12). The Catechism uses the term *"synderesis"* in this sense. It also uses "conscience" exactly as Aquinas does, where *"conscientia"* is an act, not a power, the act of reason as it applies the principles of morality to individual situations. "As such it is not, of course, the originating source of moral principles but only the medium, or 'image', of God's eternal reason, or eternal law, which, . . . is the primary and supreme rule of human behavior," Mahoney writes (188). This means that conscience's binding power comes not from any special authority of its own, but from the force of the divine precept: "Unde, cum conscientia nihil aliud sit quam applicatio notitiae ad actum, constat quod conscientia ligare dicitur vi praecepti divini" (*de Veritate*, q.17, a.3).

In taking these positions, Aquinas is more conservative than Kant, who argued that an individual's rationally sound moral judgments possess inherent authority; that reason is essentially autonomous. His position also seems to be more restrictive than what one finds in Karl Rahner's writings on concrete individual knowledge, and the individual's ability to generate personally binding and individually specific moral norms that have authority for that individual, even when they are in conflict with the general principles of Catholic morality—a subject that takes us to another part of Aquinas' teaching that has been given a major place in the *Catechism.*

Life shows that reason does not always act as it should. Frequently, it is unduly influenced by passion, vice, or the results of the Fall. Sometimes it tries valiantly, but fails to make correct applications, just as other times it fails in applying the principles of economics or physics to complex problems. In all these cases, *"conscientia"* is in error. However, in some of these, the faults involve culpability (due to laziness, indifference, malice), whereas, in other cases, the mistakes do not involve any culpability. This part of Aquinas' analysis causes him to hold that although one must always follow the dictates of *"conscientia,"* i.e., one is always obliged to do what one judges to be morally right, an individual is not always free from moral fault in following his or her conscience.

For instance, if an individual acts from a lack of knowledge that he or she ought to possess (i.e., acts from an uninformed conscience due to carelessness or indifference about morality), then the mistake is morally culpable, and he or she is held responsible for the resulting action that follows, e.g., loss of property or life. "If conscience acts from a lack of knowledge which one ought to possess, then the error is culpable and so is the conscientious behavior resulting from it," Mahoney writes. "The ignorance in question could be 'ignorance of the law of God,' that is, of a divine commandment, whether revealed or attainable by reason, 'which one is obliged to know,' and as such it would be culpable ignorance in Aquinas's terms. It could also be, however, 'ignorance of some circumstance' in its application to a particular situation, and this can happen 'without any negligence'" (192). The *Catechism* emphasizes this part of Aquinas' teaching in its lengthy remarks about Erroneous Judgment (1790–1794).

Aquinas does wrestle with the moral issues involved in Samson's suicide (*Summa Theol.* II, II, q.64, a.5, ad 4); with exactly how an action that is always immoral can cease to be so when God commands it (*Summa Theol.* I, II, q.100, a.8). However, he does not give *"conscientia"* the authority and freedom to make decisions to act in ways contrary to any of God's immutable principles. As the *Catechism*'s text shows, these aspects of Aquinas' thought are central to its remarks about the formation of conscience (1783–1785), about making choices in accord with conscience (1786–1789), and conscience's erroneous judgments (1790–1794).

### IV. More Recent Sources: Alphonsus Ligouri, John Henry Newman

The *Catechism*'s statements about conscience have been shaped by two more recent Catholic theologians: Alphonsus Ligouri (1696–1787), and John Henry Newman (1801–1890). Besides his lasting place in the history of Catholic moral theology, because of his *Theologiae Moralis,* there are special reasons to see Ligouri's influence on the contents and sequence of the *Catechism*'s remarks about conscience. According to Bernard Haring, Ligouri's unique contribution to moral theology is the role he gives to conscience, and the care with which he describes the dynamics of a sound conscience. Haring writes, "Two distinct traits of Alphonsian moral theology are the great reverence he accords each person's conscience and the equally strong appeal to each individual to form a mature conscience." Both of these emphases were given life in Vatican II's words about conscience in the *Pastoral Constitution on the*

*Church in the Modern World* (Gaudium et Spes), because Haring wrote the final draft of the *Constitution*'s section on conscience (he tells us) expressly to be a summary of the Alphonsian vision of a person's most secret core and sanctuary—and the Council's *Constitution* is (as has been stated) a major source for what we find in the *Catechism*. Given Haring's regard for Ligouri, and his influence on the Council's moral teaching, educators might provide students with lasting intellectual benefits by encouraging them to undertake research into Ligouri's life and work, his contributions to Catholic theology.

John Henry Newman's influence on the twentieth century Church's understanding of conscience has been widely acknowledged. It is explicit in the *Catechism*'s long quote from Newman's *Letter to the Duke of Norfolk* (1778). Unlike Aquinas who gave "conscience" a narrow and limited role in his psychology, Newman's writings contain several lengthy descriptions of conscience as a prismatic, many-sided and complex phenomenon that was central to his own life, and to human life in general.[5] For Newman (it has been said that no Catholic theologian ever championed conscience's authority more than him), conscience is intellectual and emotional, critical and judicial, an inner light and a personal judgment, a gift of the Creator as well as a possession of a creature, a subject of rights and the bearer of duties.

"Conscience is the aboriginal Vicar of Christ," Newman writes in his *Open Letter.* "A prophet in its informations, a monarch in its premptoriness, a priest in its blessings and anathemas, and even though the eternal priesthood throughout the Church could cease to be, in it the sacerdotal principle would remain and would have its sway." In what has been called the final flowering of Basil's notion of conscience, Newman sees conscience as "the voice of God speaking within us." And "that 'inward light,' given as it is by God . . . intended to set up within us a standard of right and truth, to tell us our duty in every emergency, to instruct us in detail what sin is, to judge between all things which come between us, to discriminate the precious from the vile, to hinder us from being seduced by what is pleasant and agreeable, and to dissipate the sophisms of our reasons." In efforts to explain the *Catechism,* students, in particular adults, will benefit from talks on Newman and his writings. Newman's life is fascinating; his thought is modern in its emphasis on conscience's dignity and freedom; it is conservative, however, in its anti-liberal emphasis on the objectivity and unity of moral and religious truth. For Newman, conscience has authority because it expresses God's law; it has rights because it has duties. In his mind, moral goodness does not depend solely upon one's efforts to realize right behavior; nor is conscience a long-sighted selfishness or a desire to be consistent with oneself. Also Newman's psychology is pre-Freudian, and thereby lacks some of the insights of contemporary psychologists, those, for instance, one finds in Walter Conn's analysis of conscience, where how "authentically" a person forms his or her conscience is more important than how an individual "faithfully" follows his/her conscience. However, Newman is quite contemporary, as James Keating argues, in emphasizing the close link between the call to holiness and the desire to be good and to choose rightly—the place of prayer ("listening") in moral decision making.[6]

We should be cautious, moreover, about using Newman's famous toast as a free-standing summary of his complex position about the relationship between conscience and the pope. "Certainly, if I am obliged to bring religion into afterdinner toasts (which indeed does not seem quite the thing), I shall drink—to the Pope, if you please—still, to conscience first, and to the Pope afterwards." "The whole of Newman's thought lies between the poles of two God-given popes," Sheridan Gilley writes in his impressive study of Newman's mind. "The private pre-emptory if fallible *pope of conscience,* the witness to the God within, creating that hunger for God which is satisfied and fulfilled by the *public pope* of the external revelation of God in scripture and tradition, as upheld in the witness of the infallible Church."[7] For Newman, the Church is the pillar and ground of truth; and conscience and the pope are unable to come into direct conflict, since both are sovereigns in their own realms. The pope proclaims the Church's moral message; conscience applies that message in the individual's life.[8]

Further, in spite of Newman's advocacy of the personal aspects of knowledge (he was accused of being a Modernist by some of his readers, including the American Catholic scholar Orestes Brownson), catechists should not see in Newman's words exactly what they find in Sidney Callahan's essays that emphasize the unique, personal, and contextual aspects of moral decision making, the role of intuition and personal energy, the necessity of giving up a one-sided rationalistic deductive model of moral decision making and replacing it with a wholistic model that acknowledges the inward as well as the outward challenges involved in this activity.[9] Nor should readers see in Newman's writings, Charles Curran's position that for "the Christian who has made a commensurate effort to form his conscience correctly, the dictate of conscience is an infallible norm of conduct," and "even though the action itself is not in objective conformity with the divine will, the Christian's conduct is pleasing to God, for it stems from a pure heart."[10] Newman grounded conscience's authority in its supernatural origins, and its role as the "voice of God" in the heart; modern theologians base conscience's authority on the dignity of the human person, and the respect due individuals in society.

## V. Contemporary Sources: Vatican II, Cardinal Ratzinger, John Paul II

Besides the sources mentioned, the *Catechism*'s four-part teaching on conscience, in particular its emphasis on "erroneous conscience," must be related to several more recent statements: Vatican II's Pastoral Constitution on the Church in the Modern World *(Gaudium et Spes);* Cardinal Ratzinger's 1991 lecture on "Conscience and Truth"; and Pope John Paul's 1993 encyclical *Veritatis Splendor.*

Vatican II's words about conscience are among its best known. They have received extensive comment.[11] Conscience, the Council says, reveals that law which is fulfilled by love of God and of neighbor and joins all humans together in the search for truth "and for the genuine solution to the numerous problems which arise in the life of individuals and from social relationships." The Council's statements, a puzzling fusion of high-sounding philosophical contradictions, according to James Gaffney, have an undeniable place in the *Catechism*'s teaching. However, other recent sources might have been no less important.

Cardinal Ratzinger's short, informal lecture is a skillful attempt to reconcile the apparent opposition between conscience and the Magisterium, between individual autonomy and teaching authority, the constraints involved in liberty of conscience and the limits imposed by objective moral truth.[12] Building creatively upon themes in Paul, Augustine, Aquinas, and Newman, Ratzinger describes conscience as "a window through which one can see outward to that common truth which founds and sustains us all," the "power of perception for what is highest and most essential," and as "the perceptible and demanding presence of the voice of truth in the subject" (4). In a return to Plato and Augustine that modern psychologists and educators will find difficult to accept, the author states that there are actually two levels in conscience: a first, named *"anamnesis",* which consists in an innate memory of, and "inner ontological tendency" toward the divine; and a second level, named *"conscientia,"* which refers to judgments and decisions, to the acts of applying basic knowledge about good and evil in particular situations. These two levels are the keys to both the authority of conscience and the Church as moral guide.

For Ratzinger, the "anamnesis" results from the godlike constitution of our being, but it is not "a conceptually articulated knowing, a store of retrievable contents. It is so to speak an inner sense, a capacity to recall, so that the one whom it addresses, if he is not turned in on himself, hears its echo from within. He sees: That's it! That is what my nature points to and seeks" (14). Ratzinger sees this "remembering" as the foundation of morality, of papal teaching authority, and the authenticity of the Church's moral traditions. "This Christian memory, to be sure, is always learning, but proceeding from its sacramental identity, it also distinguishes from within between what is genuine unfolding of its recollection and what is its destruction or falsification"(16). The second level corresponds to Aquinas' *"conscientia"*—it is the act of applying basic moral knowledge in specific situations; it has three elements: recognizing, bearing witness, and judging.

The author argues that individual moral decisions, papal moral teaching, and objective morality are interrelated not separated, in harmony not in conflict. He writes, "The anamnesis instilled in our being needs, one might say, assistance from without so that it can become aware of itself. But this 'from without' is not something set in opposition to anamnesis but is ordered to it" (16). Conscience's "innate memory" provides humanity with lasting and universal moral truths that the Church safeguards; and the individual's conscience judges rightly, i.e., his or her *"conscientia"* is correct—free from error and guilt— when it acts in accord with "the anamnesis of memory" (17–18).

While audiences will not find much support for Ratzinger's themes in current research into moral decision making, they have their roots on Aristotle and Plato, in the Western moral tradition; and (in a sense) are not too removed from David Hume's efforts to establish a universal theory of moral sentiments, or what one finds in W.D. Ross's writings on moral intuitions, the reliability of common morality, and Ross's analyses of the right and the good.

A third current source for the *Catechism*'s teaching on conscience is John Paul II's encyclical *Veritatis Splendor*. Educators might find this three-part encyclical, its long section on conscience and truth (54–64), a useful commentary on the *Catechism*'s moral teaching. However, commentators on Pope John Paul's historic document have expressed some concerns that must be noted. John Wilkins, for instance, says in his introductory remarks to *Considering Veritatis Splendor* (1994), that conscience plays a crucial role in human life, and that "Men and women in the United States and Britain inherit a particularly strong sense of the authority of conscience, and the Roman Catholic Church will not succeed in appealing to their deepest convictions unless it is seen to do full justice to that voice which Newman called, in an exceptionally daring phrase, 'the first of the Vicars of Christ'" (xiii). Wilkins notes that the pope rebuts the false, radically subjective view of conscience that is widespread in Western societies (he is also openly critical of theologians who over emphasize the "creative" character of conscience, and teach that conscience is not obliged, in every case, by particular negative precepts). However, Wilkins is concerned that the pope's emphasis on conscience's fallibility, on vincible and invincible error, on the role of the Church and its Magisterium in the formation of conscience, might dethrone the informed conscience in relation to authority. "So long as conscience means resisting totalitarianism, there is nothing but applause for it from the Pope. But as soon as conscience starts operating in the personal ethical sphere, his caution mounts," Wilkins writes. "The encyclical stresses that conscience is subject to error, needs shaping, has to work hard, requires help from the tradition and insights of the community. Yet there is no reflection of this essential dialogue in the encyclical itself"(xiii). While other writers, for instance, Joseph Selling, Louis Janssens, Bernard Haring, Jean Porter, Richard McCormick, Maura Ryan, William Spohn, and Ronald Burke, have expressed their concerns about this encyclical, Brian Johnstone has raised specific problems about the encyclical's teaching on conscience.[13]

## VI. Conclusion

The years since 1962 when Pope John XXIII opened the Second Vatican Council have seen great efforts to achieve the Council's goals. Used intelligently and creatively, adapted to cultures and audiences, the *Catechism* (like the Church's *Code of Canon Law*) has the power to play a major role in advancing Christian and world unity. The *Catechism*'s teaching on conscience, in the hands of insightful educators, will be (as Pope John Paul II said on the work's publication) a useful support to ecumenical efforts that are moved by the desire for the unity of all Christians—and a "sure and authentic reference text for teaching Catholic doctrine and particularly for preparing local catechisms."

What the *Catechism* says about conscience does not correspond with the analyses of some well-known Catholic educators and developmental psychologists, those, in particular, who see the individual as inherently autonomous, and the self 's own lived experience as the primary source of moral truth. It is conservative in its analysis; limited in its ambition. Some students will be disappointed that the *Catechism* fails to deal explicitly and openly with the freedom of Catholics to dissent from papal moral teaching; that it does not give any concrete examples where such liberty exists. Teachers will have to face difficult questions about the meaning of technical terms, the document's stress on culpable error and vincible ignorance, and its inadequate use of the insights of modern political theory and philosophy. They will have to deal, as well, with the many of the limitations mentioned by Cardinal Ratzinger in his commentary on Vatican II's statements about conscience. However, imaginative catechists who present the *Catechism*'s teaching in the light of its sources, and focus students' interests upon conscience's mysteries—on the research possibilities in Paul, Newman, Vatican II, and John Paul II —will further the Council's goals.

## Notes

[1]  For useful information about Paul's usage, Philippe Delhaye, *The Christian Conscience* (New York: Desclee, 1968), 48–49; James Gaffney, "Conscience: The Evolution of Ambiguity," in *Matters of Faith and Morals* (Kansas City: Sheed & Ward, 1987), 115–133; John Mahoney, *The Making of Moral Theology* (Oxford: Clarendon Press, 1987), 184–188.

[2]  On this subject, J. Dolan, "Conscience in the Catholic Theological Tradition," in W. Bier, editor, *Conscience: Its Freedom and Limitations* (New York: Fordham University Press, 1971).

[3]  For useful information about Aquinas' ethics, Brian Thomas Mullady, *The Meaning of the Term 'Moral' in St. Thomas Aquinas*, Studi Tomistici #27, Citta del Vaticano: Libreria Editrice Vaticana, 1986; Gaffney, op. cit., 126–127; John Mahoney, op. cit., 187–193.

[4]  Stephen R. L. Clark, *Aristotle's Man: Speculations upon Aristotelian Anthropology* (Oxford: Clarendon Press, 1975), 14–27.

[5]  On this subject, Bernard J. Mahoney, "Newman's Conscience: A Teleological Argu-

ment," in *John Henry Newman: Theology & Reform*, edited by Michael E. Allsopp and Ronald R. Burke (New York: Garland Publishing, 1992), 131–144.

[6] James Keating, "The Conscience Imperative as Prayer," *Irish Theological Quarterly* 63, 1 (1998), 65–89.

[7] Sheridan Gilley, *Newman and His Age* (London: Darton, Longman & Todd, 1990), 362.

[8] On the use of Newman's thought in recent years, Michael E. Allsopp, "Conscience, the Church and Moral Truth: John Henry Newman, Vatican II, Today," *Irish Theological Quarterly* 58, 3 (1993), 192–208.

[9] For Callahan's views, her *In Good Conscience: Reason and Emotion in Moral Decision Making* (San Francisco: Harper, 1991).

[10] Charles Curran, "The Christian Conscience Today," in his *Christian Morality Today* (Notre Dame: Fides Publishers, 1966), 13–25. For further information on Newman: Francis J. Kaiser, *The Concept of Conscience According to John Henry Newman* (Washington: Catholic University of America Press, 1958); Terrance Merrigan, "Newman the Theologian," *Louvain Studies*, 15, 2–3 (Summer-Fall, 1990), 103–118; Michael E. Allsopp and Ronald R. Burke, editors, *John Henry Newman: Theology & Reform* (New York: Garland Publishing Inc., 1992). Also, the essay on "Conscience" by Walter J. Woods, in *The New Dictionary of Catholic Social Thought,* Judith A. Dwyer, editor (Collegeville, Liturgical Press, 1994), 223–228.

[11] For instance, Joseph Ratzinger's comments on *Gaudium et Spes*, art. 16, *Commentary on the Documents of Vatican II*, Herbert Vorgrimler, general editor (New York: Herder & Herder, 1969), vol. V, 134–136; Joseph Fuchs, "Divine Law, Objective Moral Order, Magisterium—and Moral Knowledge in the Conscience," in *Vatican II: Assessment and Perspectives Twenty-five Years After (1962–1987)*, Rene Latourelle, editor (New York: Paulist Press, 1989), vol. 2, 490ff.

[12] Joseph Cardinal Ratzinger, *Conscience and Truth* (Braintree, MA: Pope John Center, 1991).

[13] Brian V. Johnstone, "Erroneous Conscience in *Veritatis Splendor* and the Theological Tradition," in *The Splendor of Accuracy*, Joseph A. Selling and Jan Jans, editors (Grand Rapids: Eerdmans Publishing Comapny, 1994), 114–135. Also: Michael E. Allsopp and John J. O'Keefe, editors, *Veritatis Splendor: American Responses* (Kansas City: Sheed & Ward, 1995).

# The Human Act and Its Moral Evaluation in the *Catechism of the Catholic Church:* A Critical Analysis

Todd A. Salzman

## I. Introduction

According to its prologue, the *Catechism* aims at presenting an organic synthesis of the essential and fundamental contents of Catholic doctrine, as regards both faith and morals, in the light of the Second Vatican Council and the whole of the Church's tradition. Its principal sources are the Sacred Scriptures, the Fathers of the Church, the liturgy, and the Church's Magisterium (11).

Implied in this statement is that each source, and perhaps the sources taken as a whole, provide the *Catechism* with a univocal, logically coherent tradition which, though it should "help to illumine with the light of faith new situations and problems which had not yet emerged in the past," remains essentially consistent and unchanged. While it may be the case that there is a dogmatic minimalistic common denominator that unites each source and/or the sources taken as a whole, to present them as such is to overlook the radical evolution and richness of the Catholic tradition(s) which has evolved and developed, especially since Vatican II, in light of "the signs of the times." It is in light of these developments that particular teachings have been disregarded, radically altered, or even reversed in some cases. Through an examination of this evolutionary process, one can frequently come to a deeper understanding of the Catholic tradition(s), its present interpretation, and perhaps directions it may move in order to further develop and facilitate the individual Christian in living out his or her journey. Unfortunately, the *Catechism* frequently presents certain topics as a synthesis of various periods and teachings without recognizing the subtle, or even blatant changes which have occurred. And while it is certainly not the purpose of the *Catechism* to sort out or attempt to

61

respond to the complex question of the development of certain doctrines and traditional teachings, through its systematic exposition it should not draw attention to these very questions. In its discussion of the human act and its moral evaluation, it has done just that.

Article 4 of Part III, entitled "The Morality of Human Acts," begins with what appears, on first sight, to be a concise and coherent definition of human acts. Following this definition, it proceeds with the first subsection, "I. The Sources of Morality," for determining the morality of such acts. Traditionally as well as in contemporary moral theology, the object, end, or intention and circumstances serve as criteria for morally evaluating the human act as either good or evil. Subsection two, "II. Good Acts and Evil Acts," describes what qualifies an act as either morally good or evil. Unlike other articles in the *Catechism* that frequently give extensive references and source documentation, there is a single scriptural reference in this article (*Mt* 6:2–4). Consequently, the reader is left to speculate as to the source or sources from where this (brief) presentation of the human act, the sources of morality, and good and evil acts are taken. On further examination, it appears that the presentation is a compilation of various sources throughout tradition to which the author(s) had recourse, and combined into a seemingly coherent presentation.

In this essay, we will examine the human act and its moral evaluation. While Pope John Paul II promises that his specially appointed commission has created a text "whose unity and coherence are assured" (p. 3), this coherence is far from evident in Article 4. In fact, upon close reading, one is left with a muddled presentation of the human act and its moral evaluation which is likely to cause more confusion than clarification amongst the *Catechism*'s intended audience.[1] This ambiguity does not facilitate the catechetical purpose to "be a sure and authentic reference text for teaching catholic doctrine," nor does it clarify the traditional ambiguity in discerning first of all, what constitutes a human act; and secondly, how that act is to be morally evaluated as either good or evil.

## II. The Human Act

"Human acts, that is acts that are freely chosen in consequence of a judgment of conscience, can be morally evaluated. They are either good or evil" (1749). This seemingly straightforward, unambiguous account of what constitutes human acts overlooks the various ways in which the human act has been understood throughout tradition which, no doubt, will affect how that act is judged morally good or evil. There is no indication of the sources to which the author(s) had recourse in formulating this definition. Thus, we must look to tradition to discern first, how the human act is understood and, secondly, how it is to be morally evaluated in light of this understanding. Three periods throughout the history of the Roman Catholic Church will be investigated which have defined the human act in a unique way relative to the theological context and purpose for discussing that act: St. Thomas Aquinas; the moral manual tradition; and Vatican II. There are indications throughout the *Catechism* and article four in particular, that the author(s) had recourse to all three of these traditions without clearly delineating any of them and the impact each has had on the conceptualization of the human act.

## II. a.  Thomas Aquinas: Acts of a Human vs. Human Acts

The first and most obvious source for the Catechism's presentation is St. Thomas Aquinas. His *Summa Theologiae* is the most authoritative and systematic of the traditional sources which defines the human act and the sources for morally evaluating that act. In the first question of the prima secundae St. Thomas begins with a distinction between two types of acts, human acts (actus humanus) and acts of a human (actus hominis). Only those acts which are of a person's own deliberate willing are properly called "human acts"; those acts which are not human acts, but are attributable to a person are called "acts of a human."[2] Morality is confined to human acts. Therefore, according to Thomas, "moral acts and human acts are the same."[3]

To illustrate the distinction between human acts and acts of a human, consider the following act descriptions. A child trips on a sidewalk, falls down, and scrapes her knee. A young woman sneezes. An old man scratches his elbow. A teenager steals a car stereo in order to purchase drugs. A woman, faced with an unwanted pregnancy, chooses to have an abortion. What is common to all of these acts is that they are done by human beings. As such, however, they are not necessarily subject to moral evaluation. The first two acts do not proceed from the reason and will of the agent and are not, therefore, voluntary acts. Such acts are not subject to a moral evaluation since they do not involve a conscious, voluntary, free choice on the part of the agent. The last two acts proceed from a deliberate will. They entail a conscious, deliberate choice on the part of the moral agent (though not necessarily a free choice in the case of a drug addict). And since human acts and moral acts are synonymous for Thomas, these two acts are subject to moral evaluation. The third act, the man scratching his elbow, could either be from a deliberate act of will or not. If he is merely responding to an epidermal agitant, it is an act of a human and therefore an amoral act. If, however, when he scratches his elbow it is a sign for his cohorts to enter the bank and proceed to remove the money at gunpoint, then it is a human act which is morally culpable. The first two acts are considered acts of a human and do not entail a moral judgment. The last two acts involve a conscious, free choice on the part of the agent, and are therefore subject to moral evaluation. These are human acts in the proper sense. The third act could either be an act of a human or a human act, depending on the voluntariness and meaning of the act. Thomas summarizes these two types of acts:

> . . . of the actions a man performs those alone are properly called human which are characteristically his as a man. He differs from non-intelligent creatures in this, that he is the master of what he does. Consequently those actions alone which lie under his control are properly called human. Now he is master through his mind and will, which is why his free decision is referred to as an ability of reason and will. Therefore those acts alone are properly called human which are of his own deliberate willing. Others that may be attributed to him may be called "acts of a man," but not "human acts," since they are not his precisely as a human being.[4]

An objection to the distinction between acts of a human and human acts which immediately comes to mind is the following: What about those acts which proceed from reason and a deliberate act of will, and yet seem awkward, even inaccurate, to declare morally good or bad? Consider the following example. A young woman approaches an ice cream shop. She faces an immediate dilemma, choosing between either bubble-gum or tutti-frutti when she only has the means to buy one scoop of ice cream. She consciously reflects upon her options and deliberately chooses bubble-gum over tutti-frutti. The criteria of an act proceeding from reason and a deliberate act of will fulfill the requirements for making this a human act. And yet, would we want to say that this act is subject to evaluation as morally good or bad? Did the girl choose badly and therefore act immorally in her choice by opting for bubble-gum over tutti-frutti? Such a deliberate act of choice seems to fall out of the confines of what we normally consider a morally good or bad act. The question remains then, how does this act differ from those previously described acts which it would be appropriate to label human acts, and therefore subject to moral evaluation?

One aspect of moral theology is concerned with determining which types of human acts are subject to moral evaluation. And though the girl choosing her favorite flavor of ice cream is a deliberate act of will guided by reason, and therefore a human act according to Thomas, it does not constitute a morally good or bad act. Or does it? It is conceivable that Thomas would argue that this act is a human act and therefore a moral act in that it is a conscious, free choice based on an inner act of the will. The goal of the act is not the mere pleasure of enjoying a particular flavor of ice cream, though this could be a good in itself (an aesthetic good), but to fulfill an appetite, hunger. This raises an important point. Thomas' notion of a human or moral act is much broader than those acts which we may consider to be within the realm of morality and subject to moral evaluation. This is so because Thomas' overall purpose for composing the *Summa* was to guide humanity to their ultimate end, friendship with God. The moral act either contributes to, or detracts from, this ultimate end, and from it, gains its moral significance. The reason that the girl's choice of ice cream could be considered a human and moral act in Thomas' approach to the moral life, whereas it would be queer in manualistic or contemporary moral theological discussions to consider it as such, is that Thomas has a much broader notion of morality. For Thomas, all human acts, i.e., acts which proceed from a deliberate act of will guided by reason, either contribute to, or detract from, one's final end. It is important to keep this in mind when considering Thomas as a source. He was not preparing a moral manual to train confessors, nor was he developing a personalist or normative ethic. Rather, he was concerned primarily with the overall goal of the Christian for this life and eternity. Human beings attain salvation through doing good and avoiding evil. All individual human acts, according to Thomas, are either morally good or morally evil.[5]

## II. b.  The Manuals of Moral Theology: Acts of a Human, Human Acts and Nonmoral Human Acts[6]

The tradition of the manuals of moral theology which emerged shortly after the Council of Trent and persisted up until Vatican II, although they rely upon St. Thomas for their form and content, have a unique understanding of the human act which is intimately tied to the purpose of the manuals themselves. There were two aspects to the manual tradition, the theoretical and the practical. The theoretical aspect was explained in the Compendium or the Institutiones of moral theology. Frequently, these treatises began with an explanation and definition of the human act. The practical aspect of the manuals was explained in the *Casus Conscientiae* (Cases of Conscience).[7] These manuals consisted of a description of certain moral dilemmas, including acts and circumstances, and the moral evaluation of those situations. The purpose of the manuals, both theoretical and practical, was to train seminarians in administering the sacrament of penance. While many manualists fell in line with Thomas' identification of the human and moral act, others distinguished between them. Whereas every moral act is a human act, every human act is not necessarily a moral act. Children who act without adequate knowledge of good and evil (e.g., prior to the age of discretion) and adults who choose to do morally indifferent actions, such as reading and writing, are nonmoral human acts. These acts qualify as human acts because they are a manifestation of a deliberate act of will. They do not, however, qualify as moral acts because of a lack of awareness (children) or a lack of moral content. Thus a third dimension was added to Aquinas' distinction between acts of humans and human acts, nonmoral human acts.[8]

Although, like Thomas, the manualists were concerned with humanity's final end, the focus of the confessional, and therefore the manuals, was on the individual human act. It was the purpose of the confessor to determine the moral nature of the individual human act, the moral culpability of the penitent and his or her appropriate penance. It is quite logical, then, that some manualists would consider it necessary not only to distinguish between human acts and acts of humans, but also between moral and nonmoral human acts. Within this distinction, the girl's choice of ice cream would fall under the auspices of a nonmoral human act. Furthermore, the human act was perceived as a static, isolated reality to be examined and analyzed in determining its moral nature, rather than an action which both formed and expressed the habitus of an individual person. Whereas Thomas had a more wholistic understanding of the human act in relation to the virtuous or vicious disposition of the individual, the manuals tended to view the act in isolation. This was a consequence of the "moral theology of the confessional," the role and function of which was to train seminarians to be good confessors; i.e., to recognize those human acts which were moral, judge the moral culpability of the penitent, level the appropriate penance, and grant absolution.

While a detailed analysis of the manualists' hermeneutic of Thomas is beyond the scope of the present work, there are significant similarities between the two including, but not exclusively, their anthropology, the focus on the physical structure of certain (primarily sexual) acts, and the analysis of the isolated act. In general, the manualists shared Thomas' definition of the human being as a rational animal endowed with free will. Implicit in this definition is a dualistic, Aristotelian anthropology. On the most fundamental level, all animals share a common nature. Particular to human beings is rationality and free will, which is added to, not integrated with, our animal nature. Thus, the acts which we share in common with animals (e.g., the sexual act) are considered according to their natural finality and purpose (procreation). And while the sexual act can be an expression of love and can nurture the relationship, this is a secondary dimension unique to the human animal. From this perception of the human act, those acts are moral which conform to their natural finality. Besides authors in this collection, Charles Curran refers to this tendency of identifying the act's natural finality with its moral nature as physicalism, and it is a characteristic common to Thomas and the moral manuals, particularly with regard to sexual acts.[9] In order to analyze the morality of such acts from a physicalist perspective, it was unnecessary to investigate the overall disposition or habits of the individual or the totality of his or her relationships. Rather, the tendency was to focus on the isolated, external act occurring in a moment of time to determine its moral nature. While St. Thomas and his *Summa* continue to function as a point of departure for much of contemporary moral theology, the anthropology which both he and the manualists share as well as their focus on the individual, physical structure of the act has been explicitly challenged in the pre- and post-Vatican II era.

## II. c.  Contemporary Moral Theology: Personalism and Normative Ethics

Vatican II's call for a more scientific approach to moral theology informed by Sacred Scripture[10] was an acknowledgment of the limitations of moral theology, especially within the manual tradition, as well as a challenge to theologians to develop a nuanced, though traditional, methodological approach to moral theology which went beyond the confines of the confessional. The scientific examination and exploration of moral theology stimulated a shift in moral theology on at least two accounts: There was a shift in moral paradigms from a natural law to a personalist paradigm; and moral theologians investigated other disciplines such as the behavioral sciences and philosophy in order to scientifically develop moral theology and clarify its methodology. Philosophical explorations resulted in normative ethics and methodology as a novel dimension of moral theology. Both personalism and normative ethics have a unique understanding of the human act which differs from Aquinas' and the manualists' notions.

### II. c. i.  Personalism: The Human Act Adequately Considered

The "Pastoral Constitution on the Church in the Modern World" (*Gaudium et Spes,* hereafter, GS) serves as a charter document for developing a personalist moral theological paradigm. While the manuals give preeminence to natural law and the ten commandments in their ethical formulations, and the moral life consisted of individual, isolated acts which either conformed to or violated these laws or commandments, in GS the groundwork was laid for establishing the human person adequately considered in his or her entirety of being in relation to the totality of reality as a foundational principle for moral theology.[11] With this transformation from natural law, rules, and commandments to the human person adequately considered as a basis for moral theology came a corresponding transformation of the nature and meaning of the human act.

From the perspective of the human person adequately considered, human acts are more or less an expression of who the human person is and strives to become. There developed what might be labeled "a human act continuum" of which certain human acts are a negligible expression of who the person is qua human, for example, brushing one's teeth, whereas other human acts may (in exceptional cases) totally express who we have chosen to be and become as human persons, for example, one's vocational choice to become a racketeer or a committed advocate for human rights. Whereas in the former case it would be appropriate to view this act as an individual, isolated human act, much like the manual understanding of the (nonmoral) human act, in the latter case, this decision, though possibly expressed in a single act, is normally the culmination of a process of discernment, dispositions, and individual acts, all of which form who a person is and his or her fundamental disposition toward reality, God, and others. Such fully human acts are considered an expression of our fundamental option, a concept which developed concomitantly with personalism and expresses a shift in understanding the human act.

As developed by Louis Monden, fundamental option entails a choice the human person makes "not with respect to specific objects but with respect to the totality of existence, its meaning and its direction.[12] The person either commits oneself to pursue justice and love or refuses to do so. To the extent that the human act is less fully human, it either manifests and affirms our fundamental option or challenges this commitment. To the extent that it is a fully human act and expresses, fundamentally, who we have chosen to become as a human being, it either alters or reaffirms and strengthens our fundamental option. From a personalist moral theological perspective, while it may be possible to pinpoint the moment of a concrete decision where a person either confirms or alters his or her fundamental option in a fully human act, to limit the fully human act to this moment in isolation from the history and lived experiences which culminated in this decision, is to view the human act as did the manualists, in an isolated, static, and perhaps physicalist sense. A personalist account of the fully human act considers the human act adequately considered.

The human act adequately considered entails a full consideration of the human person expressing himself or herself in entirety, i.e., as a unique, historical, corporeal subject in relation to God, others, oneself, and the world, and on the basis of these dimensions, attempts to discern where the human act lies on the human act continuum and, correspondingly, to what extent it is a complete expression of the human person. For instance, the day a man and woman exchange wedding vows could be described as the marital act, i.e., a human act where each spouse publicly commits himself and herself to the other unconditionally. To focus on that aspect of the marital act, which is no doubt significant, without acknowledging the months or years that went into nurturing the relationship, fostering trust, growing in love and commitment to one another, which is publicly expressed and ecclesiologically recognized in the exchange of vows on the wedding day, as well as the future development and expression of this commitment, is to give disproportional significance to what is, in actuality, a culmination of a series of events with openness to the future, which constitutes the fully human act of marriage. The human act adequately considered extends beyond the actual concrete decision and execution of the act and entails the entire lived experience which went into making a choice and living out that choice. Very rarely, if indeed ever, are acts which would qualify as fully human acts, and therefore have the capability of altering one's fundamental option, made spontaneously or instantaneously. The mere idea of such spontaneity posits against a fully human act which requires knowledge of the implications this act may have for one's fundamental option. Richard McCormick illustrates this notion of the fully human act in his description of adultery. Whereas the manuals would consider the human act of adultery, i.e., sexual intercourse with another's spouse, a mortally sinful act, McCormick expands the parameters of the human act to entail not only a physical description of what has taken place (sexual intercourse) along with a relational consideration (the spouse of another), but also "the meetings, thoughts, desires, plans, effects as foreseen, the vacillations, and so on" that culminated in an act of adultery.[13] While the human act of adultery is an event which happens in a moment of time, to focus on this moment is to ignore the course of events which led up to this act, and to view the act in an isolated sense, rather than as a process which evolves over time.

According to personalism, the human act is not morally analyzable in isolation from the historical, relational, acting person. Rather, the human act is first and foremost human. That is, it is a full consideration of those dimensions which constitute a particular human person and are freely and intentionally expressed in a physical or mental act. Through an analysis of the dimensions that constitute a human person we discern the meaning and nature of the human act in relationship to the totality of the human person and his or her existence, and judge it morally good or evil. This is by no means a simple or concise analysis. The *Catechism* recognizes the complexity of this process in its acknowledgment that particular circumstances such as "ignorance, inadvertence, duress, fear, habit, inordinate attachments, and other psychological and social factors" may diminish or even nullify a person's imputability and responsibility for an action (1735).[14] This is a pastoral approach which recognizes human finitude and the effect that finitude has on the agent's freedom and, therefore, moral culpability for an action.[15] While recognizing these limitations, however, the *Catechism* further asserts that "circumstances of themselves cannot change the moral quality of acts themselves; they can make neither good nor right an action that is in itself evil" (1754). If moral culpability is negligible due to various circumstances, in what sense can the *Catechism* maintain that an act evil in itself remains so? If the act is evil, it would seem the person executing that act has committed a morally evil act and, therefore, is morally culpable. If this is not the case, as the *Catechism* clearly states, why not? The answer lies in the normative ethical dichotomy between act and agent, the second contribution to moral theology as a science since Vatican II.

### II. c. ii.  Normative Ethics: Right and Wrong Acts

Whereas personalism understands the human act adequately considered as a composite whole, act and agent, in his or her totality of being, normative ethics deconstructs the human act into act and agent. The distinction between act and agent has arisen within the discussion of normative ethics and the foundation and formulation of ethical norms. In its evolution, normative ethical discourse has become increasingly dependent upon the distinction between the ethical terms right and good and their opposites.[16] Right and wrong are deontic ethical terms which pertain to acts, whereas good and bad are aretaic ethical terms which pertain to human acts, persons, dispositions, motives, or intentions.[17] While a human act can only be judged morally good or bad in relation to the entirety of human experience, certain acts tend to be right or wrong. It is the role of normative ethics to determine, on the basis of Scripture, Tradition, the magisterium and the "signs of the times," all of which may not agree,[18] which acts tend to be right and therefore prescribed, and which acts tend to be wrong, and therefore proscribed. These prescriptions or proscriptions are formulated into norms which function as *a priori* guiding principles for right and wrong behavior. Due to the relatively new distinction between deontic terms and aretaic terms, and the terminological ambiguity which frequently accompanies normative discussions, moral theologians have divided norms into three classes which attempt to overcome this ambiguity. Norms which prescribe or proscribe right or wrong acts are labeled concrete norms, material norms, or concrete material norms. For example, "do not tell a falsehood" is a concrete norm proscribing an act which tends to be wrong. Concrete synthetic norms prescribe or prohibit human acts, i.e., they include a description of the act and include the dispositional character or intention of the agent in their act description. "Do not tell a lie" is a concrete synthetic norm which describes an act (telling a falsehood) with a malevolent intention (to deceive). Thus, act and intention are contained within the definition. Killing and murder are another example of terms which either describe an act or a human act respectively. Whereas murder is always wrong, killing tends to be wrong, except in certain situations, e.g., self-defense. A third type of norm is the synthetic norm which prescribes or prohibits certain dispositions. For example, "be just," "be chaste," or "do not hate." These norms indicate the moral goodness or badness of certain dispositions but are contentless in the sense that they do not indicate what is a just, chaste, or hateful act.

In normative ethics, then, there is a unique understanding of the human act which distinguishes between right and wrong acts and morally good or bad human acts. While it is clear that the concrete synthetic norms which prescribe or prohibit certain types of behavior are absolute in the sense that we can never morally justify a lie or murder, it is by no means clear that concrete norms are absolute. In fact, it is sometimes the case that we can justify telling a falsehood (e.g., in order to protect an innocent person) or killing (e.g., in the case of self-defense). Concrete material norms are a priori guidelines for behavior which either prescribe or proscribe right or wrong acts. Although such acts are human acts, in that they are performed by human beings, they are premoral acts physically described in objective norms. Not until all the components of an act are known in relation to the human person does an act become a human act subject to a moral judgment.

These three periods each define the human act in a unique way relative to the theological and historical context of the discussion and the anthropological understanding of what constitutes a human person. Thomas was not preparing a moral manual for the confessional, nor was he functioning out of a personalist moral paradigm. Operating out of an Aristotelian anthropological framework, his understanding of the human person as rational animal was limited in comparison to contemporary notions of the human person.[19] Neither was Thomas developing a normative ethic. As we have seen, his notion of the human act is much broader than what we consider to be within the parameters of morality. While Thomas considered the human act as a single deliberate action, he was concerned how this individual action contributed to the formation of habits or dispositions and brought us to our final end, friendship with God. The manualists, while relying upon Aquinas extensively, had a different purpose for composing their manuals. Their purpose was to train priests to be good confessors. Thus, the human act tended to be isolated and analyzed in an often legalistic, minimalistic, and physicalist sense to discern the moral nature of that act, the guilt of the penitent and his or her appropriate penance. Both Thomas and the moral manualists tended to view the human act as a single, deliberate action.

With Vatican II and GS, the human person adequately considered became a paradigm for moral theology and with it came a unique understanding of the human act. As an expression of the human person, the human act is either more or less fully human. Fundamental option designates those fully human acts in which we either commit ourselves to the totality of reality, or reject that reality. Such fully human acts are rarely an individual, isolated act in the Thomistic or manualistic sense. Rather, they are the culmination over time of repeated acts which form dispositions and affect the totality of our relationships. From this perspective, "the human act is understood as a moral configuration of a person's life rather than as a single deliberate action."[20] Finally, on a normative ethical level, the act is either right or wrong in abstracto, whereas only the human act is evaluated morally good or evil. The various definitions of the human act are by no means synonymous. To present the human act as if its conceptualization has been consistent throughout tradition is to ignore the radical paradigm shifts (e.g., from natural law to personalism) which influence and alter the con-ceptualization of the human act. Throughout the *Catechism,* especially in section one and two of article four, "The Morality of Human Acts," one can find implicit or explicit allusions to all of these understandings of the human act. What results is confusion for the reader on how to understand the human act and its moral evaluation. We have examined the first aspect of this query; we will now proceed to the criteria for morally evaluating the human act, the traditional sources of morality.

## III.  The Sources of Morality

Part III, Chapter One, Section One, entitled "The Dignity of the Human Person," begins on a promising note. Article I, "Man: The Image of God," contains several references to GS portraying the human person in his or her dignity as "the only creature on earth that God has willed for its own sake" (1703, quoting GS 142), possessing reason and free will (1704), endowed with freedom (1705), and guided by conscience (1706). In reading this prelude, one eagerly anticipates that the theological insights inspired by GS regarding the human person, and in turn the human act, will be incorporated into the *Catechism*'s presentation on the human act and its moral evaluation. This, however, is not the case.

Similar to the human act, there is no source documentation on the sources of morality. We may speculate that, like some of the manualists who did not indicate St. Thomas' *Summa Theologiae* I–II, q. 18, aa. 2–4, as their source for defining the object, end, and circumstances, this is considered self-evident.[21] Neither does the encyclical *Veritatis Splendor* indicate a source when it discusses the object, end, and circumstances.[22] While it may not be the case that the author(s) of this article relied exclusively upon q. 18, aa. 2–4 as his source, it would be safe to speculate that Thomas' *Summa* was at least one of the sources. We concur with Jean Porter's analysis that, while Aquinas' thought may not be normative for VS or, we might add, for the *Catechism*, he "offers one of the most insightful accounts of moral judgment that is available to us, and his account, moreover, has set the framework for all subsequent moral theology."[23] Like Porter, we will take Thomas' analysis and description of the sources of morality as our point of departure. It is clear from the *Catechism*'s presentation that not only is it subject to some of the same criticisms long noted in Thomas' explanation of the object, end, and circumstances, as well as the physicalist baggage of the manuals, but it has contributed its own unique confusion to their explanation.

## III. a.  The Object

In the first paragraph the *Catechism* presents four unique and conflicting statements regarding the object of the human act. We will consider each of these in turn.

Definition one: "The *object* chosen is a good toward which the will deliberately directs itself." This statement accurately reflects a portion of Thomas' thought. In his discussion of the components of the human act (*S.T.*, I–II, qq. 6–17), Thomas asserts that all human acts begin with the apprehension by the intellect of a good, real *(bonum)* or apparent *(apparens bonum)*. This good is then presented as an object by the intellect to the will. The human act originates in the perception which is the apprehension of some good, either actual or apparent. Willing is the rational appetite *(appetitus rationalis)*, and the *objectum* of the will is the end sought, the *bonum* or *apparens bonum*.[24] According to Aquinas, exterior or material things are good in themselves, yet in relationship to the object of the act some are fitting while others are not.[25] Even those acts which are morally evil are pursued for an apparent good.[26] The fittingness of the material depends upon whether or not the object corresponds to the dictates of right reason.

In the *Catechism*'s first definition, the object is explained in an external, nonmoral, material sense where the will deliberately directs itself toward the object. So for instance, a scalpel is a good thing in itself. Furthermore, it can be used in an act of mutilation. We could describe the *exterior* object as an act of mutilation. The question remains, however, whether this mutilation was a life-saving operation due to gangrene of the removed limb, or the type of mutilation which was done as a form of torture or experiment on human beings, for instance, in the Nazi era. This depends upon the intention of the doctor either to return the patient to health through a necessary, though regrettable amputation, or to amputate merely as an experiment to satisfy certain curiosities; and the circumstance of whether the patient was a healthy individual or had gangrene of a limb that required a life-saving operation. It is with the further consideration of the meaning and purpose of the act in relation to the human person and circumstances that we understand the object to be a real good or an apparent good, and either morally good or evil. It is in considering the interior object of the will *in relation to* the exterior material object that one enters the realm of morality. The first clause, "the *object* chosen is a good," is morally meaningless for Thomas because all objects that are chosen are good, though they are not necessarily appropriate objects of choice for a particular human act and thus morally good. In this first definition, then, the object is presented in a nonmoral, material sense. This assertion is supported by the second definition.

Definition two: "[The object chosen] is the matter of a human act." In q. 18, a. 2, Thomas specifically addresses the assertion of whether or not the object is the matter of the human act. It is clear that in this article Thomas is addressing the object understood in a moral sense as is indicated in the title: Does a human act possess good or evil from its object *(utrum actio humana habeat bonitatem vel malitiam ex objecto)*? In relation to the human act, the object is comparable to that which gives a physical thing its form. In fact, throughout this article, Thomas uses the analogy between physical things and human actions to clarify what he means by the object. Just as a physical thing is specified by its form, so too, an action is specified by its object. The concrete act is the material which is specified and reduced from potency to act by the object. Hence, the object must be understood in a verbal sense as dynamic activity which deals with the material that it moves, but is not identical to that material. As Thomas succinctly states: "An object is not the material out of which *(materia ex qua)* an act is made, but the material about which it deals *(materia circa quam)*; it takes on the role of form in that it gives specific nature to an act."[27] Thomas compares the specifying character of an act by its object to a motion which receives its specifying character from its term. Hence, term and object are synonymous in their respective functions. Just as a term *(terminus)* is a state of being implied in a process of becoming, so also, the object is the origins of an act as its *terminus a quo,* what it starts from, and *terminus ad quem,* what it arrives at.[28] As an analogy, Thomas asserts that in nature there is evil when a specific form is missing. For instance, when something besides a human being is begotten. Similarly, basic evil arises in moral acts from the object. To take what does not belong to oneself is an act bad of its kind.

For Thomas, then, the object chosen is not the matter of a human act, but is the matter which it specifies as form to matter. This is the moral object. The *Catechism*'s statement reflects more the manualist physicalist sense of the object which has a tendency to identify it with the external, physical act. According to *Veritatis Splendor,* "by the object of a given moral act . . . one cannot mean a process or an event of the merely physical order, to be assessed on the basis of its ability to bring about a given state of affairs in the outside world" (78). From this, it is clear that *VS* does not consider the object "the matter of a human act," contrary to the *Catechism.* Neither does Thomas consider the object of the human or moral act the matter from which it is made *(materia ex qua)*, but the matter with which it deals *(materia circa quam)*.

Definition three: "The object chosen *morally* specifies the act of the will, insofar as reason recognizes and judges it to be or not to be in conformity with the *true* good" (emphasis added). Whereas definition one defines the object in a nonmoral sense, definition three specifically states that the object chosen *morally* specifies the act of the will. Precisely because it is moral the object can morally specify the act of the will. In this definition the object of the human act is a moral object, not a nonmoral object (definition one) or the matter of a human act (definition two). This third definition most accurately reflects Thomas' object of q. 18, a. 2, and is repeated in 1758.

1761 provides what is supposed to be another summary of the object's definition. It reads: "There are concrete acts that it is always wrong to choose, because their choice entails a disorder of the will, i.e., a moral evil." In this sentence "concrete acts" are synonymous with "the object of the choice" (1755). In her commentary on *VS* and the moral act, Jean Porter comments on 78, which specifically quotes this sentence from the *Catechism*. As she acutely points out, however, "this gets matters backwards. If the object of the act qualifies the will, surely that is *due to* the moral significance of that object."[29] That is, only because the object is moral can it morally specify the will in its choice. Definition three, 1758, and 1761 all place morality within the object of choice.

There is a subtle distinction, however, between the third definition and 1758 on the one hand and 1761. The *Catechism* has attempted to move the locus of morality from the object of the will's choice in the former case ("the object chosen morally specifies the act of the will") to the will's choice of that object in the latter case ("[the objects] choice entails a disorder of the will"). In both cases, the object is a moral object and specifies the will. In one case (the third definition and 1758), the act of the will aligns itself with the moral object; in the other case, the act of the will is disordered in its choice of that object. If the object morally specifies the will, however, it is because of the object's moral nature. Though subtle, this distinction is important because the *Catechism* utilizes it in its distinction, as we shall see shortly, between the object and intention.

Definition four: "Objective norms of morality express the rational order of good and evil, attested to by conscience." Whereas the first three definitions view the object in various relations to the agent, this definition objectifies the object in norms of morality in an ontological sense, divorced from the agent choosing the object.[30] Concrete norms prescribe or proscribe acts which tend to be right or wrong, respectively. These acts, however, are considered in an ontological sense, and are not yet moral or human acts. For instance, a falsehood tends to be wrong. If, however, a person tells a falsehood in order to protect an innocent human being from a homicidal maniac, telling a falsehood is a morally good act. Objectively speaking, the falsehood is still wrong. Morally speaking, it is good, and perhaps obligatory. This final statement associates the object with objective norms of morality and normative ethical discussions concerning right or wrong acts rather than morally good or evil human acts.

Suffice it to say that these four sentences which present the object as a source of morality in no way present a coherent or concise view of that object.

### III. b.  Intention

Similar terminological ambiguity surrounds the *Catechism*'s presentation of the end or intention, the second source of morality. The *Catechism* juxtaposes the object and intention, asserting that, "in contrast to the object, the *intention* resides in the acting subject." It further states that "the end is the first goal of the intention and indicates the purpose pursued in the action. The intention is a movement of the will toward the end: it is concerned with the goal of the activity" (1752). As stated above, one definition of the object chosen is that it "morally specifies the act of the will, insofar as reason recognizes and judges it to be or not to be in conformity with the *true* good." From this it appears that while the object and intention may contrast in terms of residence (though this claim is questionable from a previous definition of the object), in moral content and meaning, they are synonymous. If an object morally specifies the act of the will, it is because it is a *moral* object with a specific end or purpose. The will recognizes the moral object which includes the act and the end of that act, and either chooses or refuses that object. So for instance, murder is gravely illicit by reason of its object (1756). Thus the object describes the matter of a human act, killing another person, the malevolent intention of that act, and the morally relevant circumstance that the victim is innocent (as opposed to killing an aggressor in self-defense, for example). In this instance, the object described by the *Catechism* is a *moral* object and determines the purpose pursued in the action by its very definition. Obviously neither intention nor circumstances could change this gravely illicit act to a morally good act. If the intention was self-preservation with the added circumstance that one was being attacked by an unjust aggressor, this could change the moral nature of the act, but it would no longer qualify as an act of murder, but self-defense. Consequently, if a person chooses an object defined by the term murder, both the moral nature of the act and the end or intention of the agent are contained within the act's description, murder. Morally speaking, there is no contrast between the object and intention. Although the examples which the *Catechism* cites of those acts, which are always gravely illicit by reason of their object (murder, adultery, blasphemy and perjury) independently of circumstances and intentions (1756), do not facilitate any clear understanding of how the object and intention contrast each other, viewing the object from another perspective may clarify this ambiguity.

### III. b. i.  Intention and Object: Interior and Exterior Acts

In the above definition of the object, both intention and object "reside" in the subject morally because the object contains the intention of the subject in its very description. If, however, the object is considered as the "matter of a human act," which presumably is external to the acting subject, then the object may indeed contrast with the intention. Aquinas addressed this very distinction between an internal and external object in his *Summa;* the former is identified with the intention and the latter with the exterior act.

In q. 1, a. 1, Thomas asserts that what is characteristic of a human act is that it is a voluntary act whose object is the good which can be called the end of a human act: "the object of the will is the end and good. That is why all human acts must be for the sake of an end."[31] Thomas reiterates this in q. 1, a. 3. Consequently, in his discussion of an inner act of the will whereby the will chooses an end, object and end can be interchanged without changing the meaning of the statement.[32] Here, the object is the formal object of the interior act of the will. The object of the interior act of the will is what causes the will to choose the means of bringing about the end. The means are the external act to bring about the end of the inner act of the will. So, while the end is willed first in the mind, it is last in execution.[33] The will wills the end and then the means to attain that end. Thomas clarifies the apparent contradiction of the object specifying the act in q. 18, a. 2, or the end specifying the act in q. 1, aa. 1 and 3. In so doing, he makes the distinction between interior and exterior acts and their respective objects:

> In the voluntary acts are found two acts, namely the interior act of the will and the exterior act, and each of these has its own object. The end is properly the object of the interior voluntary act; the object of the exterior act is that on which it bears. Therefore, just as the exterior act is the kind of act it is because of its object, so the interior act of will is specified by the end as by its proper object. However, that which is from will is formal with regard to that which belongs to the exterior act, because the will uses the members as instruments in order to act, and exterior acts only have the note of morality insofar as they are voluntary. So it is that the species of the human act is formally taken from the end and materially from the object of the exterior act.[34]

So for instance, the exterior act of almsgiving is a right act by reason of its object. If done with the purpose or intention of alleviating poverty, helping one's neighbor, or out of love for God, it is also a morally good act. If, however, one gives alms in order to be praised by other people, St. Thomas would say that the object of the interior act of the will, the intention, is bad, and therefore the act is morally evil.[35] The interior object (the intention) and the exterior object (the exterior act) form the human act as a composite whole. In order for the human act to be morally good, the intention must be morally good and the exterior act must be right, or at least indifferent. If the intention is bad or the exterior act wrong, then the human act is morally bad. A morally good intention cannot make a wrong exterior act morally good. If this were the final word, however, then telling a falsehood (a wrong act) in order to protect an innocent human being (a good end or intention) could never be morally justified. Or, taking what belongs to another, an object bad of its kind,[36] in the case of dire need and with the good intention of self-preservation, could never be morally justified. For Thomas, however, such an act is morally justified.[37] Thus, even if the exterior object tends to be wrong, it can be morally justified in certain situations.

While Thomas' distinction between interior and exterior acts with their respective objects clarifies the *Catechism*'s claim that the object and intention contrast one another, this assertion is not reflected in the examples which the *Catechism* cites. All would agree that blasphemy, perjury, murder, and adultery (1756) are gravely illicit acts. What is open to discussion is whether or not these acts can be defined according to their object alone as the *Catechism* maintains, given its previous definitions of the object. Suffice it to say that not only is the *Catechism* extremely unclear in its presentation of the object, end, or intention, and the moral distinction between the two, but Thomas is ambiguous on this point as well. In the *Summa* he identifies acts such as murder (II–II, q. 64), theft and robbery (II–II, q. 66), fraud (II–II, q. 77), and lying (II–II, q. 110) as generic concepts designated by their object.[38] These acts, however, contain the agent's intention in their very definition. Consequently, we should not be surprised that the *Catechism* does not resolve this point. What is surprising is that it would include in its presentation this complex philosophical and theological issue.

### III. b. ii.  Intention and Fundamental Option

"Intention," the *Catechism* further asserts, "is not limited to directing individual actions, but can guide several actions toward one and the same purpose" (1752). Earlier, the human act was considered from various historical vantage points. This statement exemplifies Thomas' and the manualists notion of the human act where intention directs individual actions or a series of actions toward the goal intended by the agent's choice of the (external) object. Once the act or series of acts is complete, so is the end or intention. While the doctrine of fundamental option is not *explicitly* discussed in the *Catechism,* there is an implicit reference to it in the *Catechism*'s further definition of the intention: "it *can orient one's whole life toward its ultimate end*" (1752, emphasis added). This additional statement regarding the intention is unique to the *Catechism* and is only discussed in Thomas and the moral manuals under the auspices of the *finis ultimus,* one's ultimate end. Granted that fundamental option concerns one's basic, innermost freedom and the formation and expression of that freedom, whereas intention has to do with the *reasons* behind particular acts; if intention is expanded to include the orientation of one's whole life toward his or her ultimate end, the lines of demarcation between intention and fundamental option are broken down.

Clearly there is a distinction between these two senses of intention, yet the *Catechism* does not indicate the relationship between them.

While giving an example where the purpose of the individual act (helping one's neighbor) coincides with the purpose of one's life (love of God), it entirely skirts the issue where these two types of intention do not coincide, and the moral implications one has for the other. For instance, if a person, in a moment of human weakness, gives alms for the sake of vainglory, would it follow that this intention would alter the person's orientation toward his or her ultimate end, love of God? Ideally, one's intention in an individual act or a series of acts and one's orientation toward one's ultimate end coincide. How are we to judge cases where these two conflict? Do these different notions of intention carry the same moral weight? While "a good intention . . . [directing individual actions] does not make behavior that is intrinsically disordered . . . good or just," the question remains whether such an intention would alter one's orientation toward his or her ultimate end. This of course depends on the definition of intention and whether or not it carries the same moral weight as it is expressed in a single act or considered in relation to one's ultimate end. The *Catechism* does not address this issue, nor will it be expanded upon here. The point is that, rather than clarifying an under-standing of intention, the *Catechism* merely introduces fundamental questions which moral theologians have been struggling with for years, presumes that this is a clear, catechetical teaching, and moves on to the next agenda. The result is confusion and ambiguity as to how we are to understand the intention of the human act and its role and function in the moral evaluation of that act.

### III. c.  Circumstances

Regarding the third source of morality, the *Catechism* maintains that "*circumstances,* including the consequences, are secondary ele-ments of a moral act" (1754). As secondary elements, they may increase or diminish the moral goodness or evil of human acts or the agent's responsibility, but they cannot change the moral quality of acts, i.e., "they can make neither good nor right an action that is in itself evil." In this sense, circumstances affect the moral culpability of the agent, but cannot alter the moral quality of the act. There are several points of inconsistency with both Aquinas and the *Catechism*'s earlier statements on responsibility. We will consider each of these in turn.

### III. c. i. Aquinas on Circumstances

First of all, Aquinas, following Cicero, enumerates seven relevant circumstances attending human acts: who *(quis)*, what *(quid)*, where *(ubi)*, by what aids *(quibus auxiliis)*, why *(cur)*, how *(quomodo)*, and when *(quando)*.[39] In question 18, article 3, where Thomas specifically addresses circumstances in relation to the moral evaluation of the human act, he is interested in whether or not circumstances alter the specification from the object of the *kind* of act a moral act is (either good or bad), and if so, to what extent.

In response to this question, Aquinas uses the analogy of physical things which find their full perfection not only in the substantial form which gives a thing its specific nature, but also from supervening qualities *(accidentia)* which add to it. The same is true with moral activity writes Thomas: "For its full goodness as a whole is not constituted by what kind of act it is, but is filled out by additions which are like its qualities; such are its due circumstances. Accordingly if anything be missing in their count the act will be bad."[40] From this, he draws three conclusions. First, circumstances are external to the extent that they do not specify an act's nature. However, they do function as qualities which modify the action, and to that extent, remain internal to the act. Consequently, they are inherent qualities in the act, but do not constitute the act's essential nature. Secondly, he makes a distinction between circumstances as accidents, those which are accidental *(per accidens)* predicates, or essential *(proprium)* properties. The former are incidental to moral evaluation, whereas the latter are to be considered essentially related to, and morally relevant in, that evaluation. It is the role of moral science to examine (and determine) circumstances which are essential properties. Finally, Thomas maintains that good *(bonum)* can be applied to natural things and moral acts in both their kind and how they are qualified. That he makes this stipulation is significant in that it implies that the good of an act could be affected by the good (or bad) of the act's qualifications, i.e., its circumstances as essential properties. Furthermore, an act's qualifications must have implications for an act's moral goodness or badness; otherwise, there is no need to distinguish between the good of moral acts in their kind, and how they are qualified, for an act would be either good or bad in its specific kind, regardless of qualifications.

By qualifying circumstances as "secondary elements of a moral act," the *Catechism* ignores the case where circumstances belong to the act *per essentia,* and therefore, change the moral nature of the human act. One may speculate as to why the author(s) omits this qualification which is explicit in the *Summa*[41] as well as in the moral manuals.[42] One gets a hint from the single circumstance which is mentioned, consequences (1754). By restricting circumstances in general, and consequences in particular, to the realm of secondary elements, the *Catechism* virtually eliminates the consideration that consequences may indeed change the moral nature of a human act, and by implication, denies legitimacy to certain teleological theories which give foreseeable consequences a major consideration in the moral evaluation of that act.[43] Various traditions within Roman Catholicism have consistently taught that circumstances, including consequences, can change the moral nature of the act. By denying the moral significance of circumstances the *Catechism* is not faithful to those traditions.

### III. c. ii.  The *Catechism* and Circumstances

The first ambiguity within the *Catechism* itself concerns a consideration of circumstances and responsibility in relation to the moral act. Under Article 3, "Man's Freedom," the *Catechism* states: "*Imputability* and responsibility for an action can be diminished or even nullified by ignorance, inadvertence, duress, fear, habit, inordinate attachments, and other psychological or social factors" (1735). Specific circumstances of a human act include "environment, social pressure, duress, emergency, etc." (1756). While duress is the only common aspect between both lists, one could speculate that environment, social pressure, and emergency could come under either psychological or social factors which may diminish or nullify imputability and responsibility for an action. Thus, while asserting that circumstances can reduce, or even nullify personal responsibility, and further asserting that "circumstances of themselves cannot change the *moral* quality of acts themselves; they can make neither good nor right an action that is in itself evil" (1754, emphasis added), it is unclear in what sense the *Catechism* is using the term "moral." Surely, in order for a human act to be morally evaluated good or evil, the human person must be responsible for that act. We would not consider the act of a person who was forced at gunpoint to rob a grocery store (acting out of a fear of death) a morally bad act, even though we would consider the act itself a wrong act. The circumstances of coercion, duress, and fear in this instance nullify freedom and, therefore, moral culpability. If this is the case, then it seems that the *Catechism* must limit the term "moral" to acts. Thus robbery, in and of itself, is evil (more accurately, wrong), though it is not necessarily morally evil when certain circumstances are present. If this is the case, then it would be more accurate to say that "circumstances of themselves cannot change the *non*moral quality of acts themselves; they cannot make right an action that is in itself wrong," where nonmoral refers to acts independently of a moral subject. In its own explanation, the *Catechism* has interjected a dichotomy between act and agent, long recognized in philosophy and normative ethics, whereby even though an act may be wrong, it is not necessarily morally bad or evil. Elsewhere, however, the magisterium adamantly rejects this dichotomy.[44] Thus, the *Catechism* is left with an untenable position. Either circumstances can limit or even nullify the agent's responsibility, which is explicitly stated, and, therefore "moral" is limited to acts which, evil in themselves (wrong), cannot be made right. Or, circumstances, as "secondary elements of a moral act" cannot change the moral nature of the act, and moral refers to agent and act. This, however, is rejected by the *Catechism*'s statement concerning responsibility and the role of circumstances.

The second ambiguity pertains to the *Catechism*'s assessment of "Good Acts and Evil Acts," section II of Article 4. "A *morally good* act requires the goodness of the object, of the end, and of the circumstances together" (1755). This statement is reminiscent of Thomas' (and the manualists') reference to the aphorism of Psuedo-Dionysius in question 18, article 4: "Each single defect causes evil, whereas complete integrity is required for good." The question which is frequently begged in referring to Thomas' use of this aphorism as well as the *Catechism*'s own statement is that this pertains to *moral* goodness or evil. The question immediately comes to mind that if the circumstances cannot change the moral quality of an act, which the *Catechism* asserts in 1754, then even bad circumstances cannot change a morally good act to a morally bad act. If, however, we allow that circumstances can change the moral nature of an act, as is clear from both Thomas and the manualists, then this aphorism considers only morally good or bad circumstances whereas any other circumstances, including those circumstances defined by the *Catechism,* would not be a consideration in this aphorism. Thus, either: (1) circumstances could be eliminated from this aphorism; (2) the reference is to moral circumstances which affect the moral nature of an act; or (3) the aphorism applies to onto-logical goodness, not moral goodness. Since the *Catechism* and tradition consistently include circumstances as an essential consideration of this aphorism, and the *Catechism* explicitly states that circumstances cannot change the moral nature of a human act, we are left with option three as a viable alternative. A more plausible explanation is that whereas a (nonmorally) bad circumstance may detract from the overall ontological goodness of the act, it does not necessarily change the human act's moral character.[45] In this case, Pseudo-Dionysius' aphorism would refer to ontological goodness, not moral goodness. Thus, while each single defect may cause evil, this is an ontological evil which does not change the moral quality of the human act.

### III. d.  Good Acts and Evil Acts: The Relationship Between the Sources of Morality

As one might imagine, if the parts to a whole are ambiguous, the whole itself cannot be expected to be coherent. Such is the case with the interrelationship between the object, end, or intention and circum-stances. The *Catechism* asserts that "there are acts which, in and of themselves, independently of circumstances and intentions, are always gravely illicit by reason of their object" (1756). Acts which violate truth, such as perjury (1756) and lying (1753), are examples of those acts which are intrinsically disordered by reason of their object, regardless of intention and circumstances. Elsewhere, the *Catechism* discusses the eighth commandment and, following Augustine, asserts that "a lie consists in speaking a falsehood with the *intention* of deceiving" (2482, emphasis added). In this definition, the *Catechism* recognizes a distinction between the act (object?), telling a falsehood, and the malevolent intention, to deceive. It is difficult, if not impossible, to reconcile this definition which distinguishes between the act and intention which, combined, constitute a lie, with its previous definition which includes lying as an act intrinsically disordered according to its object. At this point one might ask where the line of demarcation lies (no pun intended!) between the object and intention? It is self-evident that a good intention cannot make behavior that is intrinsically disordered good or just if that intrinsically disordered act contains the malevolent intention in its very definition, as is the case with lying.

The *Catechism* further stipulates that the person being communicated to must have "the right to know the truth" (2483). This point is taken up in 2488, "the *right to the communication* of the truth is not unconditional," and 2489, "no one is bound to reveal the truth to someone who does not have the right to know it."[46] These further qualifications move beyond Thomas' and the manualists' focus on the individual act and its moral analysis and specifically interject the relational consideration of a human act, the human act adequately considered. Truth is not a platonic idea with which we either conform to or violate,[47] but is a manifestation of our interaction between and among human beings which has various meanings and degrees in light of those relationships. The definition of truth and the responsibility to communicate it is intimately tied to the relational considerations with those whom we interact. Granted that every person is our neighbor; the truth and the right to truth between spouses may be far different than that between employer and employee, and again, between complete strangers. Does this person with whom I am communicating, here and now, have a right to the truth? And if so, to what extent?

These questions are far removed from detailing the mere structure of the human act, its characteristics, and how they relate to one another. The judgment on the right to truth, of course, is based in part on the exercise of prudence and speculation as to how the person may use the truth (consequential considerations) and whether or not that person's use will promote the value of truth as we understand it, which is essentially a relational reality. These estimations are by no means simple or concise. As human beings, we are limited in our ability to analyze and assess a situation in its moral entirety over a period of time, let alone in the "heat of the moment." The *Catechism*'s interjection of these qualifications into the traditional definition of lying raises a primary consideration of morality, the relational element which is easily overlooked if we focus on the traditional sources of morality as those components which determine the moral nature of the human act. By introducing the relational consideration into the discussion of truth in particular, though it is an essential consideration of all moral behavior, perhaps unknowingly, the author(s) are recognizing the ambiguity in moral decision making and the tension between what is normally considered to be right or wrong (e.g., telling the truth vs. a falsehood) versus the moral response which a particular situation demands in light of our relationships, the context of the situation, and any other aspects which have an impact on our moral response.

Given these further considerations, is it morally meaningful to assert that some actions are intrinsically disordered according to their object alone, independently of circumstances or intention? Or does the focus on these aspects of the human act remove that act from reality and relationships which constitute the very core of morality? How are we to define the act of lying where a person does not have a right to know the truth? If, in a particular situation, it is clear that "being silent" or "making use of a discreet language" will not ensure "the good and safety of others, respect for privacy, and the common good" (2489), then would telling a falsehood with the intention to deceive in order to protect one of these goods be morally justified? If so, which seems indisputable given the *Catechism*'s own qualification on the right to truth, where does that leave our traditional definition and understanding of intrinsically evil acts according to their object alone, regardless of intention and circumstances? Is it coherent, consistent, or clear to rely upon the traditional sources of morality for determining a morally good or evil act?[48]

## IV.  Conclusion

With its emphasis on tradition, perhaps it would have been beneficial if the authors of the *Universal Catechism* would have followed the example of their predecessors who composed the *Roman Catechism* and had not included a discussion of the human act and the sources for morally evaluating that act. Neither the definition of the human act nor the sources which are utilized in its moral evaluation are consistently, or oftentimes coherently, defined throughout Catholic tradition(s). In fact, these topics have been, and continue to be, a major point of discussion, even contention, among the magisterium and many moral theologians. The fact is, neither St. Thomas nor tradition are entirely consistent in their terminology, and to introduce these terms into the *Catechism* is to foster confusion, rather than clarity which, presumably, is the *Catechism*'s primary objective.

# Notes

[1] The Prologue states that "this work is intended primarily for those responsible for catechesis." First and foremost are the bishops. "Through the bishops, it is addressed to redactors or catechisms, to priests, and to catechists. It will also be useful reading for all other Christian faithful." As commentaries, anthologies, and articles appear on the *Catechism,* it is becoming increasingly evident that even for scholarly theologians this text proves to be exceedingly complex and difficult reading in many areas.

[2] *S.T.,* I–II, q. 1, a. 1.

[3] *S.T.,* I–II, q. 1, a. 3; and q. 18, a. 8 (ET: Thomas Gilby, *St. Thomas Aquinas: Summa Theologiae* [London–New York: Blackfriars, 1966]).

[4] *S.T.,* I–II, q. 1, a. 1.

[5] *S.T.,* I–II, q. 18, a. 9.

[6] See, Norbert Rigali, "The Moral Act" (*Horizons* 10 [1983] 252–66). I am indebted to Fr. Rigali's insights in his article at several points in this section.

[7] See, Joseph Selling, "*Veritatis Splendor* and the Sources of Morality," Louvain Studies 19 (1994), 12.

[8] H. Noldin, A. Schmitt, and G. Heinzel, *Summa Theologiae Moralis* (30th ed.; Innsbruck: F. Rauch, 1952), vol. I, 66; and Dominic M. Prümmer, *Handbook of Moral Theology*, tr. Gerald W. Shelton (New York: P.J. Kenedy & Sons, 1957), 8. See N. Rigali, "The Moral Act," 252–53.

[9] Charles E. Curran, *Directions in Fundamental Moral Theology* (Notre Dame: University of Notre Dame Press, 1985), 127–32.

[10] "Decree on Priestly Formation" in Walter Abbott (ed.), *The Documents of Vatican II* (New York: America Press, 1966), 451–53, n. 16.

[11] For the development of a personalist methodology, and an elaboration of those dimensions which constitute the human person adequately considered, see Louis Janssens, "Artificial Insemination: Ethical Considerations," *Louvain Studies* 8 (1980), 3–15.

[12] Louis Monden, *Sin, Liberty and Law*, tr. Joseph Donceel, S.J. (New York: Sheed and Ward, 1965), 31.

[13] Richard A. McCormick, *Notes on Moral Theology: 1965 through 1980* (Washington, D.C.: University Press of America, 1981), 304.

[14] The *Catechism* does not explicitly refer to these limitations as circumstances in this paragraph. Further on, however, it explicitly states that these can be qualified as circumstances (1756). Also, under paragraph 1754, there is a cross-reference to paragraph 1735. See below.

[15] See N. Rigali, "The Unity of Moral and Pastoral Truth," *Chicago Studies* 25 (August, 1986), 224–32.

[16] See J. F. Keenan and his extensive work on the distinction between right and good: "What Is Good and What Is Right? A New Distinction in Moral Theology," *Church* 5 (1989), 22–28; "Distinguishing Charity as Goodness and Prudence as Rightness: A Key to Thomas's *Secunda Pars,*" *Thomist* 56 (1992), 389–411; and *Goodness and Rightness in Thomas Aquinas's Summa Theologiae* (Washington, D.C.: Georgetown University Press, 1992).

[17] W. K. Frankena, *Ethics* (Englewood Cliffs: Prentice Hall, 1963; 1973), 9–10.

[18] For example, on the issue of slavery. See B. Hoose, *Received Wisdom? Reviewing the Role of Tradition in Christian Ethics* (London: Geoffrey Chapman, 1994).

[19]    Rigali, "The Moral Act," 252–53.

[20]    *Ibid.*

[21]    For example, see H. Busenbaum, *Medulla theologiae moralis facili ac perspicua methodo resolvens casus conscientiae ex variis probatisque authoribus concinnata* (Palatio: 1650; new ed., 1671), 19 and 422ff. Busenbaum limits his discussion to the object or act and circumstances. This is so because, according to the traditional seven circumstances, *quid* and *cur* designate act and intention respectively. Thus, the end was discussed as one of the circumstances.

[22]    John Paul II, *Veritatis Splendor* (Vatican: Polyglot, 1993) (hereafter cited as *VS*). The encyclical does state, however, that *"The morality of the human act depends primarily and fundamentally on the 'object' rationally chosen by the deliberate will*, as is borne out by the insightful analysis, still valid today, made by Saint Thomas" (§78: Emphasis in text). Here, there is a reference to Thomas' *S.T.*, I–II, q.18, a. 6.

[23]    Jean Porter, "The Moral Act in *Veritatis Splendor* and in Aquinas's *Summa Theologiae:* A Comparative Analysis" in Michael E. Allsopp and John J. O'Keefe, *Veritatis Splendor: American Responses* (Kansas City: Sheed & Ward, 1995), 279.

[24]    *S.T.*, I–II, q. 8, a. 1; and q. 9, a. 1.

[25]    *S.T.*, I–II, q. 18, a. 2 ad 1.

[26]    *S.T.*, I, q. 5, aa. 4 and 5; q. 6, a. 1; q. 49, a. 1; q. 60, aa. 3 and 4; I–II, q. 8, a. 1; q. 72, a. 1.

[27]    *S.T.*, I–II, q. 18, a. 2, ad 2.  See also, *S.T.*, I–II, q. 1, a. 3.

[28]    Gilby (ed.), *S.T.*, I–II, vol. 18, 9, n. d.

[29]    Porter, "The Moral Act in *Veritatis Splendor*," 282.

[30]    See Gerard J. Hughes, "Our Human Vocation" in Michael J. Walsh, *The Catechism of the Catholic Church: A Commentary* (Collegeville: The Liturgical Press, 1994), 346.

[31]    *S.T.*, I–II, q. 1, a. 1.  See, Mark Van der Marck, "Ethics as a Key to Aquinas's Theology: The Significance of Specification by Object" (*Thomist* 40 [1976], 541).

[32]    Van der Marck, "Ethics," 547–48.

[33]    *S.T.*, I–II, q. 1, a. 1, ad 1.

[34]    *S.T.*, I–II, q. 18, a. 6.

[35]    *S.T.*, I–II, q. 20, a. 1.

[36]    *S.T.*, I–II, q. 18, a. 2.

[37]    *S.T.*, II–II, q. 66, a. 7.

[38]    See Porter, "The Moral Act in *Veritatis Splendor*," 284–87.

[39]    *S.T.*, I–II, q. 7, a. 3.

[40]    *S.T.*, I–II, q. 18, a. 3.

[41]    *S.T.*, I–II, q. 18, a. 10.

[42]    For example, see M. Prümmer, *Handbook of Moral Theology*, 22.

[43]    *VS*, 71–83.

[44]    *VS*, 75–76.

[45]    In reference to Thomas' use of this aphorism, the act is not simply good *(bona simpliciter)* unless it is good according to all four values:  generic, specific as directed to a proper objective, circumstances, and end. J. Gründel, *Die Lehre von den Umständen der Menschlichen Handlung im Mittelalter* (Münster, 1963), 54–55, points out that Pseudo-Dionysius' statement is metaphysical, not ethical. The "simply good," then, cannot be presumed to be synonymous with the "morally good" for Aquinas.

[46]    See J. A. Selling, "You Shall Love Your Neighbour: Commandments 4–10" in Michael J. Walsh, *The Catechism of the Catholic Church: A Commentary*, 385–88.

[47] For a discussion on the danger in ethical theory of treating values as Platonic ideas, see the exchange between R. P. George "Liberty Under the Moral Law: B. Hoose's Critique of the Grisez–Finnis Theory of Human Good," *Heythrop Journal* 34 (1993), 175–82, and B. Hoose, "Proportionalists, Deontologists and the Human Good," *Heythrop Journal* 33 (1992), 175–91, and "Basic Goods: Continuing the Debate," *Heythrop Journal* 35 (1994), 58–63.

[48] I have intentionally omitted a discussion of the frequently cited aphorism both in the *Catechism* (1753, 1756, 1759, 1761, 1789) and in *VS* (79–83), "One may never do evil so that good may result from it" (or similar versions) taken from Rom 3:8 for three reasons. First, Scriptural exegetes question the relevance of Paul's saying to moral theology (R.F. Collins, "And Why Not Do Evil That Good May Come?" in *Christian Morality: Biblical Foundations* [Notre Dame: University of Notre Dame Press, 1986] 238–53). Second, the saying itself, even if it is (mis)used within moral theological discourse, fails to distinguish between moral and premoral, nonmoral, or ontic good and evil. This distinction is a contemporary philosophical/theological one that, while by no means accepted by all moral theologians, helps clarify various aspects of moral theological discourse. See, for example, R.A. McCormick, "Killing the Patient: *Veritatis Splendor* in Focus, 3," *The Tablet* 247 [30 October, 1993] 1410–11. Third, as Gerard J. Hughes, "Our Human Vocation," in Michael J. Walsh, *The Catechism of the Catholic Church: A Commentary*, 347–48, points out, the assertion that "the end does not justify the means" begs the question as to the relationship between acts and circumstances and which circumstances can alter the act's very nature where, perhaps, the end *may* justify the means (e.g., missing Mass on Sunday to care for a loved one). As such, however, the aphorism does not function as an argument to settle controversial ethical issues. We have already addressed the relationship between the act and its circumstances and its implications on the moral nature of the act above.

# Marriage in the *Catechism:*
# Pastoral Observations

### Ann S. F. Swaner

What is the first thing one notices about the presentation of marriage in the *Catechism of the Catholic Church*? It begins with a quotation, not from Vatican II, but from the *Code of Canon Law* (1601). The Second Vatican Council provided a clear development of the Catholic understanding of marriage by emphasizing conjugal love as the foundation of marriage rather than institutions or functions. The Council drew upon the resources of personalist philosophy and biblical scholarship, took the elements of the traditional teaching, and put them in a new, less juridical perspective. The stated purpose of the *Catechism* is to present essential Catholic doctrine "in the light of the Second Vatican Council and the whole of the Church's tradition" (11); and it does repeat much of the language of Vatican II. However, this essay will show that the new *Catechism*'s treatment of marriage, what it says about sacramentality, covenant, and sexuality, mutes the personal emphases of Vatican II by its emphasis on marriage's indissolubility, and by the reintroduction of the legal language of contract and of the ends of marriage, both avoided by Vatican II. Further, I will demonstrate that because the *Catechism*'s governing understanding of marriage is a juridical one focused on the creation of an indivisible bond, it actually reverses the thrust of the Council's understanding of covenant, contract, and marriage's indissolubility.

Second, the *Catechism,* following the pattern of the *Roman Catechism* of Pius V, is structured in four parts: the profession of faith, the sacraments of faith, the life of faith, and prayer in the life of faith. The sacramentality of marriage is dealt with in part two; family life is discussed in part three under the fourth commandment; sexuality and offenses against the dignity of marriage are dealt with in part three under the sixth and ninth commandments. An unfortunate consequence of this divided and fragmented treatment of marriage and sexuality is that the *Catechism*'s positive appreciation of sexuality is not integrated into its understanding of the sacramentality of marriage. The *Catechism*'s discussion of the love of husband and wife says that "Sexuality is ordered to the conjugal love of man and woman. In marriage the physical intimacy of the spouses becomes a sign and pledge of spiritual communion" (2360). But the text places too much emphasis on the marriage's "bonds" and its "twofold end."

This essay will demonstrate each of these points so that those who use the *Catechism* will be better prepared to meet the challenges of their roles—when dealing, in particular, with those aware of the personalist and future-looking insights fundamental to the Second Vatican Council's documents, and the moral theology inspired by the Council.

## I. Human Dignity

Vatican II deals with marriage and family life in the first chapter of Part 2 of the Pastoral Constitution on *The Church in the Modern World (Gaudium et Spes)*. In article 46 of this text, the Council sets the context for the discussion of marriage as that of the dignity of the human person. Marriage is one of the urgent and complex problems of the present age which "go to the roots of the human race." The Council proposes to consider it "in the light of the Gospel and of human experience."

This rooting of the nature of marriage in the dignity of man and woman created in the image of God, rather than in Augustine's three goods, was initiated by Vatican II, continued in *Humanae Vitae,* and maintained in the writings of John Paul II. The *Catechism of the Catholic Church* also grounds its understanding of marriage in the dignity of man and woman as created in the image of God and fundamentally oriented to love (1604). The equal personal dignity of man and woman is also stressed throughout (1645, 2203, 2334, 2335, 2387). "Each of the two sexes is an image of the power and tenderness of God, with equal dignity though in a different way," the *Catechism* states. "Called to give life, spouses share in the creative power and fatherhood of God" (2367).[1] The *Catechism* shows its indebtedness to the Council's theology—its acceptance of the personalist, Biblical theology that has come to dominate Roman Catholic discussions about marriage and sexuality: "God who created man out of love also calls him to love—the fundamental and innate vocation of every human being. For man is created in the image and likeness of God who is himself love"( 1604).

## II. Sacramentality of Marriage

Vatican II attempted to elucidate the personal characteristics of marriage as a sacrament of the Church. Marriage is described in article 48 as an "intimate partnership of married life and love." The Council affirms the traditional teaching on marriage as "established by the Creator and qualified by His laws," but the emphasis on love as belonging *to the essence* of marriage as established by God is new.[2] This intimate partnership is "rooted in the conjugal covenant of irrevocable personal consent." The Council stresses that marriage is irrevocable in view of the total gift of self-sacrificing love by the couple (rather than that it must be a total self gift because it is irrevocable). In this interpersonal and communitarian view of marriage, less attention is given to its strictly juridical aspects, although these are not neglected.

The Council describes the "good" of the sacrament in very personalist terms as a meeting with Christ: "For as God of old made Himself present to His people through a covenant of love and fidelity, so now the Savior of men and the Spouse of the Church comes into the lives of married Christians through the sacrament of matrimony." The effect of this meeting with Christ is that the spouses are strengthened in their love for each other; they are led by this love to God and they are strengthened in the fulfillment of their vocations as parents.[3]

Article 49 then gives a phenomenological description of marital love: it is eminently human; it involves the good of the whole person; it is healing and perfecting. Marital love is "distinguished from every other form of friendship by the specificity of sexuality as an external symbol of what has been interiorly given, namely, one's whole self as a gift to the other." Again the Council places the faithfulness and indissolubility of marriage in the context of conjugal love, and of the equal dignity of man and woman:

> Sealed by mutual faithfulness and hallowed above all by Christ's sacrament, this love remaining steadfastly true in body and in mind, bright days or dark. It will never be profaned by adultery or divorce. Firmly established by the Lord, the unity of marriage will radiate from the equal personal dig-

nity of wife and husband, a dignity acknowledged by mutual and total love. (49)

In the *Catechism*, we find some surprising changes to the Council's teaching. Sacramentality is equated with indissolubility; the sacrament is the sanctification of the marriage bond. The richness of the personalist description of the sacramentality of marriage by Vatican II is obscured here by a stress on marriage's indissolubility. These are significant—and unfortunate—differences.[4]

To explain. The *Catechism*'s discussion of the sacramentality of marriage begins with an explanation of marriage in God's plan (1601). It emphasizes the divine institution of marriage and the laws which govern it (1602). The text asserts that the vocation to marriage is written in the nature of man and woman; that it is "good, very good, in the Creator's eyes" (1604). Further, the *Catechism* affirms that marriage is no less valuable than virginity as a Christian vocation (1620). The "order of creation" is seriously disturbed, however, by sin and is in need of God's grace (1608). However, under the law of Israel, God's people gradually came to understand the unity and indissolubility of marriage through the prophets' comparison of God's covenant with Israel to exclusive and faithful married love (1610–1611).

As one examines the text, the impression forms that marriage "in the Lord" is about love and "a great mystery" to be sure (1616), but that the *Catechism* is focused on the "unequivocal insistence on the indissolubility of the marriage bond" (1615). "In his preaching Jesus unequivocally taught the original meaning of the union of man and woman as the Creator willed it from the beginning; permission given by Moses to divorce one's wife was a concession to the hardness of hearts. The matrimonial union of man and woman is indissoluble: God himself has determined it: 'what therefore God has joined together, let no man put asunder,'" we read in 1614. Further, in the *Catechism,* the grace of the sacrament is the ability to receive this original meaning of marriage as indissoluble (1615).

The medievals had difficulty fitting marriage into their sacramental system, with its two ministers (and one a woman!) and its involvement with sexuality, which seemed incompatible with grace-giving.[5] Modern theology of the sacraments, which emphasizes the place of sacraments in relation to the mission of the Church, has no less trouble fitting marriage in. Likewise the Church's canonists had difficulties in revising the *Code of Canon Law*.[6] The scholastic notion of the "sacramental reality" is today understood as a particular relation to the Church, except in the case of marriage; the *res et sacramentum* of marriage is still the indivisible bond between two individuals. The judgment that marriage is constituted simply by the consent of the two marriage partners without regard for their families or the community contributes to this patently individualistic view.[7]

On this point, an intriguing passage in the *Catechism* refers to the differing tradition of the Eastern Church in regard to the ministers of the sacrament of marriage:

> In the Latin Church, it is *ordinarily understood* [emphasis added] that the spouses, as ministers of Christ's grace, mutually confer upon each other the sacrament of Matrimony before the Church. In the Eastern liturgies the minister of this sacrament (which is called "Crowning") is the priest or bishop who, after receiving the mutual consent of the spouses, successively crowns the bridegroom and the bride as a sign of the covenant. (1623)

Are there exceptions to this ordinary norm in the Western Church? The Council of Trent was very careful in its canons on matrimony not to condemn the teaching of the Eastern Church on divorce and remarriage. An openness to the Eastern tradition with its much more communal understanding of both marriage and divorce is welcome. Perhaps the interrelation of the personal and communal aspects of marriage might be celebrated by a recognition that, while the marriage partners are ministers of the sacrament, the participation of the whole Church, signified by the person of the priest or deacon, is also essential to the sacrament.[8]

### III. Covenant

One of the key developments in Vatican II's treatment of marriage is the shift from the concept of marriage as a contract to that of marriage as a covenant.[9] The Council variously describes marriage as a "community of love," "mutual gift of two persons," as "pact," and as "covenant," but not as "contract." Paul Palmer has provided a classic description of the differences between the concepts of covenant and contract:

> Contracts deal with things; covenants with people. Contracts engage the services of people; covenants engage persons. Contracts are made for a stipulated period of time; covenants are forever. Contracts can be broken, with material loss to the contracting parties; covenants cannot be broken, but if violated, they result in personal loss and broken hearts. Contracts are secular affairs and belong to the market place; covenants are sacral affairs and belong to the hearth, the temple, or the Church. Contracts are best understood by lawyers, civil and ecclesiastical; covenants are appreciated better by poets and theologians. Contracts are witnessed by people with the state as guarantor; covenants are witnessed by God with God as guarantor. Contracts can be made by children who know the value of a penny; covenants can be made only by adults who are mentally, emotionally, and spiritually mature.[10]

By choosing to deal with marriage as a covenant, Vatican II took the discussion out of the impersonal legal language of objects and rights, and placed it into the language of persons and interpersonal relationships.[11]

Now the first section of the *Catechism* dealing with marriage in God's plan uses the covenant language of Vatican II to describe the development from creation through the history of Israel to the Christian understanding of sacramental marriage, and of "moral conscience concerning the unity and indissolubility of marriage" (1610). The *Catechism*'s opening statement on the sacrament of matrimony reads: "The matrimonial covenant, by which a man and a woman establish between themselves a partnership of the whole of life, is by its nature ordered toward the good of the spouses and the procreation and education of offspring; this covenant between baptized persons has been raised by Christ the Lord to the dignity of a sacrament" (1601). "Covenant" is used frequently in subsequent sections. However, the scholastic and juridical discussion of matrimonial consent (1625–1631) raises the suspicion that the word "covenant" has simply been standing in for "contract." For instance, the contract language is explicit in the section on consent and validity:

> "The parties to a marriage covenant are a baptized man and woman, free to *contract* marriage . . ." (1625, emphasis added)

"The consent must be an act of the will of each of the *contracting* parties . . ." (1628, emphasis added)

"This is the reason why the Church normally requires that the faithful *contract* marriage according to the ecclesiastical form." (1631, emphasis added)

As I have intimated earlier in this essay, there is evidence from a comparison of the texts that Vatican II stated that the indissolubility of marriage is inherent in the covenantal nature of the mutual gift of self-bestowal; and that John Paul II further developed this teaching in *Familiaris Consortio,* cited here by the *Catechism* (1643). But, in the latter's juridical discussion of the effects of the sacrament, it is implied that the *covenant arises from* the metaphysical, indissoluble *bond,* a reversal, in fact, of the Church's current teaching.[12]

For instance. "Thus *the marriage bond* has been established by God himself in such a way that a marriage concluded and consummated between baptized persons can never be dissolved. This bond, which results from the free human act of the spouses and their consummation of the marriage, is *a reality* [emphasis added], henceforth irrevocable, and *gives rise to a covenant* [emphasis added] guaranteed by God's fidelity" (1640). Surely Vatican II would have the bond arising from the covenant, not the covenant from the bond! This is a serious revision of recent Catholic moral and sacramental theology—a reversal that merits correction.

Another example. In the discussion of offenses against the dignity of marriage in Part Three, adultery and divorce are defined as offenses because they break the contract on which marriage is based (2381, 2384). Conjugal fidelity is also equated with indissolubility: "The covenant they freely *contracted* imposes on the spouses the obligation to preserve it as unique and indissoluble" (2364, emphasis added). Here again, we find that contract surpasses covenant.

There is, of course, no absolute opposition between covenant and contract. The language of marriage as a contract arose out of a concern for justice and freedom of consent, as Orsy et al. make plain. Love and covenant values are not opposed to justice and freedom but presuppose them. Use of the contract language, however, even alongside the covenant language, puts the consideration of marriage back in the realm of laws and institutions rather than of persons and relationships. It also has ecumenical implications for Protestant-Catholic dialogue.

## IV. Sexuality

From *"Casti Conubii"* in 1930 until Vatican II, the Church's magisterium had been preoccupied by the problem of the hierarchy of the "ends" of marriage; this teaching was heavily dependent on the formulations of canon law. The Second Vatican Council, discussing the "various benefits and purposes" of matrimony, consistently refrained from using the language of primary and secondary ends or purposes. The traditional emphasis on the value of procreation was maintained but not held to be more important than conjugal love: "By their very nature, the institution of matrimony itself and conjugal love are ordained for the procreation and education of children and find in them their ultimate crown" (*Gaudium et Spes,* 48). The good of "mutual help and service" then is presented not as subordinate to procreation but in its own intrinsic significance:

> Thus a man and a woman, who by the marriage covenant of conjugal love "are no longer two, but one flesh," render mutual help and service to each other through an intimate union of their persons and of their actions. Through this union they experience the meaning of their oneness and attain to it with growing perfection day by day. As a mutual gift of two persons, this intimate union, as well as the good of the children, imposes total fidelity on the spouses and argues for an unbreakable oneness between them. (48)

Recent Catholic theology has developed the Council's position, as we see in Lisa Sowle Cahill's 1986 summary of recent ethical literature on sexual morality and on the Christian meanings of marriage and family: "In marriage and sexuality, experience in our time shows more clearly that commitment is grounded in the affective dimensions of relationship, though it also requires for its stability social and ecclesial institutionalization. Thus love is the foundation and the inclusive 'end' of the partnership which is marriage, while the nurturing of children is an important outgrowth of that partnership."[13]

The discussion of sexuality in Part Three of the *Catechism of the Catholic Church,* under the Sixth Commandment, begins with a holistic description of sexuality as affecting the whole person (2332); an assertion of the equal though different dignity of men and women (2334); and a strikingly positive presentation of chastity (2337–2359).

Sexual difference and complementarity are oriented to the goods of marriage and family. Chastity "means the successful integration of sexuality within the person" which makes possible the gift of an integral self in marriage; it is "a school of the gift of the person" (2346). Further, the *Catechism* takes the realistic position that the development of the virtue of chastity is a lifelong task which progresses through stages (2342–2343). Offenses against chastity are seen as violations of human dignity and of the orientation of sexuality to the goods of marriage (2351–2356). Homosexual activity, however, is described as a violation of natural law (2357).

In the discussion of the love of husband and wife, love and sexual pleasure are affirmed (2360–2361), but the "bond" again becomes focal and the pre-Vatican II language of the "ends" of marriage is re-introduced, alongside the language of meaning, value, and gift. For instance:

> The spouses' union achieves the twofold *end* [emphasis added] of marriage: the good of the spouses themselves and the transmission of life. These two meanings or values of marriage cannot be separated without altering the couple's spiritual life and compromising the goods of marriage and the future of the family. (2363)

> Fecundity is a gift, an *end of marriage* . . . (2366)

Here again, as William Spohn has argued in connection with the *Catechism*'s moral vision, one has the impression that the *Catechism* owes more to the concerns that produced the *Catechism of the Council of Trent* than to the initiatives of Vatican II, or the positive developments in Roman Catholic moral theology since the Council.[14]

Finally, in speaking about sexuality, the *Catechism* presents (as one would expect) the Church's magisterial teaching on the immorality of artificial contraception (2370), on sex outside of marriage (2400), on homosexual activity (2357–2359), and other offenses against chastity. It follows the reasoning of *Humanae Vitae* about the inseparable connection between the unitive and procreative "significances" of the marriage act (2366–2379)—all in keeping with the Church's traditional view of morality as a kind of practical knowledge that involves actions, choices, character, and beatitude (1700).

To recap. Leaving aside the fact that the *Catechism*'s commandment structure gives the impression that morality is simply a matter of obedience to laws, the most disappointing aspect of the treatment of conjugal sexuality is that it is not integrated into the sacramentality of marriage. The emphasis on sexuality as oriented to the goods of marriage is a natural law understanding, not a sacramental one. The structure of the *Catechism,* in which the sacramentality of marriage is treated in Part Two and sexuality in Part Three, contributes to the fragmentation and lack of unity. But the identification of sacramentality with indissolubility and of fidelity with indissolubility contributes even more. Where sacramentality is specifically mentioned in Part Three it refers to the bond: "Marriage *bonds* [emphasis added] between baptized persons are sanctified by the sacrament" (2360).

Finally, the suggestion that a marriage without sex is a solution to irregular second marriage situations (1650)—a solution that is being formalized in pastoral-practice guidelines in American dioceses—reinforces the idea that sexuality has not been properly (let alone fully) integrated into the "intimate partnership of married life and love," that rather, the canonical right to sexual acts can and should be separated from the relationship of love between the partners.[15] Vatican II suggested that sexuality be seen as a sign of the "friendship distinctive of marriage" (*Gaudium et Spes,* 49). The statement is made in the *Catechism* (but not developed) that chastity is related to friendship:

> Chastity is expressed notably in *friendship with one's neighbor.* Whether it develops between persons of the same or opposite sex, friendship represents a great good for all. It leads to spiritual communion. (2347)

People entering marriage today expect a spiritual communion that might be called friendship. To reconcile the friendship dimension of marriage with the meaning of sexuality and to explicate how that is "a great good for all" is an urgent task for any pastorally sensitive theology of marriage. This leads me to my next and final subject.

## V. Marriage in the Modern World and in the *Catechism*

Vatican II recognized that in the modern world marriage is an urgent and complex problem. Marriage and family life have lost many, if not most, of the institutional social functions that they had in pre-industrial society. The family is no longer primarily an economic, educative, child-producing unit. Now it is a chief locus of meaning, identification, emotional and psychological support, intimacy, warmth, and understanding. The weakening of other social institutions has placed more burdens on marriage and family relationships while providing them with less support.

Demographic factors such as longer life-spans and lower infant mortality rates affect expectations for marriage and family life. A marriage in which spouses can expect to live into their eighties and in which therefore child-rearing will occupy only a relatively short period, involves different demands, expectations, and rewards than one which can be expected to end by the death of one of the spouses before the child-rearing years are over. Almost everywhere, as we move into the twenty-first century, the expectations, motives, and goals for marriage are personal rather than social. Discussion of sexuality today focuses on its meaning for human persons. It is common to speak of sexuality as a language, a means of interpersonal communication. Pope John Paul II exhibits this worldwide trend. For instance, in a General Audience on December 19, 1979, the pope said: "The whole biblical narrative, and in particular the Yahwist text, shows that the body through its own visibility manifests man and, manifesting him, acts as intermediary, that is, enables man and woman, right from the beginning, 'to communicate' with each other according to that *communio personarum* willed by the Creator precisely for them."[16]

Sexuality is also seen as an integrative force which helps to humanize and personalize human relationships. The conscious integration of sex and love is seen as a distinctive contemporary possibility. The call is for a positive evaluation of sexuality based on human and personal values and for a sexual morality based on personal responsibility.

Yet the Church and society have generally agreed in refusing to consider marriage and sexuality as purely personal and private matters, insisting that sexuality is related to marriage and that marriage is also a social institution. Sexuality and marriage have been regulated in every culture, as in laws of exogamy and prohibition of incest, in the interest of the survival of the society and of individuals. Some question today whether survival requires such regulation any longer; whether society has any need to regulate that which is not necessary for survival. This issue is at stake (I believe) in the current debate about "homosexual marriage."

It is however a mistake to regard the social aspects of marriage as opposed to, or even in addition to, the personal. The private, individual, personal model of interpersonal relations as a basis for marriage has its own problems against an overly juridical model. Church leaders and others are not wrong to insist that a marriage model based on a mutually fulfilling, self-justifying, interpersonal relationship which is incapable of or unconcerned with commitment to anything beyond itself can be profoundly depersonalizing. The privatization of marriage does not necessarily lead to its personalization. Human persons are inherently social. Although a paradox, the social is essential precisely because it is part of marriage *as personal*. Social values can be personal if the personal is not confined to the individual; the social is not reduced to the juridical.[17]

The Roman Catholic Church's view of marriage has tended to neglect the personal, while being overly individualistic; to see the social mainly in institutional and juridical terms. This perspective is inadequate to the present situation where what is needed is a revisioning of the communal/social dimension to keep the personal from being reduced to the private and divorced from the social. In order to be relevant in the daily lives of married Christians today, the Church's teaching must better reconcile the personal and the social, in less individualistic and less legalistic ways. Perhaps, as Ladislaus Orsay has stated, "about the doctrine and law of Christian marriage; we ought to think afresh."[18]

The social dimension may be less institutional, certainly less juridical, but it is no less essential to the personal meaning of marriage. For example, for the Church's teaching on divorce to be helpful in a cultural situation in which more than half of all marriages, including Catholic marriages, end in divorce, it is not enough to remind people that they are living in public adultery (2384). To develop the personal characteristics of indissolubility might be to emphasize its character as promise, possibility, gift, even as moral demand, rather than as law or as metaphysical bond. A more social view would recognize the contribution of the community and of the Church to the breakdown of marriages; this sorry situation cannot be attributed simply to a failure of will in individuals.

People want their marriages to last forever; they need to hear how entering into a sacramental marriage can offer or enable that possibility. That message requires the development of an understanding of the distinctive form of friendship that is marriage and the integration of sexuality into that understanding. Thus, one of the most fundamental questions about marriage raised in contemporary culture is that of the correlation between the personal and social dimensions of marriage, in view of the loss of many institutional functions of marriage and family and the changes in expectations and motives for marriage.

A sacramental vision of marriage which places the personal relationship that constitutes a marriage at the heart of the Church's mission suggests an answer to that question. The teaching of Vatican II moved in the direction of that kind of vision in its attempt to develop the personal content of the sacramentality of marriage, its description of marriage as a personal covenant, its recovery of the view of the family as domestic church, and its appreciation of a distinctive kind of friendship in marriage, symbolized by sexuality. It deemphasized the juridical without losing sight of the social; the very placement of the discussion of marriage in the Council's Constitution on the *Church in the Modern World* underscored this. What is needed now is to further elucidate the personal characteristics of sacramental marriage and to define more clearly and concretely its place in the mission of the church. Unfortunately, the *Catechism* has not done this.

## VI. Conclusion

The *Catechism* follows Vatican II in rooting the nature of marriage in human dignity and the vocation to love; in seeing marriage as not less than celibacy as a Christian vocation; in viewing love as no less important than procreation; and in its description of the family as domestic church. However, its move back to a more juridical stance hinders the crucial task of reconciling the personal (not necessarily private) and social (not necessarily legal) aspects of marriage in ways that make sense to married Christians at the end of the twentieth century. The *Catechism* has missed a significant opportunity to develop and advance the Church's theology.

The understanding of God's relationship with God's people and the model of the marriage relationship have mutually reflected and reinforced each other since the time of Hosea. As the Vatican II Church struggled to understand itself less juridically and more in terms of its life of love, a more personal, relational approach to marriage was pointed to and given shape. Now, as the 1990s Church seeks to express its teachings in a "universal catechism" (which will be the basis of catechesis for years ahead), the approach to marriage is again—sadly and unnecessarily—more juridical and objective.

## Notes

[1] For the background to these developments, Edward Schillebeeckx, *Marriage: Human Reality & Saving Mystery* (New York: Sheed & Ward, 1965). Also, Michael G. Lawler, *Secular Marriage, Christian Sacrament* (Mystic: Twenty-Third, 1985).

[2] On the place of love as the key to the whole of the marriage relationship, John R. Connery, "The Role of Love in Marriage: A Historical Overview," *Communio* 11 (1984), 244ff.

[3] For further on this subject, Michael G. Lawler, "Marriage, Sacrament of" in *The New Dictionary of Sacramental Worship*, Peter E. Fink, editor (Collegeville: Liturgical Press, 1990), 805–818.

[4] For an important discussion of this subject, Ladislas Orsy, "The Issue of Indissolubility: An Inquiry," *Thought* 59 (1984), 360–372. Also the same author's earlier study, "Faith, Sacrament, Contract, and Christian Marriage: Disputed Questions," *Theological Studies* 43, 3 (September 1982), 379–398.

[5] On this subject, James A. Schmeier, "Marriage, Ministers of," in *The New Dictionary of Sacramental Worship*, 801–803.

[6] For a valuable commentary on the revisions of the canon law on marriage, Francis Morrissey, "Revising Church Legislation on Marriage," *Origins* 9 (1979), 209–218.

[7] Another problem exacerbated by an overly individualist, juridical understanding of the sacrament, which is not dealt with by either the *Catechism* or Vatican II, is the problem of baptised unbelievers.

[8] On the Western and Eastern theologies of marriage, Alexander Schmennan, "The Indissolubility of Marriage: The Theological Tradition of the East," in *The Bond of Marriage: An Ecumenical and Interdisciplinary Study*, edited by William W. Bassett (Notre Dame: University of Notre Dame Press, 1968), 97–116.

[9] On this subject, Denise Lardner Carmody, "Marriage in Roman Catholicism,"*Journal of Ecumenical Studies*, 22 (1985), 28–40. Also: Lawler, Orsy, etc.

[10] Paul F. Palmer, "Christian Marriage: Contract or Covenant?" *Theological Studies* 33 (1972), at 639. Also, Wilfrid J. Harrington, *The Promise to Love: A Scriptural View of Marriage* (New York: Alba House, 1968).

[11] On this subject, Michael G. Lawler, "Faith, Contract, and Sacrament in Christian Marriage: A Theological Approach," *Theological Studies*, 52, 4 (December 1991), 712–731.

[12] For Aidan Nichols' comments on this section of the Catechism, *The Service of Glory*, 89–95, 213–214.

[13] Lisa Sowle Cahill, "Notes on Moral Theology," *Theological Studies* 47, 1 (March 1986), 117.

[14] See: Willian C. Spohn, "The Moral Vision of the Catechism: Thirty Years That Did Not Happen," *America* 3 (March 1990), 189–192.

[15] On the important issue of the place of the sacraments in the life of the divorced and remarried, besides Lawler, Orsy et al., Matthäus Kaiser, "Why Should the Divorced and Remarried (Not) Be Admitted to the Sacraments?" *Theology Digest*, 41 (1994) 8–14.

[16] John Paul II, *Original Unity of Man and Woman: Catechesis on the Book of Genesis* (Boston: St. Paul Editions, 1981), 97.

[17] On the need for a new vision of marriage, Joseph Martos, "A New Conceptual Framework for Thinking about the Sacramentality of Marriage," *New Theology Review* 9, 1 (1996), 42–57.

[18] Orsy, *Theological Studies*, 398.

# Homosexuality and the *Catechism* of the Catholic Church

**Robert Nugent**

## I. Introduction

The single entry for homosexuality in the *Catechism of the Catholic Church* is found under the heading "Chastity and homosexuality" in Part Three ("Life in Christ"), Section Two, ("The Ten Commandments in Brief"), Chapter Two, ("You Shall Love Your Neighbor as Yourself"), and Article 6, ("The Sixth Commandment").[1] The *Catechism*'s teaching on homosexuality is the Roman magisterium's 4th major pronouncement since 1975.[2] Three prior Vatican documents discussed theological, pastoral, and sociological aspects of homosexuality, indicating slight but significant developments in the Church's understanding of the sensitive and complex reality of homosexuality.[3] Apart from these Roman documents, national episcopal magisterial sources have addressed various aspects of homosexuality from within local ecclesial settings in various parts of the world.[4]

## II. Definitions and Distinctions

The opening section of the *Catechism* defines homosexuality as *relations* between men or women, but does not further specify in what these relations consist. The word was first used by the Vatican in 1975 in a context which referred specifically to sexual or genital relations.[5] Even if that narrow or limited meaning is still intended in the *Catechism,* and it seems that it is, it is important for educators not to reduce the definition of homosexuality to sexual behavior. A more nuanced and balanced definition needs to make clear that in contemporary understandings the reality of homosexual identity comprises and affects much more than sexual/genital acts.[6] A commonly accepted distinction is that between homosexuality as *orientation* and homosexuality as *genital acts*. It is crucial to be aware of this distinction in educational and therapeutic endeavors and to understand its implications, both positive and negative, for a more accurate and balanced presentation of contemporary Church teachings on homosexuality.[7] The distinction itself is not without internal tensions both theoretically and pastorally and has been critiqued by philosophers, theologians and, more tellingly, by homosexual people who do not see it as doing justice or adequately representing their personal experience of sexuality.[8]

It is important to realize that when we use the general term "homosexuality" we can mean either same-sex genital *acts* or a *homosexual orientation*. Likewise, when we use the term "homosexual relationship," we might be using it to mean, more broadly, an interpersonal *relationship of friends* characterized by same-sex orientation and identity but not involving genital expression. In talking about homosexual relations it should be made clear to audiences that the term need not be solely identified with or limited to sexual acts, but that it can refer to a wider range of human experiences affected by an individual's sexual orientation which is but one component of personal sexual identity.[9] Furthermore, this broader understanding of homosexual relations can be seen as related to the magisterium's definition of sexuality which, based on scientific research, says that "the human person is so profoundly affected by sexuality that it must be considered as one of the factors which give to each individual's life the principal traits that distinguish it."[10] Even more directly, the U.S. Catholic bishops stress that sexuality is a "relational" power, not merely a capacity for performing specific acts. They cite the Vatican's Congregation for Catholic Education which claims that sexuality is a "fundamental component of personality, one of its modes of being, of manifestation, of communicating with others, of feeling, of expressing and living human love."[11]

It is this appreciation of the homosexual orientation as related to feelings and expressions of human love and interpersonal intimacy rather than simply with genital acts that marks a significant advancement in the Church's understanding of homosexuality and its pastoral ministry to gay and lesbian people. The identification of gay and lesbian individuals with their sexual orientation and the additional identification of their sexual orientation with genital behaviors are serious obstacles to a realistic understanding of homosexuality and, hence, to effective pastoral ministry. Both socially and pastorally such reductions help perpetuate discrimination and injustice against this group of individuals.[12]

The second and more precise segment of the *Catechism*'s definition of homosexuality speaks of men and women who experience "an exclusive or predominant sexual attraction towards persons of the same sex." Once again, as with the term "relations," the *Catechism*'s use of the term "sexual attraction" ought not be automatically identified simply with sexual attraction much less with sexual acts. Sexual attraction normally includes erotic feelings, physiological responses, and the desire for some kind of intimacy with the object of attraction. But sexual attraction can also be part of a deeper human desire and need for emotional intimacy and bonding as well—attractions which can be acknowledged and dealt with without recourse to any form of specific genital embodiment. Sexual attraction, then, including homosexual attraction, can be a positive basis for certain forms of friendship, bonding, and commitment. Intimacy might also be part of such a relationship provided such intimacy is understood in a broader sense which need not be expressed in any overt genital activity.[13]

If, on the pastoral level, the Church were to acknowledge and support the possibility of such relationships as morally sound and psychologically helpful for gay and lesbian people, this would be a significant and positive step toward healing the sense of alienation that many homosexual people experience.[14] For many lesbian and gay Catholics, however, such a step, while certainly welcomed, would still be judged as not speaking directly or realistically to their basic convictions about the goodness of their loving relationships including genital expression. The subjective meaning and value of these kinds of relationships for themselves and, increasingly, for family members and friends, stand in tension with the objective teaching of the Church on the fundamental meaning and purpose of human sexuality as heterosexual, unitive, and procreative and within a covenanted relationship. While this situation cannot be ignored, it would be pastorally harmful to focus on it to the exclusion of other areas of mutual agreement and common ground which could be utilized for dialogue and even cooperative projects.[15] At the same time, the full truth of the Church's teaching on the objective immorality of homosexual acts and the objective disorder of the homosexual inclination must be presented with pastoral sensitivity and according to the ability of the learners to understand and absorb it.

By including the words "exclusive" or "predominant" sexual attraction in their definition of homosexuality, the *Catechism* recognizes that

humans are not easily dichotomized into simple categories of homosexual and heterosexual. Human sexuality can be conceptualized as a
continuum of feelings, desires, attractions, and behaviors ranging
between exclusive heterosexuality and exclusive homosexuality.
Understandings about human sexual reality from scientific studies can
contribute to the refinement of Church teaching on various moral
questions. In 1986, when speaking specifically of homosexuality, the
Vatican acknowledged that the Church "is in a position to learn from
scientific discovery."[16] The U. S. bishops also acknowledge the role that
the sciences have in helping us discover moral truth. New scientific data
and theories about the origins of sexual orientation, for instance, while
far from unanimous or conclusive, need to be pursued even though they
can be separated from Church judgments on the homosexual
orientation.[17]

### III. Human Sexuality Studies

Although the *Catechism* does not specifically reference the ground-
breaking but controversial studies of the Kinsey Institute in the late
1950s and early 1960s, it does reflect some of the language of Dr.
Alfred Kinsey in its definition of homosexuality. From his research with
thousands of subjects, Kinsey developed a six-point scale to illustrate
the variability of human sexual attraction and behavior. On the basis of
their same-sex genital behavior and erotic responses during certain
periods of their adult lives, Kinsey classified some individuals as
*exclusively* or *predominantly* homosexual. Individuals in category six
of his six-point scale, for example, are those whose sexual attractions
and behaviors involve only those of the same gender. Those in category
five are individuals who, although having a significant amount of
heterosexual experience and attraction (perhaps even heterosexually
married), are oriented *primarily* to members of their own sex. This
distinction between exclusive and predominant homosexual orientation
impacts on two important issues involving scientific research on
homosexuality and societal and religious responses to homosexuality:
(1) the definition of a homosexual person and the statistical frequency
of homosexual individuals in any given population; and (2) the controversial issue of whether or not sexual orientation can be radically
changed or even substantially modified.

While Kinsey's studies have provided invaluable data for increas-
ing our understanding of homosexuality, they are not without their

methodological problems, one of which is the kind of populations selected for the survey, which includes significant numbers of prison inmates and prostitutes. Aside from personal and ideological attacks on Kinsey, more reputable professional criticisms of the studies have surfaced which at least question the methodology and some of the interpretations of the data.[18] Despite some valid criticisms and methodological flaws, the overall value and influence of Kinsey's research remains.

Perhaps the major criticism of Kinsey's work, at least from the vantage point of the contemporary understanding of homosexuality today, is his definition of a homosexual person. Kinsey classified as homosexual anyone who has engaged in any same-sex behavior or who has any same-sex arousal during his or her lifetime. Such a definition is too strongly weighted in the direction of a behavioral approach and results in much too broad a definition of a homosexual person to be scientifically useful.

Today's more common understanding of a homosexual orientation gives more importance to the psychological and emotional components of sexual attraction and the individual's self-identification as "gay" or "lesbian" as more reliable indicators of sexual orientation than genital arousal and expression. Since scientific studies and anecdotal evidence indicate that many individuals experience some same-sex attractions and/or behaviors in the course of their lives (especially in same-sex environments like prisons, boarding schools, etc.), the factors of behavior and arousal alone seem less than adequate in defining homosexual orientation. In other words, the *primary* element in identifying sexual orientation is not necessarily the gender of the person one is sexually *attracted* to, but rather the gender of the person with whom one tends to *fall in love*.

Even here the issues are not always clear-cut. Males generally become aware of their fundamental sexual orientation at an earlier age than females and, usually, through the experience of overt sexual behavior which persists through adolescence rather than emotional or romantic involvements. Women, on the other hand, perhaps because of socialization factors, come to an awareness later in life (sometimes even after marriage) and usually through strong emotional and romantic attractions and involvements. The phenomenon of heterosexually married gay and lesbian individuals who really do love their spouses, but whose most deeply felt psychologically or emotionally fulfilling sexual relationships involve same-sex partners, indicate the complexity of human sexuality.

The *Catechism* alludes obliquely to the question of the incidence of homosexually oriented individuals when it simply states, "The number of men and women who have deep-seated homosexual tendencies is not negligible."[19] Apart from the use of the word *tendencies* rather than *orientation,* which we will discuss below, the *Catechism* carefully and wisely avoids taking any position on the number of homosexual people in society or the Church. It is impossible to estimate the precise number of gay men and lesbian women in any social grouping or attempt to do so on the basis of a scientific random sample. A true random sample would require that all homosexual people in a given group be willing to identify themselves as such. For many reasons, such a survey is not possible at this time, at least in the general population.

## IV. Changing Sexual Orientation

The second issue related to the exclusive/predominant distinction has to do with the possibility of changing or significantly modifying sexual orientation. Whether a homosexual orientation can be changed is dramatically impacted by the definition of who is a homosexual person. A number of studies claim a statistically significant success rate in *changing* or *converting* homosexual people to heterosexuality by psychological, behavioral, or even spiritual means. When examined closely, however, it appears that these studies have included in their initial treatment population individuals who would be more accurately rated a three on the Kinsey scale—those sometimes called *ambi* or *bi*-sexuals.[20] In some cases change-oriented programs accept individuals who are predominantly, but not exclusively, *heterosexual* (a Kinsey two), i.e., a person who has experienced a significant amount of homosexual behavior or arousal, but who is predominantly heterosexual. In this case, therapy designed to strengthen the heterosexual component could be facilitated by incorporating those heterosexual experiences and attractions. Whether one can be changed from a Kinsey six to a Kinsey one is doubtful. Claims of changing homosexuality need to be scrutinized rather carefully to determine whether the change is of external sexual behavior or function only or a change in internal erotic and emotional attractions and feelings. The latter change cannot be empirically verified.

## V. Theoretical Conceptions of Homosexuality

Underlying the questions of definition, prevalence, and malleability of sexual orientation is a larger theoretical question: Is there really such a thing as homosexual orientation defined as an *essential* component of human sexual identity whose causes are as yet unknown, whose origin is involuntary, and whose fundamental direction is radically unchangeable? The *essentialist* academic or clinician answers this question in the affirmative. Essentialists believe there have always existed homosexual individuals throughout all of human history and in all cultures, a fact which allows us to speak of and study a valid "gay history."[21] Opposed to this view are the *social constructionists* who believe that human sexual identity, like all social realities, is, in large part, socially and culturally constructed with the individual's own response to homosexual behaviors and attractions playing some part also.[22]

The ongoing debate (for the most part, an academic exercise) between the two understandings does have ramifications in related fields such as history, law, and theology. The *Catechism* itself appears to be sympathetic to the social constructionist position when it says that homosexuality "has taken a great variety of forms through the centuries and in different cultures." The majority of mainline Christian denominations in the United States, including the Roman Catholic Church, however, have accepted the essentialist position. Church statements, studies, and policies all seem grounded on essentialist assumptions. There are, however, echoes of the social constructionist position in some Vatican documents. For example, they prefer to speak about homosexual *impulses, temptations,* and *tendencies* rather than sexual *orientation* as a fixed scientific category or a given reality. These terms are much less definitive or determined than orientation and seem to imply some possibility not only of resistance, but actual change on the part of the individual.[23]

On the other hand, the Vatican, as early as 1975, distinguished between individuals whose homosexuality is more of a transitory and changeable reality and those who are *definitively such* (i.e., the constitutional homosexual) because "of some kind of innate instinct." If the phrase "innate instinct" were interpreted as natural, it would then seem to side with an essentialist understanding of homosexuality.[24]

## VI. Origins of Homosexuality

The search for the origins of homosexuality has implications for both theological and pastoral efforts by the churches and also for cultural attitudes and societal policies toward gay and lesbian citizens. One commonly accepted truth in discussions of the origins of homosexuality is the almost universal acceptance that a person's sexual orientation is not a matter of free choice. The struggle for gay civil rights for example, has been aided enormously by the comparison of gay and lesbian people with other groups such as African-Americans and women who are afforded protection on the basis of an involuntary human characteristic like gender and skin color. In arguing against civil rights for homosexual people, however, the Vatican rejects the argument that sexual orientation can be legitimately compared with race and gender and used as a basis for any legal claims to non-discrimination because "homosexuality" is identified primarily with sexual behavior and behavior which is objectively immoral.[25] Immoral behavior can never be the basis of human civil rights. Nor can the orientation be validly compared with other human characteristics such as race or gender because these latter are morally neutral whereas the homosexual orientation is an "objective disorder."

The *Catechism* wisely abstains from taking a position on the question of causality. In 1983 a document on sex education from the Vatican's Congregation for Catholic Education did venture to name some of the supposed causes of homosexuality, although none of them are repeated by the CCC.[26] The *Catechism* reveals a certain bias in the issue of causality when it says that the *psychological genesis* of homosexuality remains largely unexplained. Some stress environmental ("nurture") causes such as learned behavior, parental conflicts, lack of gender role models, imprinting of early sexual experiences, etc. Current research in the field of genetics seems to point to some underlying genetic predisposition to homosexuality. But the vast majority of researchers and theorists reject the simplistic and outdated either/or (nature/nurture) controversy in favor of the more complicated theory that there is a combination and interaction of both environmental and biological factors. Nor can environment be limited to external social factors since internal genetic components are affected by their own unique environments (e.g., hormones) which act upon them. Nature and nurture are two sides of one coin and cannot be neatly separated.

In their 1990 document on human sexuality, the U.S. bishops echo the more complex theory: "The medical and behavioral sciences do not yet know what causes a person to be homosexual. Whether it is related to genetics, hormones, or some variation in psycho-social upbringing, the scientific data presently seems inconclusive. There may be a combination of factors involved."[27]

## VII. Biblical Texts

In a surprisingly few brief lines the *Catechism* summarizes the magisterium's major biblical and theological arguments against homosexual acts and seems to close the door firmly to the possibility of any further discussion or development.[28] It should be remembered, however, that the *Catechism*'s purpose and format is to summarize and present the fundamentals of authentic Church teaching and not to respond in any detail to new scientific information and questions, developments in the area of pastoral ministry, and questions raised by current theological discourse.

The *Catechism* asserts that the twin foundations for the magisterium's judgment on homosexual acts are Sacred Scripture and tradition. It describes homosexual acts as "acts of grave depravity" and in footnote #140 refers the reader to four scripture passages: Genesis 19:1-29; Romans 1:24–27; 1 Corinthians 6:10; and 1 Timothy 1:10. The description of homosexual acts as depravity reflects language used in the 1975 *Declaration on Certain Questions Concerning Sexual Ethics*. The use of *depravity* is an unfortunate choice because of its harsh judgmental tone and strong emotional connotation. Given these two factors, the word can lead people to believe that such acts are uniquely despicable and harmful to society and the people who engage in such acts, likewise depraved and despicable. Although the word might sustain a less emotional tone in a more technical anthropological or philosophical explanation, it has been used in some quarters to heap opprobrium and hostility on gay and lesbian people. This is something which the magisterium ought not to contribute in any way, even if unintentionally by its choice of language. Fortunately, the language does not appear in other more balanced and sensitive presentations of Church teachings, especially those by certain individual bishops and regional or national groupings.[29]

Three of the four scriptural passages which the *Catechism* cites come from the New Testament. Three of the four passages were also referenced in the 1975 document. The additional reference to Genesis 19:1–29 comes from the CDF's 1986 *Letter* to the bishops which also uses Genesis but only 19:1–11 to argue against homosexuality. There are a few minor differences between the scriptural references in the *Catechism* and those in the 1986 *Letter:* the citation from Leviticus 18:22 and 20:13 found in the previous document, but it is not included in the *Catechism;* Genesis 19:1–11 is cited in the 1986 *Letter* rather than 19:1–29, which appears in the *Catechism;* 1 Cor. 6:9 is cited in the *Letter* as opposed to 1 Cor 6:10 in the CCC; finally, *Letter* cites Romans 1:18–32 while the *Catechism* cites Romans 1:24–27. A close examination of the texts does not reveal substantial differences in their use. It is noteworthy that in the classical Leviticus text (18:22), which for many, at least, is the most clear, an unambiguous moral condemnation of male anal intercourse is omitted.

The magisterium realizes that the long-standing and traditional interpretations of all of the standard texts used to support a biblical rejection of homogenital acts have been challenged both in scholarly biblical criticism and in more popular presentations.[30] In the 1986 *Letter,* the magisterium acknowledged that biblical literature owes a good deal of its varied patterns of thought and expression to the different epochs in which it was written. The world in which the New Testament was written was quite diverse from that of the Old Testament. In the face of this remarkable diversity, nevertheless, the *Letter* still maintains that there is a "a clear consistency within the Scriptures themselves on the moral issue of homosexual behavior."[31] In the face of biblical scholars and others who offer new understandings of biblical texts which might weaken or undermine their ability to carry the weight of an absolute and universal condemnation of all homogenital acts, the magisterium points to a "constant Biblical testimony" which "forms a solid foundation for the Church's teaching."[32] In order for the new interpretations to be correct, the interpretation of Scripture must be in substantial accord with that tradition.

## VIII. Tradition and Theology

The meaning of *tradition* as one of the two principal sources of Christian revelation is also raised in the *Catechism*'s presentation of homosexuality when it says "tradition has always declared that 'homosexual acts are intrinsically disordered.'"[33] The statement is documented by footnote #41, which refers the reader to paragraph 8 of

*Declaration.* In that document, the phrase *intrinsically disordered,* however, is connected with a discussion of biblical data rather than Church tradition. Those who suffer from this anomaly, the *Declaration* says, are not personally responsible for it, but the *scriptural* judgment attests to the fact that homosexual acts are intrinsically disordered. The technical language of intrinsic disorder arises neither from Scripture nor the living tradition of the Church, but is actually a rather recent theological or philosophical concept. Thus, the claim that homosexual acts have always been declared in the tradition (understood either as Scripture or Tradition) as intrinsically disordered is somewhat problematic given the fact that the language itself is a relatively recent addition to theological discourse. The Catholic Theological Society of America (CTSA) touches on the scripture/tradition dynamics in its paper on the ordination of women: "When the Council of Trent declared that certain traditions deserve equal veneration with scripture, it specified that such traditions must have the Gospel as their source, must have been received by the Apostles from the very mouth of Christ, or have been revealed to them by the Holy Spirit, and have been preserved without interruption in the Catholic Church."[34] It seems doubtful at least that the Vatican is claiming such authority for the theological judgment that describes homosexual acts as intrinsically disordered. Furthermore, the intense debate among Catholic moralists about the methodology employed in defining any particular human act as intrinsically disordered and the debate's implications for moral decision making at least makes one cautious in claiming a long tradition for this particular terminology.[35]

In addition, the *Catechism* states that homosexual acts are contrary to the *natural law* without explaining or clarifying its understanding of natural law.[36] Some idea of its reasoning, however, is found in its claim about the inability of homogenital acts to be biologically procreative since they "close the sexual act to the gift of life" and the related claim that they do not involve biological and psychological or affective *complementarity.* Both of these assertions have been examined in recent years even by moderate Catholic theologians who point to what some believe is an internal inconsistency in the Church's acceptance of sexual acts in a heterosexual marriage incapable of biological procreation due to sterility or advanced age.[37]

The adequacy of a theological anthropology of sexual complementarity which is based solely or primarily on biological differences is also a subject of debates among theologians.[38] A study commissioned in the 1970s by the Catholic Theological Society of America, though severely criticized by both the Vatican and the U.S. Catholic Bishops' Committee on Doctrine, moved beyond the biological procreative and psychologically unitive principles of sexuality which, in the Catholic moral tradition, ground marital genital acts. The CTSA report argued for the moral possibility of same-sex genital acts within the context of stable, faithful, and committed same-sex union by expanding the meanings of both unitive and procreative.[39]

## IX. Pastoral Initiatives

Seeming to anticipate a discussion of pastoral care which would incorporate some of these new biblical and theological insights, the CCC says under no circumstances can such homogenital acts be approved. Here again the language is similar to that of the 1975 *Declaration* which says that homosexual acts can in no case be approved. The question of approval of homosexual acts on the pastoral level was dealt with in 1975 when the CDF stated explicitly that "no pastoral method can be employed which would give moral justification to these [homosexual] acts on the grounds that they would be consonant with the condition of such people."[40]

In a 1972 document dealing with pastoral care of homosexual persons, a committee of the Catholic Bishops of England and Wales stressed the need in pastoral ministry to apply the clear-cut heterosexual, marital norm of sexuality to specific situations. The example they give to illustrate a pastoral application of a general norm is that of two homosexual individuals in a relationship who, while acknowledging the Church's normative teaching on heterosexuality, find it impossible to lead a celibate life. The stability of their same-sex union, they argue, outweighs the disorder of any homosexual acts that take place within the relationships. In this case, say the English bishops, "the goodness or badness of such acts can only be judged morally in practice when consideration has been given to intention and circumstances."[41] The Bishops of England and Wales cannot be accused of justifying homosexual acts because they hold the norm that such acts are objectively morally unacceptable and the intentions and circumstances do not change the fundamental nature of the act. But, as Richard McCormick notes, the bishops do seem to be giving moral justification in this individual circumstance—not on the grounds that such acts are consonant with the homosexual orientation, but because the stability of the union outweighs the disorder of homosexual acts which take place within it.[42] This line of reasoning is also echoed in the pastoral plan from the Archdiocese of San Francisco.[43]

Paragraphs 2358 and 2359 address the issue of pastoral care. The first significant comment acknowledges the involuntariness of the homosexual orientation: "They do not choose their homosexual condition." The magisterium first spoke of the lack of choice in its 1975 *Declaration* when it described a group of homosexual persons who are "definitely such because of some kind of innate instinct" as opposed to others whose homosexual condition is transitory or, at least, not incurable. The use of *incurable* and *condition* rather than *orientation* bespeaks a medical model of homosexuality fraught with both linguistic and conceptual problems. The validity of the medical model has been criticized by both theologians and philosophers especially following the 1973 decision by the American Psychiatric Association to declassify homosexuality as an emotional or mental disorder.[44]

In a more questionable claim for which no empirical evidence is offered, the *Catechism* says that for most homosexual persons their homosexuality is a trial. But, one might inquire, in what does this trial precisely consist for the individual? For many gay and lesbian persons the trial is not in accepting their homosexual orientation, but in the negative or hostile judgments and behaviors of certain segments of society and religion and in the social discrimination, ridicule, and marginalization many of them encounter. Furthermore, when these judgments are internalized by the gay or lesbian person, then the trial could involve lack of self-esteem, poor self-image, or even intense self-hatred to the point of self-destructive behaviors in the more extreme cases.[45] But in this scenario, the source of such trials for most gay and lesbian individuals comes from outside themselves rather than from the orientation itself.

In one of the most positive statements about gay and lesbian people, the *Catechism* says that they "must be accepted with respect, compassion and sensitivity."[46] Similar sentiments were also expressed in the 1986 *Letter* which characterized homosexual people as often generous and giving of themselves. But some of the language and reasoning of that document and the circumstances in which it was heard, unfortunately, made it difficult for many to experience it as really fostering genuine respect, compassion, and sensitivity for lesbian and gay people. The statement evoked mostly negative reactions from many quarters of the Church including some bishops.[47]

## X. Social Justice and Gay Civil Rights

Violence in word and action was also strongly denounced in the 1986 document and characterized as a "kind of disregard for others which endangers the most fundamental principles of a healthy society." While the magisterium teaches officially that the "intrinsic dignity of each person must always be respected in word, in action and in law," a subsequent statement in 1992 by the Vatican pertaining to gay civil rights seemed to many to compromise the spirit of this teaching.[48]

The *Catechism* strongly opposes discrimination when it says that "every sign of unjust discrimination in their regard should be avoided."[49] The use of the word unjust is key to understanding this position. In 1992 the question of discrimination and gay and lesbian civil rights was the subject of a document released by the Vatican which, in effect, actually justified certain forms of discrimination against lesbian and gay people in certain situations where it would not only be considered just but even necessary.[50]

The document, which was originally not made public, drew sharp criticism from individuals and groups including Catholic bishops who viewed it a serious departure from the Church's long tradition of social justice teachings.[51] One U.S. moral theologian charged the Vatican with rewriting the classical rules of moral theology by encouraging the toleration of a lesser evil act (positive discrimination) not because of the inevitability of a greater evil occurring, but only because of what *might* happen in society if it were not allowed to discriminate against homosexual people.[52]

In what is a surprising reference to non-Christian homosexual persons, the *Catechism* urges them simply to "fulfill God's will in their lives." Such advice seems to leave them an opening to discern to the best of their abilities what exactly is God's will for them. In a similar vein in 1995, England's Cardinal Basil Hume reminded gay and lesbian Catholics that they, like heterosexual people, are expected by God to keep his law and to work toward achieving a difficult ideal even if it can be realized only gradually: "In all circumstances and situations of life," Hume advised, "God calls each person, whatever his or her sexual orientation, to fulfill that part of his created design which only that person can fulfill."[53] This approach resonates with the subjective convictions of many gay and lesbian individuals who sincerely feel that precisely as a gay or lesbian person they are part of God's created design and that they can only be faithful by living out their lives as gay or lesbian individuals.

The *Catechism,* however, offers another view. When Christian gay and lesbian people encounter difficulties from their sexual orientation, they are advised to unite themselves with the sacrifice of the Lord's cross. This advice is a traditional form of Christian spirituality that has helped many Christians endure untold sufferings and grow in a deep appreciation of and identify with the suffering Christ. It can, however, also be too quickly and superficially advised. No pastor, for example, would advise a woman to remain in an abusive relationship and suggest that in so doing she can offer her sufferings in union with the sacrifice of the Cross. Where sufferings can be alleviated rather than endured passively, sound spirituality requires an individual to take steps to do so.[54]

## XI. Chastity

The solution of chastity is raised in the final section of the *Catechism*'s discussion of homosexuality. Homosexual persons are called to the virtue of chastity and to virtues of "self-mastery that teaches them inner freedom, at times by the support of disinterested friendship, by prayer and sacramental grace."[55] The phrase *disinterested friendship* is coded language for a platonic friendship that does not include genital expression as has been suggested earlier in this chapter. Cardinal Hume made the same point when he said: "Sexual loving presupposes friendship, but friendship does not require full sexual involvement."[56]

In addition, the *Catechism* refers to the traditional approaches to ministry to homosexual Catholics as including "prayer and sacramental grace." Commonly understood, the two sacraments which hold priority of place in such a ministry are those of reconciliation and Eucharist.[57] The traditional approach to ministry with homosexual people also includes ongoing spiritual direction and various kinds of support groups. One model of ministry is the organization called *Courage.*[58]

The *Courage* model of ministry can be helpful to many people and, because of its faithful adherence to magisterial teaching on homogenital acts and inclination, often enjoys support and encouragement from bishops in some dioceses. It views the homosexual orientation as a developmental disorder and encourages individuals to "come out" of their homosexuality either fully by becoming heterosexual or partially by resisting homosexual temptations and living a chaste life. Testimonies abound as to the success of the group's efforts.

Another Catholic organization called *Dignity* which was established in 1969 also emphasizes the centrality of the Eucharist in the lives of gay and lesbian Catholics as well as community support. But unlike *Courage, Dignity* views the homosexual orientation as a created gift of God which can be lived out in a morally good way, including sexual-genital expression.[59] It is organizations like these and many other developing ministries in dioceses throughout the United States which have brought homosexual Catholics back to the Church and fostered the values of personal dignity and responsibility, though they often differ radically in their stances toward Church teaching on acts and inclination and even on the concept of pastoral care and the need for civil rights.

In light of this diversity of ministries, it is important to remember what the pastoral plan of the Archdiocese of San Francisco says: there can be no one ministry for all homosexual men and women. Because of the diversity of gay and lesbian Catholics, they need and will benefit from a variety of ministries with the understanding that all these models conform to the teaching of the Church. Intensive spiritual support groups like *Courage* and *Dignity* may not always constitute a realistic avenue of development for many gay and lesbian Catholics. The Church should support other larger organizations insofar as they enhance and further the values of the gospel.[60]

## XII. Conclusion

The treatment of homosexuality in the *Catechism* represents significant developments both in concepts and terminology over previous statements of the Roman magisterium. There are a number of non-doctrinal claims, however, which require additional discussion and clarification if they are to be sustained or defended as true to the pastoral experience of many ministers and helpful in the task of reconciliation. While there is an apparent openness to incorporating recent scientific knowledge in some areas and to decrying discrimination and fostering "respect, compassion and sensitivity" for gay and lesbian people, the precise understanding of these terms and their practical applications in the life of the local Church as it relates to its gay and lesbian members require much more study, research, and dialogue in the public forum.

The *Catechism* is not meant as an exhaustive treatment of the topic. Nevertheless, it is unfortunate that there is a lack of acknowledgment of the reality of homosexual clergy, words of support for the struggles of Catholic parents of gay and lesbian children, encouragement of responsible theological discussions, and an awareness of the many developing official and public diocesan and pastoral ministries in various countries. These lacunae conspire to make the *Catechism*'s treatment of homosexuality less than complete or current.

On the pastoral level, then, it is important for educators and counselors to be in touch with gay and lesbian people, their parents, their families and to avail themselves of the many resources that are presently available.[61] In this way, they best utilize the *Catechism* by supplementing its understanding with sociological data and analyses, theological commentaries and approved models of pastoral ministry that already exist in many dioceses of the United States.

## Notes

[1] There are two cross-references in the section on homosexuality: 2333 which deals with the anthropological nature and theological implications of male and female differences and 2347 which deals with chastity.

[2] The three previous Vatican documents include "Declaration on Certain Questions Concerning Sexual Ethics," *Origins,* 5 (January, 22, 1976), 1 ff; "Letter to the Bishops of the Catholic Church on the Pastoral Care of Homosexual Persons," *Origins,* 16 (November 13, 1986), 379–382; "Some Considerations Concerning the Response to Legislative Proposals on the Non-Discrimination of Homosexual Persons," *Origins,* 22 (August 6, 1992), 174–177.

[3] For a good example of how organic development proceeds, see James R. Pollock's "Teaching in Transition" in Jeannine Gramick and Robert Nugent (Eds.), *The Vatican and Homosexuality* (New York: Crossroad, 1998), 179–188, and *Building Bridges: Gay and Lesbian Reality and the Catholic Church,* Jeannine Gramick and Robert Nugent, Mystic, CT: Twenty-Third Publications, 1993.

[4] The most extensive anthology of Catholic documents is contained in *Voices of Hope: A Collection of Positive Catholic Writings on Gay and Lesbian Issues,* Jeannine Gramick and Robert Nugent (Eds.) (New York: Center for Homophobia Education, 1995).

[5] Although the 1975 *Declaration* spoke in general terms of "homosexual relations between certain people," and "homosexual relations within a sincere communion of life and love analogous to marriage," it defined homosexual relations as *acts* which lack a certain finality, i.e., the biological finality of procreative potential.

[6] For a helpful discussion of several components of sexual identity, including expla-

nations of gender and erotic orientations, see *Becoming a Sexual Person,* Robert T. Francoeur (New York: MacMillan Publishing Company, Second Edition, 1991), 431–461.

[7] The two important distinctions in the 1975 Vatican *Declaration* are between "transitory" and "permanent" homosexuality and between a homosexual "tendency" and homosexual "acts."

[8] The U.S. Catholic bishops recognize a certain ambiguity about this distinction when they say that while the distinction is helpful in the education and pastoral arena, it is "not always clear or convincing." *Human Sexuality: A Catholic Perspective for Education and Lifelong Learning* (Washington, D.C.: United States Catholic Conference, 1990), 56.

[9] "It is very important to keep in mind a point made earlier: that one's sexual orientation is integral to one's very self. In other words, one's homosexual orientation does not simply encompass sexual desires, but influences (although it does not determine) the ways one thinks, the ways one decides, the ways one responds, the ways one relates, the ways one creates and structures his or her whole world. Gerald D. Coleman, "Homosexuals and Spirituality," Chicago Studies, (Vol. 32), 1993, 229 in *Voices of Hope, op. cit.,* 223.

[10] *Declaration, op. cit.,* 3.

[11] *Human Sexuality, op. cit.,* 8–9.

[12] Gerald D. Coleman stresses the importance of avoiding this reductionism in his *Homosexuality: Catholic Teaching and Pastoral Practice,* New York: Paulist Press, 1995. In another place he writes: "When homosexuality is understood principally as an orientation to certain sexual or genital justice is not done to homosexual persons . . . homosexual orientation is not an orientation to sexual *activity* as such any more than definitive heterosexuality." "Homosexuals and Spirituality," *art. cit.,* 229.

[13] James Hanigan examines this point in his *Homosexuality: The Test Case for Christian Sexual Ethics* (New York: Paulist Press, 1988).

[14] A first step in this direction has been taken by Cardinal Basil Hume's "Note on Church People Concerning Homosexual People," *Origins* (Vol. 24: No. 45), April 27, 1995, 767–769. The pastoral plan of the Archdiocese of San Francisco also says that "It is this need for closeness and intimacy that leads the homosexual person to seek a stable relationship with another person. Homosexual people fall in love. And as long as this is so, sexual activity might occasionally occur." *Voices of Hope, op. cit.,* 107.

[15] Collaborating in ministry to persons with AIDS is one of the ways Richard L. Smith discusses in his *AIDS, Gays and the Catholic Church,* Cleveland: Pilgrim Press, 1994.

[16] "Letter to the Bishops of the Catholic Church on the Pastoral Care of Homosexual Persons" in *The Vatican and Homosexuality,* Jeannine Gramick and Robert Nugent (Eds.), (New York: Crossroad, 1988), 1.

[17] Cardinal Ratzinger said that people objected to the use of "innate" in the *Catechism* to describe a homosexual orientation because the word left the origin and, therefore, the basis for a moral judgment of homosexuality too open. He said the *Catechism* does not presume to know all the origins of homosexuality and has left room for all the hypotheses whether innate or developed under certain circumstances. But the *Catechism* does recognize that the inclination is deep-seated in the individual's subconscious and is not simply a matter of choice or will. See "Catechism Takes Harder Line of Death Penalty," *National Catholic Reporter* (19 September 1997), 12. A not too technical and readable overview of current genetic research on sexual orientations can be found in *A*

*Separate Creation: The Search for the Biological Origins of Sexual Orientation* by Chandler Burr (New York: Hyperion, 1996).

[18] For a recent critical biography of Kinsey's life and research, see *Alfred C. Kinsey: A Public/Private Life* by James H. Jones (New York: W. W. Norton and Company, 1997). See also "Kinsey's Science," a letter to the editor from James H. Jones defending Kinsey's work in the *New York Times Book Review* (30 November 1997).

[19] 2357.

[20] Clinicians representing this approach include Elizabeth Moberly and Joseph Nicolosi. See "Survey of Sexual Orientation Changes by the National Association of Research and Therapy of Homosexuality (NARTH)," Encino, CA, 1997.

[21] *Christianity, Social Tolerance and Homosexuality, Gay People in Western Europe from the Beginning of the Christian Era to the Fourteenth Century,* John Boswell (Chicago: University of Chicago Press, 1988).

[22] *The Construction of Homosexuality,* David S. Greenberg (Chicago: University of Chicago Press, 1988).

[23] For further discussion of this point, see "Sexual Orientation in Vatican Thinking," Robert Nugent in *The Vatican and Homosexuality, op. cit.,* 48–58.

[24] While this might be true, it does not mean that the Vatican would consider the orientation "natural" in the sense that it could be acted upon in a morally good way: "no pastoral method can be employed which would give moral justification of these acts on the grounds that they would be consonant with the condition of such people." *Declaration,* #8. In the Italian version of the *Catechism* the word "innate" was used to describe the inclination. In the English version this was rendered "deep-seated," which is less likely to be construed as natural. The objection by some, including Fr. Harvey, to the use of innate, according to Cardinal Ratzinger, was that it made people think that homosexual tendency was already present at the moment of birth or conception. Ratzinger was quoted as saying that many experts said this has not been proven. John Harvey argues that innate cannot be understood as natural and that when it was used in the original text of the 1975 *Declaration* the Latin said "quasi innatus" or "as if innate."

[25] For an analysis and critique of this argument, see "The Civil Rights of Homosexual People: Vatican Perspectives," Robert Nugent, *New Theology Review* (Vol. 7. No. 4, November, 1994), 72–86; and "Homosexual Rights and the Catholic Community," Robert Nugent, *Doctrine and Life* (Vol. 44, No. 3, March, 1994), 165–173.

[26] Among the theories named were "lack of healthy family life, weakness of absence of the father, or a dominant mother; inadequate education; lack of effective peer relationships; arrested emotional development; lack of normal sexual development; narcissism and others." *Educational Guidance in Human Love,* Sacred Congregation for Education, Rome, 1983, excerpted in *Homosexuality and the Magisterium,* John Gallagher (Ed.) (Mt. Rainier, MD: New Ways Ministry, 1983), 91.

[27] *Human Sexuality, op. cit.,* 55.

[28] For comments on the Vatican's use of Sacred Scripture, see "Homosexuality: The New Vatican Statement," Bruce R. Williams, *Theological Studies,* 48 (June, 1987), 259–277.

[29] *Voices of Hope* contains Catholic writings on homosexuality, none of which refer to it as a "depravity."

[30] A recent work which summarizes current biblical scholarship critizing traditional interpretations of certain texts related to homosexuality is Daniel A. Helminiak's *What the Bible Really Says About Homosexuality* (San Francisco: Alamo Square Press, 1994).

[31] *The Vatican and Homosexuality, op. cit.,* 2.

[32] *Ibid.,* 3.

[33] 2357.

[34] "Scholars Question Vatican," *Catholic Messenger,* Davenport, Iowa, June 13, 1996, 1.

[35] For an enlightening discussion of this issue, see Jean Porter's "The Moral Act in Veritatis Splendor and in Aquinas's *Summa Theologiae:* A Comparative Analysis" in *Veritatis Splendor: American Responses,* Michael E. Allsopp and John J. O'Keefe (Eds.) (Kansas City: Sheed and Ward, 1995), 278–295.

[36] An overview of the discussion of natural law in Catholic moral theology including various definitions and its relationship to Catholic moral teachings can be found in *Natural Law and Theology,* Charles E. Curran and Richard A. McCormick (Eds.) (New York: Paulist Press, 1991).

[37] "The good of procreation is not unrelated to the unitive good, but it is also not essential to it. The mere fact of an intentional and biological inability to procreate can no longer be considered a moral barrier to sexual intimacy where the integral goodness of the unitive end of sexuality is possible of realization—at which point in the developing theological tradition the morality of homosexual acts and unions is open for moral re-evaluation." Hanigan, *op. cit.,* 46. In an article published in *L'Osservatore Romano,* Piero Schlesinger characterizes the argument that denial of civil marriage to homosexual couples and not to sterile couples as "captious." Yet he says the question requires further study to show how denial is in no way related to discrimination. But, he adds, since marriage has shown "flexibility" over the ages including forms which are profoundly different if not in opposition, it is logical to ask the question "whether the limitation of hetero-sexuality could eventually be overcome." N. 22–28 May, 1997, 10.

[38] For two examples, see Margaret Farley's "An Ethic for Same Sex Relations" in Robert Nugent's (Ed.), *A Challenge to Love: Gay and Lesbian Catholics in the Church* (New York: Crossroad, 1983), 93–106; and Daniel Maguire's "The Morality of Homosexual Marriage," *Ibid,* 118–134. For the position of the Church on same-sex marriages, see *Same-Sex Unions and Marriage: A legal, social, and theological analysis,* A Resource Paper by the Office of General Counsel, Secretariat for Doctrine and Pastoral Practices, Secretariat for Family, Laity, Women, and Youth, National Conference of Catholic Bishops, United States Catholic Conference (Washington, D.C., July, 1997).

[39] *Human Sexuality: New Directions in American Catholic Thought,* Anthony Kosnik et al., (Eds) (New York: Paulist Press, 1977).

[40] *Declaration, op. cit.,* #8.

[41] *An Introduction to the Pastoral Care of Homosexual People,* Catholic Social Welfare Commission, Catholic Bishops of England and Wales (Mt. Rainier, MD: New Ways Ministry, 1981), 8, 9.

[42] See "Homosexuality as a Moral and Pastoral Problem," Richard McCormick in *The Critical Calling: Reflections of Moral Dilemmas Since Vatican II* (Washington, D.C.: Georgetown University Press, 1989), 289–313.

[43] ". . . it is likewise important to carefully interpret the meaning of sexual activity in this person's life: that is, to understand the pattern of life in which such activity takes place and to take into consideration the meaning that these sexual acts have for different people . . . While the Church teaches that homosexual activity is objectively inconsistent with the meaning of human sexuality, it never wants to evaluate this activity totally divorced from the person or circumstances in which the activity takes place." "Ministry

and Homosexuality in the Archdiocese of San Francisco" in *Voices of Hope, op. cit.,* 106,108.

[44] For a penetrating philosophical critique of the medical model, see Gareth Moore's *The Body in Context: Sex and Catholicism* (London: SCM Press, 1992). The 1986 *Letter* characterized the homosexual orientation as an "objective disorder." That language generated heated discussions about its precise meaning (still unclarified) and its potential for pastoral harm. Initially the *Catechism* did not include the disorder language leading many to think that the Church had quietly dropped the term. With the definitive publication of the Latin edition of the *Catechism,* however, seven words were changed in the section dealing with homosexuality. The original version said: "The number of men and women who have deep-seated homosexual tendencies is not negligible. They do not choose their homosexual condition; for most of them it is a trial." The amended version reads: The number of men and women who have deep-seated homosexual tendencies is not negligible. This inclination, objectively disordered, is a trial for most of them."

[45] Richard A. Isay, a psychoanalyst, has written extensively on the destructive impact of self-rejection in *Becoming Gay: The Journey to Self-Acceptance* (New York: Pantheon Books, 1996).

[46] 2358.

[47] For the full text and analyses of this document see *The Vatican and Homosexuality, op. cit.*

[48] For analysis of how various bishops used this document in dealing with local gay rights cases, see: Robert Nugent, "The U.S. Catholic Bishops and Gay Civil Rights: Four Case Studies," *The Catholic Lawyer* (Vol. 38, No. 1 1998), 101–124.

[49] 2358.

[50] "Some Considerations Concerning the Response to Legislative Proposals on the Non-Discrimination of Homosexual Persons" in *Voices of Hope, op. cit.,* 229–233.

[51] For critical responses to this document, see *Voices of Hope, op. cit.,* Part Three, "Responses to the 1992 Vatican Statement on Non-discrimination of Homosexual Persons," 175–227.

[52] "The CDF and Homosexuals: Rewriting the Moral Tradition," John F. Tuohy, *America* (September 12, 1992), in *Voices of Hope, op. cit.,* 212–215.

[53] "Note on Church Teaching Concerning Homosexual People," Cardinal Basil Hume, *art. cit.,* 769. Whether intentional or not, Hume's language of "created design" reflects the same language used by the CDF in the 1986 *Letter* to argue against homosexuality.

[54] In their response to the Congregation for the Doctrine of the Faith's concern about the pastoral statement on admitting divorced and remarried Catholics to the Eucharist issued by three German bishops, the tension between doctrine and pastoral realities is highlighted. The bishops state that what is at stake in these pastoral problems is "to rightly determine the relationship of generally valid norms to the personal decision of conscience.... the force of the objective norm can only be brought to bear convincingly in the long run if we take into account not just people's very complex life situations, but also the individual person's unique personal dignity as it is expressed in an educated conscience." This "core problem" of the relationship between norms and conscience in ministry with the divorced and remarried is also "the key to many other conflicts of contemporary pastoral practice." Certainly among these could be included the issue of homosexuality. "Response to the Vatican Letter," *Origins* (Vol. 24, No. 20 October 27, 1994), 344.

[55] 2359. It is important not to confuse chastity with celibacy. The U. Bishops remind us that: "Chastity for the single person, is not synonymous with an interior calling to perpetual celibacy," *Human Sexuality, op. cit.,* 51. Also Coleman writes: "A very important and crucial question to be faced in this whole discussion is the relationship between homosexuality and celibacy. Celibacy is a vocation which should never be confused with mere abstinence and it should not be applied *a priori* as a category to the situation of the homosexual. The Catholic Church calls homosexual people to a life of chastity, as it calls all unmarried persons. But this does *not* mean that every homosexual person is capable of living the vocation of celibacy." Gerald D. Coleman, "The Homosexual Question in the Priesthood and Religious Life," *The Priest* (December, 1984), 18.

[56] "Note on Church Teaching," *art. cit.,* 767.

[57] "Homosexuals have the same need for the Sacraments as the heterosexual. They also have the same right to receive the Sacraments. In determining whether or not to administer Absolution or give Communion to a homosexual, a pastor must be guided by the general principles of fundamental theology that only a certain moral obligation may be imposed. An invincible doubt, whether of law or fact, permits one to follow a true and solidly 'probable opinion' in favor of a more liberal interpretation." *An Introduction to the Pastoral Care of Homosexual People,* Catholic Bishops of England and Wales, Catholic Social Welfare Commission, 1979, in *Voices of Hope, op. cit.,* 70; 71.

[58] See John F. Harvey's *The Truth About Homosexuality* (San Francisco: Ignatius Press, 1996).

[59] Dignity's public and official position is that "gay men and lesbian women can express their sexuality in a manner that is consonant with Christ's teaching. We believe that we can express our sexuality physically in a unitive manner that is loving, life giving, and life affirming. We believe that all sexuality should be exercised in an ethically responsible and unselfish way."

[60] The National Association of Catholic Diocesan Lesbian and Gay Ministries serves as a clearinghouse for efforts on diocesan, parish, and grassroots ministries with gay and lesbian Catholics.

[61] The most current resource from the U.S. bishops is their 1997 document from the Committee on Marriage and Family entitled "Always Our Children."

# Catholic Social Teaching in the *Catechism*

## John T. Pawlikowski

While the section titled "Social Justice" in the *Catechism* (1928–1948) is quite brief, issues related to this theme are in fact discussed more extensively under other headings. Most notable are the treatment of the seventh commandment (2401–2463), the paragraphs on "Safeguarding Peace" included in the consideration of the fifth commandment (2302–2317; 2327–2330), and the presentation on "The Human Community" (1877–1927). References to social justice themes are also to be found scattered throughout the *Catechism,* including the sections on "The Visible World," which treats creation (337–354), article 8, which focuses on the meaning of sin, and discussion of the "seven petitions" of the Lord's Prayer (2803–2854).

Clearly the teachings of the social encyclicals have found their way into the *Catechism*. A study of the references will show a decided preference for Vatican II's *Gaudium et Spes* ("The Church and the Modern World") and Pope John Paul II's *Centesimus Annus*. The least frequently cited are Pope John XXIII's *Mater et Magistra,* and *Pacem in Terris,* and Pope Paul VI's *Populorum Progressio*. The question before us in this study is how well the major themes of the modern social encyclicals have been articulated in the *Catechism,* allowing, of course, for the necessary brevity that the catechism format requires. It is to this examination that we now turn, beginning with an overview of the major emphases in the social encyclicals. This will provide catechists with a handy summary of the major themes in these statements, as well as a sense of the key developments within the Church's teaching, both of which are invaluable if the *Catechism*'s message is to be correctly communicated.

### I. Twentieth Century Catholic Social Teaching

In my studies on official modern Catholic teaching on social justice, particularly the research I undertook in connection with the publication of the United States Catholic Conference's volume *Justice in the Marketplace*[1] (which appeared as a companion piece to the U.S. Bishops' Pastoral Letter on the Economy), I have been increasingly struck by the basic consistency in outlook that runs through the social encyclicals from Leo XIII to John Paul II. While there certainly have been marked shifts in certain areas of papal teaching (e.g., toward a more egalitarian social vision beginning with John XXIII, toward a greater emphasis on solidarity and toward increased criticism of war as an instrument of justice), five themes have remained central since Leo XIII. They are: (1) no absolute rejection of private property; (2) no support of class struggle; (3) no formal endorsement of Capitalism; (4) a preferential option for the rights of workers; and (5) firm support of unionization.

The publication of the first papal social encyclical *Rerum Novarum* was in many respects a startling event when one considers the previous history of Catholicism and the personal background of Pope Leo XIII. No real precedent existed in the Church for such a declaration. Catholic social thought was still largely grounded in a Medieval view of society in which there existed little basis for human rights claims, including economic ones.[2]

The path that led to the development of *Rerum Novarum* was rather complicated. It began with a prophetic address to the upper classes of Paris in 1868 by the future Cardinal Mermillod. In his speech he tried to convey to the ruling elites something of the awful conditions faced by the majority of laborers whom he described as abandoned and exploited. Eventually, in 1881, Cardinal Mermillod with the support of Leo XXIII became the spiritual leader of a largely lay group of Catholic leaders (almost all European) who came together to discuss the application of central themes in Thomistic thought to the new social realities in Western Europe in response to the cardinal's warning about the possibility of widespread social collapse. This group became known as the Fribourg Union.

The Union met once a year between 1885 and 1891. Though the members shared a common commitment to social ideals, their political outlook varied greatly. Some remained entrenched in the aristocratic mindset while others had become committed partisans of newly emergent democratic trends. In the course of their discussions several issues emerged as central. The first was the importance of a just wage. The Union strongly affirmed it in principle and acknowledged the right of workers to organize to secure it. In general, they remained cautious about state intervention in terms of a just wage, but did recognize its necessity if an employer flatly refused to negotiate with workers. *Rerum Novarum*'s stance on this question closely parallels that of the Union.

The Fribourg Union also steered a middle course when it came to private property. The basic right was strongly affirmed. But having established private property as a basic human right, the Union qualified it a bit by emphasizing as well each person's right to subsistence, which was eventually termed a "primordial" right. It is clear when one examines the Union's papers that its members remained uncomfortable with the way in which the liberals had elevated private property to the pinnacle of the human rights ladder. In the end the Union remained somewhat ambivalent on this question, something that is true as well for the papal encyclical.[3]

The principal focus of the Union was the creation of a viable alternative both to Capitalism and Socialism. The economic model it eventually devised, known as the "regime corporatif," was described by the Union as rooted in natural human groups that correspond to natural interests and common social functions. This model was to find its way into the first two papal social encyclicals. Both the Union and the pope involved fervently hoped that this new social model, rooted in Medieval visions of a just and tranquil social order, would prevail and help overcome the chaos then rampant in Europe, a social situation they attributed to the combined influence of rationalism, Capitalism, and above all Protestantism, which in their minds had generated a major decline in political authority and the rapid spread of individualism.

Ultimately the Fribourg Union must be said to have chosen the road of social reform rather than social revolution. The appeal of its work to Leo XIII and his aristocratically inclined advisors lay in the fact that the social reform the Union proposed was tied to a social model firmly grounded in the scholastic tradition.[4] As Normand Paulhaus has correctly stated, the Union's purpose in proposing the establishment of a corporative system "was simply to reform the contemporary socio-economic order and rid it of its worst defects. The Medieval *spirit,* not its institutions, served as the 'old wine' which they now tried to pour into 'new wineskins.'"[5]

Forty years after the publication of *Rerum Novarum,* Pius XI released the second major social encyclical, *Quadragesimo Anno.* It picked up on many of the themes originally set forth in *Rerum*

*Novarum:* the dignity of labor; the rights of workers to organize and even to participate in some measure in ownership, management, and profit; the belief that Communist and even more moderate Socialist economic theories inherently contradict basic Christian moral principles. *Quadragesimo Anno* also added some new dimensions to Catholic social teaching. Economic concentration had become far more pronounced in the 1930s than it was in the time of Leo XIII. So Pius XI gave this matter special attention. In a number of addresses prior to the encyclical itself, he denounced those who had accumulated invested funds and were using them solely for the sake of personal dominance. The pope insisted that such activities were destroying the free marketplace and rendering the economic system harsh and cruel. To counter this trend, his encyclical gave special emphasis to a theme that would become central to Catholic social teaching in subsequent years, namely, *subsidiarity.* Though this theme has roots in *Rerum Novarum,* it received its classic formulation from Pius XI:

> Just as it is wrong to take away from individuals what by their own ability and effort they can accomplish and commit to the community, so it is an injury and at the same time both a serious evil and a perturbation of the right order to assign to a larger and higher society what can be performed successfully by smaller and lower communities. This is a fixed and unchangeable principle most basic in social philosophy, immovable, and unalterable. The reason is that all social activity, of its very power and nature should supply help to the members of the social body, but may never destroy or absorb them.[6]

Commenting on this principle, David Hollenbach insists that it justifies governmental intervention primarily to undergird persons and smaller communities. But in pursuing such intervention, says Hollenbach, governments must take cognizance of the fact that the family, the neighborhood, religious institutions, and professional and labor groups have an internal dynamic that ought to be respected.[7]

Seen in historical perspective, the principle of subsidiarity appears as a response to the growing economic concentration in Western capitalist countries that so concerned Pius XI as well as to the challenge of state centralization advocated by various forms of Socialism. In recent years the principle's attractiveness has waned somewhat as it has become part of an ideological struggle within Catholicism regarding the social vision demanded by the roots of the Christian faith.[8] The principle has tended to become the backbone of the conservative Catholic attack on the liberal welfare-state and on any form of governmental intervention in the economy. This abandonment has elicited a sharp rebuke from Andrew Greeley and John Coleman.[9] Msgr. George Higgins has attempted to defuse the ideological battle surrounding subsidiarity by stressing both the respect that state institutions must show toward individuals and voluntary associations and the fact that in certain circumstances state institutions take precedence over voluntary associations because there are programs required by the common good that "are beyond the competence of individual citizens or groups of citizens."[10] Archbishop Rembert Weakland has put forth a similar view.[11]

While I remain convinced of the principle of subsidiarity's basic value, I think it would be best today to cast its substance within the framework of the principle of participation which has become a cornerstone of recent Catholic social teaching. The past several popes, including John Paul II, have placed far greater emphasis on this principle than on subsidiarity itself. The notion of "participation" embodies the most important features of the original principle of subsidiarity while not lending itself quite as much to political manipulation by those forces opposed to any form of governmental intervention in the social sphere.

The years immediately following the appearance of *Quadragesimo Anno,* marked as they were by the scourge of Fascism and Nazism, left Catholic leadership little time for any comprehensive analysis of social issues. Pope Pius XII did deliver a series of radio addresses at Christmas which began to shape a vision of a new world social order which was later to serve as a basic starting point for Pope John XXIII.[12] The horrible realities of World War II had convinced Pius XII of the need for a total overhaul of the international social order.

We must appreciate the profound implications of this call for a new social order in the pope's Christmas messages from the early forties, for there are Catholic social commentators today who have mistakenly claimed that Pius XII contributed little to the advance of the Catholic social vision in the twentieth century. This is simply not the case. While I have critiqued his view of ecclesiology which contributed to his highly reserved public response to the victimization of Jews, Poles, and others by the Nazis,[13] in his Christmas messages Pius XIII boldly withdrew any further Catholic support for efforts to preserve the old social barriers and aristocratic privileges in Europe. He was willing to make a move which the Fribourg Union, Leo XIII, and Pius XI all had resisted. A subtle revolutionary spirit emerges from these Christmas addresses. For Pius XII, nothing short of a fundamental reconstruction of the international economic order would bring about human dignity for all, a dignity which everyone has as a birthright and whose ultimate source is God. This vision inspired many of the leaders who set Europe on a new course after World War II with the establishment of the European Steel and Coal Community out of which has emerged the present European Union.

Specific themes which appear in the Christmas sermons include the following: (1) the economically advantaged nations must assume major responsibility for creating a new economic order devoid of the disequilibrium of past systems; (2) the religious dimensions of human existence cannot be fully grasped apart from an understanding of the profound impact of economic realities on this existence; (3) no analysis of war can bypass an appreciation of its economic dimensions; and (4) subsidiarity ought to remain central in a reconstituted international economic system. Clearly here was the seedbed for many of the principal themes of the social encyclicals which have appeared in the fifty years since the end of World War II.

The election of John XXIII opened up a whole new era in Catholic social teaching on economic matters. While the first two social encyclicals had basically tried to enhance the rights of the working classes in Europe within the prevailing social system, John XXIII took up the challenge put forth in Pius XII's Christmas sermons. John's first social encyclical *Mater et Magistra* (1961) begins with an important analysis of the role of private property in Catholic social thought. It speaks of the need for an increased awareness of the social dimensions of property in light of the growing interdependence of the world community.

John felt the need to refine the Catholic approach to private property in order to respond to changed international conditions. In his encyclical, he focuses on "private initiative" more than on private property as such and places great emphasis on the responsibility incumbent upon public authorities to guarantee the effective output of necessary consumer goods and their availability to all citizens.[14] The pope appears to regard a government's "overseer" responsibility as highly as he does the principle of private property. And this "overseer" role has a certain permanency about it: it is not something government exercises only occasionally in situations of "last resort." Only in this way can human sustenance be assured on a worldwide basis.

Both *Rerum Novarum* and *Quadragesimo Anno* had placed some limitations on the use of private property. But observance of these limits was essentially left to individual decision. In *Mater et Magistra* a significant shift occurs. The basic decision making now lies much more with state authorities. As the late Joseph Gremillion put it, while John XXIII retained previous papal teaching on private property, he placed it more directly in relation to the common good. For John, according to Gremillion, "the *common good*" is not the glib phrase of a political campaign: It forms the bedrock of Catholic social doctrine, more fundamental than property, because its goal and measure is man and his perfection.[15]

Private property is not the only area where we see a marked turn toward an ongoing governmental role under John XXIII. Faced with a doctrinaire form of European Socialism, Leo XIII was extremely cautious about granting government any significant role in the conduct of economic affairs. Pius XI was a bit more relaxed in this regard, but still fundamentally reserved. For John XXIII economic problems had reached such global proportions that he could see no way out of the present morass without a substantial role for governments. While voluntary groups retained a vital role in their resolution, John urged that government was at times obliged to act on its own initiative if economic justice was to be realized.

With the papacy of John XXIII the focus of the Catholic Church has shifted from the working classes of Europe and North America to the millions in the Third World living in conditions of intense economic oppression. John turned Catholic attention toward a restructuring of the economic system on a global level which would provide basic sustenance for the impoverished millions of the world. Nothing in the pope's writings suggests that he favored a wholesale abandonment of the prevailing Capitalist system in this restructuring process. However, he did call for a major overhaul of this system that went beyond reformist impulses of Leo XIII and Pius XI.

John XXIII's writings clearly recognize the need to adjust economic programs to specific conditions prevailing in a given nation. The Church cannot endorse one economic model for all social settings.

John papacy brought to an end the effort launched by the Fribourg Union and the first two papal social encyclicals to create a distinctively Catholic alternative to existing economic theories. This approach has been continued in the main by his successors, though John Paul II has restored some of the specific condemnations of Socialism and Capitalism found in the earlier documents.

John XXIII also contributed mightily to international social thought through his other major social encyclical *Pacem in Terris* (1963). Addressed to the world community, this document emphasized human rights not only in general but in specific terms, including the right to religion and conscience, the right to cultural and moral values, and the right to emigrate and immigrate. He also added a list of corresponding duties, including the need for mutual collaboration. This list of rights represents the boldest statement of its kind found anywhere in papal social teaching.

This encyclical recognizes the absolute need for public authority on a national, and increasingly, on an international level. While all public authority must serve the common good, John views government as an indispensable agent of justice. There is need for greater support of the United Nations and other multilateral institutions.

*Pacem in Terris* is also significant for its strong condemnation of the arms race. Speaking in the immediate aftermath of the Cuban Missile Crisis and the erection of the Berlin Wall, John's message was both clear and prophetic. He argued that justice, right reason, and human dignity demand an immediate halt to the international arms race which generates a climate of fear and harms social and economic progress, especially in the Third World.[16]

In his declaration on social questions, Paul VI borrowed extensively from the writings of John XXIII. At times, however, he pushes a notion of his predecessor beyond prior limits. A case in point is his stance on economic pluralism. Paul VI clearly did not regard Catholic social teaching to be wedded to any specific social system rooted in natural law. Nor did he believe it was possible to speak of Catholic social doctrine as such, *only* of Catholic social teaching or the social teachings found in the Scriptures. Paul's *Octogesima Adveniens* issued for the eightieth anniversary of *Rerum Novarum* underscores this point:

It is with all its dynamism that the social teaching of the Church accompanies men in their search. If it does not intervene to authenticate a given structure or to propose a ready-made model, it does not thereby limit itself to recalling general principles. It develops through reflection applied to the changing situations of this world, under the driving force of the Gospel as the source of renewal when its message is accepted in its totality and with all its demands.[17]

Another important feature of Paul VI's approach to economic justice was his emphasis on the centrality of political participation in the process. Economic inequalities were not merely the result of technical flaws in the economic system according to him. Rather they were the direct result of the lack of meaningful participation and power in the political system. Paul thus continued in the footsteps of John XXIII in the focus on *participation* as a vital dimension of the struggle for significant reforms in the international economic order.[18]

There is little doubt that one of the most controversial aspects of Paul VI's teachings on economic justice in *Populorum Progressio* and *Octogesima Adveniens* had to do with his outlook on private property. He went considerably beyond his predecessors in speaking about legitimate restrictions on private property. *Populorum Progressio* acknowledges the right of the state to expropriate certain property which is underused, poorly used, whose present use results in hardship for the people, or whose use is detrimental for the overall well-being of the nation. It also regards as morally unacceptable the practice of the rich transferring their wealth outside their own country without any regard for the detrimental effect this may have on the national economy.

Paul VI's "socialist" reputation was further enhanced in the eyes of some by his general hostility toward the renewal of liberal ideology in economic affairs in the name of economic efficiency. This was seen by many as the most trenchant critique of the Capitalist system ever to appear in a papal document. While many Catholics, especially those in the financial world, took strong exception to what they considered a virtual endorsement of Socialism, other Catholics, especially those in the developing countries, saw it as an endorsement for their personal involvement in movements of Capitalism.

Paul VI also gave final approval to two central documents from the Vatican II Council that bear directly on the shape of Catholic social policy. The first is the document on "The Church in the Modern World" known by its Latin title *Gaudium et Spes.* The second is the "Declaration on Religious Freedom" on whose formulation the American hierarchy and theologian John Courtney Murray, S.J., had a significant impact. The first provides a comprehensive overview of the responsibilities incumbent upon the Church and its members in the latter part of the twentieth century. It is firmly rooted in the theological belief that the Church cannot be fully itself without direct involvement of its members in the everyday affairs of the world. A living faith, activating people to justice and love, is needed to overcome suspicion of religion. Following the same train of thought found in the social encyclicals of Paul VI, *Gaudium et Spes* insists that Catholicism is not bound to any particular political, economic, or social system. Further, this document gives special attention to the role of culture in social life. It states that cultural pluralism is a gift of God that the Church must use to spread the gospel, and that authentic freedom is integral to the preservation and development of cultural life. *Gaudium et Spes* expresses a firm commitment to the reservation of cultural rights and strongly encourages greater participation by women in cultural activities.

On the economic front, the Council's pastoral constitution underlined the centrality of people in any economic system and insisted that human labor is superior to other elements of economic life. Government has the responsibility to safeguard society from uses of private property that are detrimental to the common good.

*Gaudium et Spes* speaks boldly of the need to confront the arms race. While it does not canonize non-violence and conscientious objection, it certainly declares them valid moral options in a more forceful way than previous Catholic social documents. It rules out the targeting of population centers with weapons of mass destruction and expresses great reservation about the efficacy of deterrence policy. Disarmament is presented as an important priority for Christians.

*Dignitatis Humanae,* Vatican II's statement on religious freedom, while more limited in scope than *Gaudium et Spes,* significantly reoriented Catholicism's outlook toward the state. As a compromise document that had to respond to the variety of Catholic political experiences throughout the world, the conciliar declaration is a document of what John Courtney Murray called "very modest scope." One clear implication of this document is its commitment to the democratic "constitutional" state as the best model for preservation of authentic religious freedom. Though Murray himself regarded *Dignitatis Humanae* as a "modest" document, he claimed without hesitation that it had buried classical Catholic consciousness on the subject. There is little doubt that Pope John XXIII's strong endorsement of the "constitutional" model in his encyclical *Pacem in Terris,* issued in the midst of the ongoing, often acrimonious, conciliar debate on *Dignitatis Humanae,* played a major role in making possible this decided shift in Catholic thought.

Thus, the Council's "Declaration on Religious Freedom" must be seen as an important new step in the effort of Roman Catholicism to grapple with the realities of the modern world. It marks the end of any expectation on the part of Catholics that governments will serve (or are *in principle* to serve) as defenders of the faith. In the secular, constitutional state the highest value that both state and society are called upon to protect and foster is the personal and social value of the free exercise of religion. John Courtney Murray wrote of the significance of the Declaration in this vein:

> Thus the Declaration assumes its primary theological signifi-cance: formally, it settled only the minor issue of religious freedom. In effect, it defines the church's basic contemporary view of the world—of human society, of its order of human law and the functions of the all too human powers that govern it. Therefore, the Declaration not only completes the Decree on Ecumenism, it also lays down the premise, and sets the focus, of the church's concern with the secular world.[19]

Mention also needs to be made of two other Paul VI–era documents. The first is the 1971 Statement of the Synod of Bishops in 1971, "Justice in the World," which represents a major example of post–Vatican II episcopal collegiality and further refines previous papal social teachings in light of *Gaudium et Spes.* Two points in particular stand out in this document. The first is the clear affirmation that work for justice and involvement in the transformation of the world are integral elements of authentic gospel proclamation which must be oriented toward the redemption of the humanity and its liberation from every form of oppression. The second point is the reality of "structural injustice" which some have termed "social structural sin."

This synod document is also strong on the right to human development, on the central importance of participation by those who suffer injustice, on the critical value of maintaining respect for human rights within society and within the Church, and on the need for the Church to reflect a basic commitment to justice in its own lifestyle. The document also affirms the deep links between liturgy and justice.

The other document from this period is from Paul VI himself. Titled in Latin *"Evangelii Nuntiandi"* (Evangelization in the Modern World), its principal focus is on the Church's approach to mission. But in so doing, the pope declares that combating injustice and preaching liberation constitute essential ingredients of true evangelization. Following Vatican II, he affirms the importance of cultural preservation in the evangelization effort and underscores the importance of maintaining religious liberty as a fundamental human right. He continues in the tradition of a papal social teaching by excluding violence as a valid option for the attainment of justice.

Pope John Paul II has issued three major social encyclicals. They are *Laborem Excercens, Sollicitudo Rei Socialis,* and *Centesimus Annus.* In addition, his very first encyclical, *Rdemptor Hominis,* though it did not focus primarily on social issues, did lay down an overall theological framework which the pope employed in arguing his case for greater papal letters.

In *Redemptor Hominis,* John Paul argued for the Christological basis of human dignity. Concern for human dignity is a way of manifesting Christological reality in human society. This is an essential component of the Church's supernatural mission, not merely a "humanitarian" add-on. Picking up on his basic theme, John Paul posits an integral relationship between faith and economic life in *Laborem Exercens* which Richard McCormick has described as an ongoing philosophical meditation on human work in its varied dimensions.[20] Three themes important in the *Catechism*'s social teaching emerge as central in this first of John Paul's social encyclicals. The first is the centrality of work to the whole social question. And work is examined in two respects. The first is quite traditional—exploitative working conditions are immoral. This immorality stands out even more when one considers the dignity of every human person in the light of Incarnational Christology. Any economic system that reduces work to a mere instrument is to be condemned. While the way of stating this relationship may be somewhat unique to John Paul II, it is consistent with the tradition that has prevailed since Leo XIII.

The second major point made by John Paul II is the more creative one—work is considered not only for its potential to dehumanize, but as the means whereby the human person assists in the sanctification of creation. Thus, work becomes a vehicle for exercising human co-creatorship.

*Laborem Exercens* continues on the path set by John XXIII and Paul VI in emphasizing that a just wage does not exhaust the justice due to workers. John Paul II calls for new forms of profit-sharing, co-management, and co-ownership of productive property as an inherent part of workers' rights. Companies have not satisfied their justice obligations to their employers merely by paying a just wage. Some appropriate form of worker participation in ownership and decision-making is also required in the papal vision.[21]

John Paul II's more recent social encyclicals focus far more directly on particular socioeconomic questions than the more theological reflections resented in his first. In both of these documents the pope strongly defends the principle of participation in economic life. Without such participation an economy ultimately not only stagnates, but also likely results in forms of economic concentration that leave millions in, or near, the brink of poverty. When set against the totality of his teaching on economic justice, it is clear that John Paul II is no uncritical champion of Capitalism. There is no need to prepare a ticker-tape parade for him down Wall Street. In *Centesimus Annus,* he explicitly warns Western nations against any premature euphoria regarding their economic systems. While the market economy remains basic, major structural adaptations are required if it is ever to attain its true potential of sustaining a system of global justice. And the pope is clear about his belief that these adjustments are not apt to occur merely as a result of the market's internal dynamics. There is a role for the state in such readjustment, though on this point he is definitely less specific than Paul VI.

For John Paul II the basic questions to be asked about Capitalism (or any economic system) are what is its basic impact on people throughout the globe, and increasingly, how has it affected the realm of nature? This is the ultimate papal barometer. And it is his position that by these standards of measurement Capitalism continues to fail the test to a large extent despite its acknowledged philosophical superiority over other economic systems.

In an address on May 15, 1991, shortly after the release of *Centesimus Annus,* Pope John Paul told a group of international economic and political experts gathered in Rome to commemorate *Rerum Novarum*'s one hundredth anniversary that growing economic imbalances among the nations of the world brought on by large concentrations of wealth must be ended. He also cited the ravaging effects of pollution in the same speech. Coming as it did so soon after the release of his encyclical, this address may be seen as a Vatican counterbalance to those who inaccurately interpret the encyclical as endorsing the triumph of Capitalism.[22]

The same can be said for a major statement on the Church's social teaching which John Paul II delivered on September 9, 1993, at the University of Latvia in Riga. Here he offers his own explicit interpretation of his two major social encyclicals in terms of Capitalism. The pope emphasized that Catholic social doctrine cannot be viewed as "a surrogate for Capitalism." While the Church has consistently condemned "Socialism," it has likewise "distanced itself from capitalistic ideology, holding it responsible for grave social injustices." John Paul II underlined that, even after the collapse of Communism, grave doubts have to be raised about the validity of Capitalism. While he believed in the "market economy," such an economy acquires legitimacy only if it is circumscribed with a strong juridical framework which enables it truly to promote the freedom of all people. The pope also stressed that Catholicism is not tied to any specific political or economic system, but primarily offers a social theology which evaluates all concrete systems in the light of human dignity, moral law, and the divine plan for the human community.[23]

Increasingly John Paul II has also expressed reservation about Capitalism's lack of ecological concern. This is clearly the case in the two most recent social encyclicals and it surfaced even more explicitly in his 1990 World Day of Peace message which focused on ecology. In that message the pope said the following:

> It is manifestly unjust that a privileged few should continue to accumulate excess goods, squandering available resources, while masses of people are living in conditions of misery at the very lowest level of subsistence. Today the dramatic threat of ecological breakdown is teaching us the extent to which greed and selfishness—both individual and collective—are contrary to the order of creation, an order which is characterized by mutual interdependence.[24]

Two other themes have emerged in John Paul's writings of late. One is a growing concern about the relationship between militarization and the economy. Part of the pope's strong objection to the Gulf War stemmed more from the continued negative impact of military spending on human development across the globe than from any direct application of just war criteria or from any concern for the Church's strategic interests in the region. The importance given this theme in *Centesimus Annus* is good evidence of this. The second theme is the development in awareness in John Paul's writings of the dangerous effect of "Capitalist-generated" culture on human consciousness. Cultural renewal is certainly necessary in the papal view if the Capitalist system is ever to reach an acceptable moral standard internationally. In saying this, John Paul is clearly following the emphasis on culture found in the Council's *Gaudium et Spes*.

## II. The *Catechism* and Social Teaching: Where They Come Together

The task of synthesizing all of Catholic teaching, including the social encyclicals, into a single volume certainly was a daunting task. Hence it has to be recognized at the outset that the *Catechism* could not encompass all facets of more than a century of Catholic social teaching. Conscious of that inevitable limitation, we may still ask, however, whether it presents, albeit succinctly, the principal features of that teaching. The answer is *only partially*. In some areas the *Catechism* does a commendable job of highlighting the thrust of papal and conciliar teaching. In other areas it must be judged deficient.

References are included to many of the major Vatican social documents of the past century with a decided preference shown for *Gaudium et Spes* followed by *Centesimus Annus* and *Sollicitudo Rei Socialis*. Both *Rerum Novarum* and *Quadragesimo Anno* are virtually ignored as resources, while John XXIII's *Mater et Magistra* and *Populorum Progressio* are cited only very infrequently. *Pacem in Terris* is used a little more, but mostly in relation to the issue of authority in society rather than its central themes of human rights and world peace. The 1971 Synod Document on "Justice in the World" is not cited at all.

The *Catechism* does strongly reaffirm some of the major components of the papal/conciliar tradition. In the first place, it underlines the fundamentally social nature of the human person. The human person "needs to live in society" (1879). Society cannot be seen as extraneous to humanity but rather as a constituent dimension of authentic personhood. It is only through mutual service and dialogue with others that people develop their potential according to the *Catechism*, echoing the perspective of the Council's pastoral constitution.

The profoundly communitarian nature of human existence is further underscored in the *Catechism* in four paragraphs devoted to human solidarity (1939–1942). Citing both *Sollicitudo Rei Socialis* and *Centesimus Annus,* these paragraphs emphasize that solidarity among people is integral to any proper understanding of human life, whether cast in more secular or more explicitly theological terms. Theologically speaking, solidarity has its roots in Christ's redemptive sacrifice on the Cross. This sense of solidarity is absolutely critical for the resolution of the socioeconomic problems facing the world today. This sense of solidarity should impel Christians to champion greater equality among nations in terms of resources and economic capability. This is especially the case with regard to dismantling the "perverse mechanisms" that block the development of less advanced nations. In what has to be considered one of the *Catechism*'s strongest statements on social justice (2439), it is explicitly stated that wealthy nations have a grave moral responsibility to assist economically deprived countries, especially where there is a history of seizures of natural resources without fair payment. This is a duty rooted in solidarity and charity, and in the latter case in justice as well. The *Catechism* also speaks of a sense of spiritual solidarity that can serve as the backbone of enduring social commitment. Solidarity, although a popular term now, has rich potential for catechesis.[25]

Having affirmed the strongly communitarian outlook of Catholic social teaching, the *Catechism* goes on to underline the difference between "communitarianism" and "collectivism." In the spirit of the rather consistent rejection of the socialist option commonplace in the social encyclicals, the text stresses that "the principle of subsidiarity is opposed to all forms of collectivism" (1885). Certainly this position must be judged in keeping with the general direction of Catholic social teaching. Nevertheless it would have been useful to indicate that in both *Populorum Progressio* and *Sollicitudo Rei Socialis* we find a greater willingness to accept any social system (including presumably the socialist) provided that the particular system guarantees genuine participation on the part of the people who fall under its influence.

While there is little question that subsidiarity has been a focal point of Catholic social teaching from the time of *Quadragesimo Anno,* and hence the *Catechism* is quite right in giving it the emphasis it does, a cautionary note should have been sounded lest any Catholic interpret this commitment to subsidiarity as an unqualified endorsement of a "government is best which governs least" policy. As has already been noted in this analysis, respected Catholic commentators such as Msgr. George Higgins have insisted that there are times when the small effective agent of social policy is in fact the government. The desegregation legislation of the sixties and seventies is a case in point. And it is clear, beginning with *Mater et Magistra,* that the governmental role is viewed as integral and permanent in the process of implementing Catholic social teaching. John XXIII projected an indispensable "overseer" responsibility for government which he saw as something to be exercised on a continual, rather than an occasional, basis. In no way did he envision the role of the government as one of "last resort." In its presentation of subsidiarity and the corresponding role of government the *Catechism* has failed to capture fully the dynamic relationship posited originally by John XIII and repeated by Paul VI and John Paul II.

One area where the *Catechism* can be given a high grade is in dealing with war/peace issues. From its strong emphasis on the biblical injunction of "love of enemies" as a centerpiece of Christian spirituality to its explicit criticisms of the arms race and mass destruction through armed conflict, it has captured well the spirit prevailing in social documents, especially *Pacem in Terris* (which unfortunately it does not appeal to directly) and *Gaudium et Spes* (which it relies upon extensively). It also echoes the words of Paul VI when it describes peace as not merely the absence of war, but the result of justice (2304).

In the section focusing on "the duties of citizens," rather than in the one devoted to safeguarding peace and avoiding war, the *Catechism* adds a dimension to this question which is especially pertinent in many parts of the Third World: armed resistance in the face of oppression by political authority. The Catechism strictly conditions the right to engage in armed resistance (basically adapting the classical just war criteria). However, it does acknowledge the legitimacy of such resistance in certain grave situations, thus at least slightly moderating the strong opposition to violence generally characteristic of Catholic social teaching. The *Catechism* is to be commended for acknowledging the need at times for political liberation through armed resistance through citizen, rather than governmental, military action. If a criticism is to be made, it is that something should have been said on this point as well within the primary section on war/peace issues lest people understand the contemporary vision of peace in a way that excluded this moral option.

My final point of commendation concerns the strong linkage the *Catechism* establishes between spiritual conversion and the quest for justice and peace. This linkage has been emphasized in a special way during the past few decades of Catholic social teaching. It picks up in a way on the famous maxim of Nicolas Berdyaev that "bread for myself is a physical problem; bread for my neighbor is a spiritual problem." This linkage is especially well-stated in paragraph 2831, part of a reflection on the meaning of the Lord's Prayer. The text speaks as follows: "The drama of hunger in the world calls Christians who pray sincerely to exercise responsibility toward their brethren, both in their personal behavior and in their solidarity with the human family. This petition of the Lord's Prayer cannot be isolated from the parables of the poor man Lazarus and of the last Judgement." In this paragraph one senses the passion for justice that often marks *Gaudium et Spes* and the papal social encyclicals but which, regrettably, is generally lacking in the *Catechism*'s presentation of Catholic social teaching.

### III. The *Catechism* and Social Teaching: What Is Missing or Underplayed

Several of the *Catechism*'s weaknesses relative to its articulation of Catholic social teaching have already been mentioned. There are others, somewhat more serious, that also must be aired.

First to the most glaring omissions. The most striking is the failure of the Catechism to present the quest for justice as absolutely central to the authentic proclamation of the gospel. While the reader of the *Catechism* certainly receives some understanding of central aspects of the Church's social teaching, this teaching can appear to be no more than one of the many dimensions of the Catholic faith. This stands in sharp contrast to the emphasis on human liberation through social commitment as part of the very core of genuine gospel preaching and evangelization in such documents as the 1971 Synod of Bishops statement on "Justice in the World" and Pope Paul VI's apostolic exhortation *Evangelii Nuntiandi*. Not a trace of this bold linkage between gospel proclamation and human liberation can be found in the section dealing with "Mission" (849–870).

The *Catechism* is also deficient in not clearly surfacing the continuing critique of Capitalism that has been a constitutive dimension of the social encyclicals since 1891. While, as John Paul II has said, Capitalism may be the system which we will have to employ, this does not mean that the Church does not have serious concerns about how this system has functioned in terms of justice. The *Catechism* is quite specific in its rejection of "collectivism." It should have been just as specific in restating the critiques of Capitalism in both the earlier and more recent social encyclicals as well as in a host of other statements made by Pope John Paul II. Only on a few occasions does the *Catechism* make reference to troublesome economic structures which by implication can be understood as capitalistic structures.[26]

There are also areas where the *Catechism* treats topics much too briefly and incompletely, given their importance in Catholic social teaching. One of these areas is that of social structural sin. At the very end of the section on sin (1869), there is an acknowledgment of this reality in an analogous way. This is far removed from the prominence given to the central impact unjust social structures have in aiding and abetting sin in human society by several of the post-Vatican II social documents such as the 1971 Synod document. John Paul II has also given considerable emphasis to such sinful situations, especially in his many regional statements on social justice during his travels.

Another problematic area is the ecological. While admittedly statements on ecology are rather recent in terms of official pronouncements, sections in *Laborem Exercens* on human co-creatorship, in *Centesimus Annus* on the necessity for humanity to be "conscious of its duties and obligations to future generations" (37), and in Pope John Paul II's World Peace Day message which focused on ecology, could certainly have provided a basis for a clear statement on Catholic ecological responsibility. There are several paragraphs dealing with the order and beauty of creation, but these remain highly philosophical and theological in their approach, lacking specific moral direction (e.g., 337–348). In a brief section entitled "Respect for the Integrity of Creation" (2415–2418): the text does condition human dominion over animals and nature. But nowhere does one find a clear presentation of the far-ranging dimensions of the ecological crisis and the pastoral and moral challenge it presents in so many countries in the world.

It is also regrettable that the *Catechism* omits the challenging charter of human rights found in *Pacem in Terris*. This was a tremendous breakthrough in Catholic thought and has a direct impact on the ongoing work of Vatican II, particularly religious freedom. This bold declaration carried on the ongoing work of Vatican II, particularly in the area of religious freedom. This bold declaration caught the imagination not only of the Catholic community, but of people throughout the world. Its succinctness would have made it an ideal fit for the *Catechism*.

One notes a certain weakness as well in the section dealing with "The Political Community and the Church." Fundamentally these paragraphs (2244–2246) are in harmony with the basic outlook evident in the documents of Vatican II and the social encyclicals. What is missing is any clear indication that at Vatican II, especially in the document on religious liberty, the Catholic Church made a decisive change in its approach to its relations with the state. In accepting the democratic pluralist state as its preferred model over the classical church-state integration model, Vatican II altered Catholic expectations of the state in terms of Catholic morality as John Courtney Murray has emphasized. This changed perception is critical to the public discussions in which the Church now finds itself. Hence it would have been beneficial to Catholic self-understanding to have the implications of Vatican II on this vital point clearly stated. Teachers will have to take up this subject with students.

It is also possible to fault the *Catechism* in terms of its treatment of Capitalism. As we have seen, Catholicism's stance on Capitalism is generally critical even though *Centesimus Annus* does indicate that it likely provides the only viable starting point for economic discussions today. Because we have seen some significantly distorted interpretations of this encyclical's remarks about Capitalism, something that John Paul himself has critiqued in several addresses subsequent to the encyclical, the *Catechism* should have included an explicit statement on the Church's perennial difficulties with Capitalism. If the response is that such a topic is too specific, my response is that the *Catechism* is quite specific on sexual sins. So why not in the area of economic justice.

One of the most severe criticisms of the *Catechism* has to do with its weak, and I would even be prone to say misleading, treatment of a matter of worldwide significance for Catholicism: migration and immigration. *Pacem in Terris* declared immigration/emigration to be a basic human right. Several Vatican documents in recent years have spoken strongly about the need for the Catholic community to respond compassionately on this issue, whether in California, Texas, Mexico, Uganda, Swaziland, Austria, Germany, Poland, etc. Unfortunately this increasingly central pastoral, moral, and political topic is discussed under a single number (2241). And the emphasis is almost as much on the right of political authorities to circumscribe immigration and the gratitude immigrants are to show to host countries than it is on the natural right of emigration/immigration as set down by John XXIII and several Vatican documents dealing with the issue. The *Catechism's* treatment of this subject has fallen far short of presenting the full trust of Catholic social teaching.

Finally, a critique such as this could not conclude without some mention of the sexist language throughout the *Catechism,* a topic that other contributors to this collection also note. Surely the forced retranslation was a violation of human equality. While there may be room for legitimate discussion of the language issue when one approaches strictly theological issues, the social justice sections of the *Catechism* generally do not involve such directly theological matters. Hence it is morally jarring to read continually "exclusive" language only with minimal exception in the text.

In summary, we can say that the *Catechism* provides an adequate starting point for teaching Catholic social doctrine. But there is definite need to supplement it with readings from the relevant Vatican II documents and papal social encyclicals.

## Notes

[1]  Byers, David M., editor. *Justice in the Marketplace: Collected Statements of the Vatican and the United States Bishops on Economic Policy, 1891–1984.* General Introduction and Document Introductions by John T. Pawlikowski (Washington, DC: USCC Publications, 1985).

[2]  See David O'Brien and Thomas Shannon, editors. *Renewing the Earth* (Garden City, NY: Doubleday, 1977), 21–22.

[3]  For further reading on the Fribourg Union, Normand Paulus, "Fribourg Union," in *The New Dictionary of Catholic Social Thought*, edited by Judith A. Dwyer (Collegeville: Liturgical Press, 1994), 404-405.

[4]  The ideas of the Fribourg Union received papal approval in a January, 1888, meeting between Union leaders and Leo XIII.

[5]  Normand J. Paulhaus. "Social Catholicism and the Fribourg Union," *The Annual of the Society of Christian Ethics* (1980), at 79.

[6]  See *Acta Apostolicis Sedis* (1931), 185, 211.

[7]  As quoted by George Higgins in "Religion and National Economic Policy: A Catholic Perspective," in Eugene J. Fisher and Daniel F. Polish, editors. Formation of Social

Policy in the Catholic and Jewish Traditions (Notre Dame, IN: University of Notre Dame Press, 1980), at 85.

[8] David Hollenbach. *Claims in Conflict: Retrieving and Renewing the Catholic Human Rights Tradition* (New York: Paulist Press, 1979), at 157. Also, the essay on "Subsidiarity, Principle of" by Michael E. Allsopp in *The New Dictionary of Catholic Social Thought*, 927–29.

[9] Greeley, Andrew. "American Catholicism: 1909–1984," *AMERICA* 150 (June 23–30, 1984), 487–492; Coleman, John. *An American Strategic Theology* (New York: Paulist Press, 1982), 102.

[10] Higgins, George. "Religion and National Economic Policy," 92.

[11] Weakland, Archbishop Rembert. "Catholic Social Services: Future Directions," *Origins* 25, 1 (May 18, 1995), 14–15.

[12] See: Yzermans, Vincent A. *The Major Addresses of Pope Pius XII*, vol. 2 (St. Paul, MN: North Central Publishing Co., 1961). Also, Steven M. Avella, "Pius XII," in *The New Dictionary of Catholic Social Thought*, 741–744.

[13] Pawlikowski, John T. "The Vatican and the Holocaust: Uresolved Issues," in Marvin Perry and Frederick M. Schweitzer, editors, *Jewish-Christian Encounters Over the Centuries: Symbiosis, Prejudice, Holocaust, Dialogue* (New York: Peter Lang, 1994), 293–310.

[14] See: Gremillion, Joseph, editor. *The Gospel of Peace and Justice* (Marynoll, NY: Orbis Press, 1975), 154. Also, Hans Lagendorfer, "John XXIII," *The New Dictionary of Catholic Social Thought*, 490–491.

[15] See: Gremillion, Joseph, *The Gospel of Peace and Justice*, 33. Also, David Hollenbach, "Common Good," in *New Dictionary of Catholic Social Thought*, 192–197.

[16] For further reading on this encyclical, Kenneth P. J. Hallahan, *"Pacem in Terris,"* in *The New Dictionary of Catholic Social Thought*, 696–706.

[17] *Octogesima Adveniens*, 24.

[18] For further reading on this encyclical, Bernard F. Evans, *"Octogesima Adveniens,"* in *New Dictionary of Catholic Social Thought*, 683–692.

[19] Murray, John Courtney. "The Declaration on Religious Freedom," in Thomas F. Stranksy, editor, *Declaration on Religious Freedom of Vatican II* (New York: Paulist Press, 1967), 131.

[20] McCormick, Richard, "Notes on Moral Theology, 1981," *Theological Studies* 43, 1 (March 1981), 92–95.

[21] For further reading on this encyclical, Gregory Baum, *"Laborem Exercens,"* in *The New Dictionary of Catholic Social Thought*, 527–535.

[22] See: "Pope, Criticizing Capitalism Laments Widening Rich-Poor Gap, Ecological Damage," *National Catholic Reporter,* 27, 31 (May 31, 1991), 8.

[23] John Paul II, "What Church Social Teaching Is and Is Not," *Origins* 23, 15 (September 23, 1993), 257.

[24] John Paul II, "Peace with All Creation," *Origins,* 19, 28 (December 14, 1989), 465–468.

[25] For further reading on this subject, Matthew L. Lamb, "Solidarity," *The New Dictionary of Catholic Social Thought*, 908–912.

[26] For further reading on this subject, Oliver F. Williams, "Capitalism," *The New Dictionary of Catholic Social Thought*, 111–123.

# Assisted Suicide in Light of the *Catechism*

## B. Andrew Lustig

Recent polls of both the general public and doctors in this country reveal growing support for the legalization of "physician assistance in dying" in response to difficult clinical cases. These poll data are perhaps not surprising, given the manner in which the public discussion has generally been conducted. There are a number of separable strains in the arguments by proponents of physician-assisted suicide, which, in their cumulative effect, have increased public support. First, for some, the so-called "right to die" should include both a negative right (i.e., the right to withhold or withdraw unwanted medical interventions, including life-sustaining treatment) and a positive right to assistance from another (ideally a physician or knowledgeable professional).[1] Second, there are a number of recent cases of assisted suicide that have drawn the attention of national media. Dr Jack Kevorkian, touted by some as a crusader for assisted suicide as the "ultimate" extension of patients' rights, has become a household name. Other more moderate physicians (e.g., Timothy Quill) have exhibited greater compassion and greater sobriety in mustering a limited defense of physician-assisted suicide for difficult cases that involve significant pain and suffering at the end of life. Howard Brody, for example, discusses the limited need for physician-assisted suicide as a "compassionate response to medical failure."[2]

Third, some commentators, while finding parochial reasons for concluding that physician-assisted suicide is morally or religiously wrong, nonetheless argue that such warrants, while compelling to particular communities, cannot be generally binding as grounds for public policy to limit the liberty interests of individuals in a secular pluralistic society. H. Tristram Engelhardt, in a typical argument, reduces the policy questions implicated by physician-assisted suicide to the matter of whether the state has any legitimate authority to intervene against this "final choice" exercised by citizens as autonomous moral agents.[3]

Opponents to any change in present social policy on assisted suicide offer a number of arguments in turn. According to some commentators, the integrity of medicine itself is at the heart of the issue. Willard Gaylin, for example, speaks passionately about the fundamental meaning of medicine as a practice and a profession that is implicated in the discussion of physician-assisted suicide. As Gaylin observes:

> The very soul of medicine is on trial. For this is not one of those peripheral issues about which pluralism and relativism can be tolerated, about which a value-free stand on the substance can be hedged around with procedural safeguards to ensure informed consent or "sound decision making." Nor is this an issue . . . that touches medicine only as a trade. This issue touches medicine at its very moral center; if this moral center collapses, if physicians become killers or are even merely licensed to kill, the profession—and, therewith, each physician—will never again be worthy of trust and respect as healer and comforter and protector of life in all its frailty. For if medicine's power over life may be used equally to heal or to kill, the doctor is no more a moral professional but rather a morally neutered technician.[4]

Other opponents, while expressing compassion for the plight of patients in hard cases, emphasize the range of deleterious consequences likely to follow in the wake of legalizing physician-assisted suicide.[5] These arguments, generally designated as "slippery slope" concerns, come in two versions. A first version emphasizes the empirical likelihood that assisted suicide, if legalized, might become less than fully consensual, especially among patients already vulnerable and marginalized by the present health care system.[6] A second version focuses less on empirical judgments about likely consequences than on the legal logic that underlies arguments for legalizing physician-assisted suicide. This approach is based on the conviction that the values basic to the arguments by proponents of physician-assisted suicide—viz., patient autonomy and the relief of suffering—seem equally compelling as justifications for active euthanasia at the patient's request for harder cases involving competent patients unable to end their lives (such as quadriplegics). Moreover, if autonomy and relief of suffering are the primary values operant in efforts to legalize assisted suicide, it is conceptually suspect to limit respect for those values to cases involving patients diagnosed as *terminal*. Why should a patient's autonomous wish to die be restricted to the circumstance of a terminal prognosis? Similarly, why is relief of suffering limited to forms of suffering linked to a terminal prognosis? There are, after all, many types of non-terminal illness—including mental anguish—for which patients might wish to have their suffering terminated through assistance in death.[7]

As a third argument, some opponents conclude that legalizing physician-assisted suicide represents a Rubicon that should not be crossed without greater attention to alternatives to assistance in dying, including greater public and medical commitments to "tending the process of dying" well, through extension of palliative efforts in both tertiary and hospice settings.[8]

Against the background of this volatile, highly charged public debate, I will consider recent Roman Catholic discussion of assistance in suicide, with a number of issues in mind. First, the Catholic position, as elaborated briefly in Part Three of the recent *Catechism*, draws upon the tradition's arguments against suicide more generally. The context of clinical medicine, which serves in much of the secular discussion to distinguish physician-assisted suicide from judgments about suicide and assisted suicide in extra-clinical circumstances, does not alter the deontological features of traditional Roman Catholic arguments. I will look first, then, to the core arguments against suicide developed in the tradition, both for their cogency as general norms and for their relevance to context of clinical medicine.

Second, I will consider the various modes of discourse found in the tradition, both in the *Catechism* and elsewhere. Ethicist James Gustafson has recently developed a compelling typology of the species of moral discourse one finds at work in bioethics, which he labels as prophetic, narrative, ethical, and policy modes. I will suggest that the Roman Catholic position, as developed in a number of recent statements, is "multi-modal"; i.e., it includes elements of all four of Gustafson's modes. At the same time, given the complexity of the Catholic position, the various warrants at work in discussion make our analysis of their respective force more difficult. How is the Roman Catholic position best understood? Is it compelling on its own terms? Is it internally consistent as an "ethical" approach? Is it telling as a "prophetic" denunciation of larger social and cultural trends, of which the effort to legalize physician-assisted suicide is but one reflection?

In offering brief answers to the foregoing questions, I will limit myself to an overview of the substantive theological and anthropological convictions at work in the Roman Catholic position and a brief consideration of Catholicism's characteristic moral method. (Obviously, a comprehensive assessment would require a much more elaborate discussion and critique of both principles and method than I will offer here.) For example, it has often been argued that, absent specifically religious premises, no absolute proscription of suicide (or, by extension, assisted suicide) can be justified on *strictly* philosophical grounds.[9] Because recent Roman Catholic arguments appeal to different warrants—primarily Scripture and natural law—the central question that emerges concerns the cogency of that *mixed* position for individuals, groups, and institutions that do not share the theological values which inform the more general natural law appeals in Roman Catholic arguments. Functionally, the question here concerns the cogency of particular modes of moral discourse as *separable* strands of a multi-modal discussion.

I will suggest that Gustafson's analysis of moral discourse is helpful not only in its typological and descriptive function but in its power to illuminate the normative choices that religious persons and individuals confront in seeking to respond effectively to cultural, economic, and political challenges to their fundamental convictions, of the sort that the effort to legalize physician-assisted suicide represents. Here, I will be concerned to elaborate several shared values that might ground a consensus of opposition to physician-assisted suicide as a change in social, legal, and moral practice.

Finally, I will briefly consider the relevance of Roman Catholic appeals to the larger policy discourse on physician-assisted suicide. Whatever the moral logic at work in the larger, often determinedly secular, debate, and whatever the outcomes of upcoming judicial and legislative choices, Roman Catholic opposition to assisted suicide will retain, at the least, its prophetic function in a society that often settles for "moral minimalism" as its preferred discourse. Moreover, the principles basic to a distinctive Roman Catholic presence in health care delivery will continue to shape decisively the practices of Catholic care institutions and the identity of professionals who work in such institutions.

## I. The Arguments in the Tradition Against Suicide

The brief discussion in the *Catechism* of suicide, and assisted suicide, occurs in Chapter Two of Part Three. The primary warrant that undergirds this discussion is expressly theological: *"human life is sacred* because from its beginning it involves the creative action of God and it remains forever in a special relationship with the Creator, who is its sole end (2258). In light of the lordship of God, the *Catechism* draws a fundamental (and exceptionless) moral conclusion: "no one can under *any circumstance* [emphasis mine] claim for himself the right directly to destroy an innocent human being" (2258).

The warrants here are primarily those of special revelation. Exodus 23:7 is invoked as the Scriptural basis of the comprehensive prohibition: "Do not slay the innocent and the righteous" (2261). However, other warrants are also invoked: "The deliberate murder of an innocent person is gravely *contrary to the dignity of the human person, to the golden rule,* and to the holiness of the Creator" (2261). While the context for such warrants may be found in both Scriptural and extra-Scriptural sources, it is worth noting here, for purposes of our later discussion that such warrants, by being available to those who would justify them in non-revelational terms, may also provide a justificatory common ground upon which to develop a consensus beyond the theological warrants that function as primary in the *Catechism* discussion.

The *Catechism* distinguishes the blanket proscription against taking innocent human life from forms of justified homicide, which include "legitimate defense" (2263–2265) and, "in cases of extreme gravity," the death penalty as a means of "preserving the common good of society" (2266). However, all forms of *"direct and intentional killing,"* which include abortion (2270–2275), euthanasia (2276–2279), and suicide (2280–2283), are deemed "gravely sinful" (2268).

I focus here on the discussion of suicide in the *Catechism,* for by extension, what is morally illicit *in se* (suicide) will also be so if the assistance of a third party is required in order to be effected (assisted suicide). In large measure, the *Catechism* rehearses the three arguments developed in the tradition and first found in that form in Thomas Aquinas. However, a comparison of Thomas's arguments with those in the *Catechism* is instructive in two respects: (a) the order of arguments in the two discussions differs; and (b) the greater nuance in the *Catechism*'s discussion makes it less vulnerable to criticisms that can fairly be raised against Aquinas's own formulation of the arguments.

In the *Summa Theologica,* Aquinas offers three arguments for the illicitness of suicide: (1) since "everything naturally loves itself [and] . . . everything naturally keeps itself in being," suicide is "contrary to the inclination of nature, and to charity whereby every man should love himself"; (2) since "every man is part of the community, . . . [one who kills himself] injures the community"; and (3) "because life is God's gift to man, . . . whoever takes his own life, sins against God . . . as he who usurps to himself judgment of a matter not entrusted to him" (II, II, Q. 64, Article 5).[10]

In the *Catechism,* the order of arguments is different. Thomas's third argument becomes the first in the *Catechism* discussion, with Thomas's first and second arguments then following as the second and third arguments respectively. In addition, Thomas's primary metaphor of life as God's "gift" has been amplified, or rather replaced, by the *Catechism*'s use of the language of God's sovereignty and our stewardship: "Everyone is responsible for his life before God who has given it to him. It is God who remains the sovereign Master of life. We are obliged to accept life gratefully and preserve it for his honor, and the salvation of our souls. We are *stewards, not owners,* of the life God has entrusted to us. It is not ours to dispose of " (2289).

A moment's reflection clarifies why the shift in language here from Thomas's metaphor of life is less vulnerable to the criticisms that can be leveled at Aquinas. The metaphor of gift suggests, *simpliciter,* that what is given is indeed the recipient's to use, or to set aside, as he or she deems best. We generally deem gratitude by a recipient the appropriate response for a gift that is given, and we tend to judge indifference to a gift an attitude worthy of censure. But the language of gift, per se, does *not* lodge a continuing right or power in the gift-giver over subsequent use or disposition of the gift. In both trivial and non-trivial ways, we are all familiar with occasions when either the exchange of one gift for another, or the renunciation or even the destruction of a gift no longer deemed useful, emerge as appropriate choices, within the strict context established by the language of gift-giving itself.

To be sure, Thomas's own use of the metaphor of gift is linked to God as Life-Giver. Hence there may be other arguments that might function, in conjunction with gift language, to make a stronger case for the illegitimacy of "terminating" the gift of life prematurely. Indeed, such arguments function directly in the *Catechism* discussion. It is because God is, in the strict sense, the owner of our lives, and because we are called to be His faithful stewards, that His purposes retain their moral force in the use and disposition of His resources. The notions of sovereignty and stewardship combine, then, to offer a far more compelling theological context for concluding that suicide and, by extension, assisted suicide, are morally illicit.

The second and third arguments in the *Catechism* mirror the first and second arguments that Thomas offers; viz., "Suicide contradicts the natural inclination of the human being to preserve and perpetuate his life. It is gravely contrary to the just love of self. It likewise offends love of neighbor because it unjustly breaks the ties of solidarity with family, nation, and other human societies to which we continue to have obligations. Suicide is contrary to love for the living God" (2281).

As with Thomas's own account, much more would be required to develop these second and third arguments in thoroughgoing fashion. As they stand, they both remain subject to serious question. It may well be that suicide contradicts a "natural inclination" to "preserve and perpetuate life." Yet biological life, as an intrinsic value, is a necessary but not sufficient condition for rendering a moral judgment regarding an act purposively related to that natural end (i.e., for determining the specific moral relevance of that natural inclination). The Roman Catholic tradition, after all, is especially rich in casuistry regarding the subjective values that function in assessments of ordinary and extraordinary means of treatment. There is, surely, a "natural inclination" to preserve life, but the relevance of that inclination to the specification of moral duty remains context-dependent. The tradition speaks straightforwardly about two fundamental criteria to be invoked in assessing whether means are to be considered ordinary or extraordinary: whether or not a given intervention offers a "reasonable" chance of success, and whether or not the treatment, in particular circumstances, is deemed proportionate or disproportionate relative to its benefits and burdens. Thus, in light of the centrality of the language of ordinary and extraordinary means to Roman Catholic casuistry, the moral force of a "natural inclination" to preserve life is not intuitively obvious. *A fortiori,* the blanket proscription of suicide solely on that basis requires more than the argument appears to provide on its own terms.

The third argument, which recasts the Aristotelian/Thomistic language of persons as "parts of the community" in terms of an "unjust" rupture of ties of solidarity again would require greater elaboration to be fully persuasive on its own terms. Only in the expressly theological context provided by the first and primary argument regarding sovereignty and stewardship does the language of "solidarity" carry implications that a choice of suicide or assisted suicide is *necessarily* a denial of solidarity. Indeed, if restricted to non-theological arguments, one might, without perversity, argue to precisely the opposite conclusion: viz., that under conditions of duress, and the undue costs often associated with end-of-life clinical care, suicide might emerge not as a denial, but an expression, of solidarity. I believe such logic to be suspect, but the language of solidarity, taken on its own terms, is insufficient to serve as an independent warrant to proscribe suicide or assisted suicide in all cases, unless linked to expressly theological themes.

However, the primacy of the theological principle of God's sovereignty (with the anthropological correlate of our stewardship) explains the *Catechism*'s recourse to the language of the "inalienability" of the "right to life of every innocent human individual" (2273).[11] Given the brevity of the *Catechism*'s discussion, it may be useful to amplify its analysis at this point by considering the analysis of the same issues found in John Paul II's recent encyclical, *The Gospel of Life*. Here there are 11 emphases the pontiff develops that reinforce and further clarify the position set forth in the *Catechism*.

(1) John Paul notes that both abortion and euthanasia are characteristic of a "new cultural climate" which "gives crimes against life *a new and—if possible—even more sinister character*" (John Paul II, 1995, p. 15). That sinister character derives from the justification offered for such practices as expressions of individual autonomy.[12] Thus,

> Broad sectors of public opinion justify certain crimes against life in the name of the rights of individual freedom, and on this basis they claim not only exemption from punishment but even authorization by the state, so that these things can be done with total freedom and indeed with the free assistance of health-care systems (15).

(2) In the wake of this profound shift in public attitudes toward the

taking of human life—ostensibly in the name of individual freedom—the integrity of the medical profession itself is under siege. Hence,

> Choices once unanimously considered criminal and rejected by the common moral sense are gradually becoming socially acceptable. Even certain sectors of the medical profession, which by its calling is directed to the defense and care of human life, are increasingly willing to carry out these acts against the human person. In this way, the very nature of the medical profession is distorted and contradicted, and the dignity of those who practice it is degraded (15).

(3) This shift in cultural and political attitudes involves a

> *war of the powerful against the weak:* [i.e.], a life which would require greater acceptance, love and care is considered useless, or held to be an intolerable burden, and is therefore rejected in one way or another (27).

(4) Specifically in reference to assisted suicide and euthanasia,

> In a social and cultural context which makes it more difficult to face and accept suffering, the *temptation* becomes all the greater *to resolve the problem of suffering by eliminating it at the root,* by hastening death so that it occurs at the moment considered most suitable (30).[13]

(5) More generally stated, the above noted "temptation" is often linked to, or expressive of, a "certain Promethean attitude which leads people to think that they can control life and death by taking the decisions about them into their own hands" (31).[14]

(6) That attitude in turn is linked to the cultural and moral emphasis on freedom which is extreme in its subjectivism. Thus,

> the roots of the contradiction between the solemn affirmation of human rights and their tragic denial in practice lies in a *notion of freedom* which exalts the isolated individual in an absolute way ... While it is true that the taking of life not yet born or in its final stages is sometimes marked by a mistaken sense of altruism and human compassion, it cannot be denied

that such a culture of death, taken as a whole, betrays a completely individualistic concept of freedom, which ends up by becoming the freedom of "the strong" against the weak who have no choice but to submit ( 36).

(7) That extreme understanding of subjectivity, which leads to what John Paul describes as a "culture of death," reflects the loss of essential moorings endemic to what has been described as the "post-modern" context. Within this atmosphere of unprincipled license,

freedom negates and destroys itself, and becomes a factor leading to the destruction of others, when it no longer recognizes and respects its *essential link with the truth*. When freedom, out of a desire to emancipate itself from all forms of tradition and authority, shuts out even the most obvious evidence of an objective and universal truth, which is the foundation of personal and social life, then the person ends up by no longer taking as the sole and indisputable point of reference for his own choices the truth about good and evil, but only his subjective and changeable opinion or, indeed, his selfish interest and whim ( 37).

(8) At the "deepest roots of the struggle between the 'culture of life' and the 'culture of death,'" one finds

the heart of the tragedy being experienced by modern man: *the eclipse of the sense of God and of man,* typical of a social and cultural climate dominated by secularism . . . Those who allow themselves to be influenced by this climate easily fall into a sad vicious circle: *when the sense of God is lost, there is also a tendency to lose the sense of man,* of his dignity and his life (39–40).

(9) That "eclipse of the sense of God and of man inevitably leads to a *practical materialism,* which breeds individualism, utilitarianism, and hedonism (42)."

(10). In such a context,

suffering, an inescapable burden of human existence but also a factor of possible personal growth, is "censored," rejected as useless, indeed opposed as an evil, always and in every way to be avoided. When it cannot be avoided and the prospect of even some future well-being vanishes, then life appears to have lost all meaning and the temptation grows in man to claim the right to suppress it (42).

(11) Finally, assisted suicide as a response to another's suffering represents "an injustice which can never be excused":

Even when not motivated by a selfish refusal to be burdened with the life of someone who is suffering, [such an action] must be called a *false mercy,* and indeed a disturbing "perversion" of mercy. True "compassion" leads to sharing another's pain; it does not kill the person whose suffering we cannot bear (109).

In these 11 arguments, John Paul II appeals to a range of values: the value of a freedom linked to objective standards of right and wrong; the value of justice, in light of which assisted suicide is seen as a violation of the rights of the most vulnerable in our midst under the guise of a misplaced compassion; and the value of the integrity of medicine as an oathed profession. But the fundamental perspective throughout his discussion remains explicitly theological. The eclipse of God's purposes results in the devaluing of life, a thoroughly subjectivist account of human freedom and agency, an attitude of unconstrained technical control of the circumstances and timing of death, an impoverished understanding of the meaning of suffering, and a social climate of materialism and hedonism. As we consider these various appeals in subsequent discussion, it will be instructive to consider how such explicitly theological premises might function in the public, determinedly secular, discussion of assisted suicide.

## II. Modes of Moral Discourse in the Debate About Assisted Suicide

I turn now to a consideration of James Gustafson's analysis of the modes of moral discourse prevalent in bioethics discussions.[15] It may be useful, at this point, to elaborate the details of James Gustafson's typology, for Gustafson argues that each mode of discourse—narrative, prophetic, ethical, and policy—is necessary to the moral deliberations of particular communities and society at large, but none is, of itself, sufficient (127).

These days, ethical discourse may be the mode most familiar to us—the appeal to rules and principles, the invocation of various rights, the vocabularies of consequentialism and deontology. Ethics is an important language, for it serves to frame our reflections as we justify choices in a pluralistic society where a common narrative cannot be assumed. But ethics, according to Gustafson, also tends to be micro-focused, small in scale, working within the bounds of the status quo, seldom concerned with the larger cultural or social picture (127–130).

Prophetic discourse, by contrast, is often quite passionate in its sweeping indictments of larger cultural trends and social sins. Such discourse tends to make up in vision what it lacks in precision. It forces us to notice the forest through the trees, to see those large-scale background features that the ethical mode in the foreground tends to underplay (130–136). The discourse of narrative is the language of story, the story that forms a community—in the Christian tradition, the centrality of the good news, the complexity of the parables, the attitudes and ethos shaped by the story the community tells, the faithfulness of the community to its own shaping narrative. Narrative is not the language of argument, of precise moral reasoning, of premises and conclusions. Instead, narrative is more full-blooded, less skeletal. The bare bones of arguments so dear to secular philosophers are covered with the sinews and flesh of tradition. Narrative, before all else, is about inspiration, about the formation of character. We are shaped by the stories we tell (136–139).

And finally, there is policy discourse. Policy discourse, rather than focusing on ideal theories or grand conceptions, usually functions within the constraints of history and culture. It works with the values already embedded in the choices that we have made. It seldom, if ever, is prophetic; its horizon is limited. It generally asks not "What is the good or the right choice?" but, within a range of alternatives, "What is the reasonably good and feasible choice?" (139–141).

In light of Gustafson's distinctions, then, two questions are especially important in regard to Roman Catholic arguments against suicide and assisted suicide: (1) In which modes are the arguments developed? and (2) How might they function in the current public debate about the moral and legal legitimacy of assisted suicide? These questions are a particular instance of a general problematic for theological ethics, Roman Catholic and otherwise: (1) the relations between theologically grounded appeals and general moral prescriptions; and (2) the relations that should obtain between morality (whatever it warrants) and law and public policy.

The arguments in the *Catechism* and especially in *The Gospel of Life* exemplify, to varying degrees, all four of Gustafson's modes. As narrative discourse, the discussion, particularly in *The Gospel of Life,* invokes a number of appeals within the tradition—the normative model of Jesus himself for believers, the authority of the Church Fathers, the shaping power of Gospel values upon the formation of Christian character and moral agency. But even more pronounced in *The Gospel of Life* is the prophetic mode of discourse. Much of the moral authority of that encyclical derives from a broad-based and fundamental critique of larger trends in culture and society, especially the tendencies of secularism toward subjectivism and unconstrained personal autonomy, as well as its hedonistic assumptions about the nature and possible purpose of suffering.

However, in contrast to narrative or prophetic modes of discourse, which some might dismiss as parochial appeals, the Roman Catholic tradition also offers recommendations for the public order based on appeals to natural law and right reason. According to the *Catechism,* and indicative of the tradition historically, human beings can attain knowledge of both God and common morality by their natural capacities. Thus, quoting *Dei Verbum,* the *Catechism* observes that

> "Our holy mother, the Church, holds and teaches that God, the first principle and last end of all things, can be known with certainty from the created world by the natural light of human reason." Without this capacity, man would not be able to welcome God's revelation (36).

At the same time, the *Catechism* reflects the tradition's awareness of the difficulties that beset the natural capacities of reason, both in relation to knowledge of God and of moral truth. Number 37, for example, reflects on the obstacles to such natural knowledge by quoting with approval from Pius XII's *Human Generis:*

> Though human reason is, strictly speaking, truly capable by its own natural power and light of attaining a true and certain knowledge of the one personal God . . . and of the natural law written in our hearts by the Creator . . . yet there are many obstacles which prevent reason from the effective and fruitful

use of this inborn faculty. For the truths that concern the relations between God and man wholly transcend the visible order of things, and, if they are translated into human action and influence it, they call for self-surrender and abnegation. The human mind, in its turn, is hampered in the attaining of such truths, not only by the impact of the senses and the imagination, but also by disordered appetites which are the consequences of original sin (37).

A clear tension emerges, then, between our natural capacities and the obstacles to their exercise. The *Catechism* again quotes from *Humani Generis:*

[That] is why man stands in need of being enlightened by God's revelation, not only about those things that exceed his understanding, but also "about those religious and moral truths which of themselves are not beyond the grasp of human reason, so that even in the present condition of the human race, they can be known by all men with ease, with firm certainty and with no admixture of error" (38).

Later, in Article One of Chapter Three in Part Three, the *Catechism* elaborates further on the epistemological tension at the heart of the natural law appeal. On the one hand,

The natural law, the Creator's very good work, provides the solid foundation on which man can build the structure of moral rules to guide his choices. It also provides the indispensable moral foundation for building the human community. Finally, it provides the necessary basis for the civil law with which it is connected, whether by a reflection that draws conclusions from its principles, or by additions of a positive and juridical nature (1959).

On the other hand, the obstacles to the knowledge of natural law make it necessary that higher sources of moral authority be invoked:

The precepts of natural law are not perceived by everyone clearly and immediately. In the present situation sinful man needs grace and revelation so moral and religious truths may be known "by everyone with facility, with firm certainty and with no admixture of error." The natural law provides revealed law and grace with a foundation prepared by God and in accordance with the work of the Spirit (1960).

Given this *need* for the clarification of natural law by supernatural sources of authority, however, the central problematic emerges for Catholic arguments when offered as ethical or policy discourse. For moral discourse in the ethical or policy modes must withstand scrutiny on its own terms, absent the "clarifying" functions of Revelation or interpretations offered by the Church's magisterium. Otherwise, the *raison d'etre* of natural law as a *via media* between merely parochial or sectarian warrants is called into serious question, or even subverted; i.e., the natural law appeal, if amendment or clarification from supernatural sources is required, becomes merely another parochial appeal.

Thus, one way to consider the relevance of Roman Catholic arguments as ethical or policy discourse is to assess their cogency as strict "rational" appeals. This is, to be sure, a problematic judgment, at the levels of both theory and practice, for the status of rationality in moral discourse has been subjected to serious and sustained criticism. However, there are two telling responses to be made here. First, the possibilities for policy consensus—on everything from child welfare and family law to choices in international affairs—suggest that forms of practical rationality are indeed available to provide a shared basis for public discourse and policy formation. Second, the law itself quite straightforwardly supports what is called the "rational basis" test for particular policy choices. Thus, in crafting public policy, a number of appeals, including those to widely shared intuitions, values, or "common morality," can provide clear warrants for collective choice.

## III. Roman Catholic and Other Arguments in Opposition to Assisted Suicide

One way to trace the conceptual and practical affinities between Roman Catholic policy recommendations and the arguments made by secular opponents of assisted suicide is to identify the basic concerns that animate secular discussion, and to appreciate their resonance with key arguments developed in the Catholic discussion, independent of specific theological commitments.

While the traditional Roman Catholic distinction between "killing" and "letting die" is best understood as a deontological constraint based on theological premises, there are also non-theological arguments which support that distinction, although, without theological commitments, such appeals may be more suggestive than binding. A number of theorists in the natural law tradition, for example, based on considerations of practical reason itself and independent of theological premises, have concluded that it is always morally wrong to choose *directly* against any basic good, including the good of life itself. Thus suicide or assisted suicide, as choices directly intended against the good of life, are morally proscribed.[16] Other opponents, while skeptical of natural law as a coherent moral epistemology, nonetheless point to quasi-metaphysical considerations as the basis of their opposition. Daniel Callahan, for example, argues for the validity of the distinction between killing and letting die on strictly secular grounds:

> At the center of the distinction between killing and allowing to die is the difference between physical causality and moral culpability. To bring the life of another to an end by an injection is to directly kill the other. Our action is the physical cause of the death. To allow someone to die from a disease we cannot cure (and that we did not cause) is to permit the disease to act as the cause of death. The notion of physical causality in both cases rests on the distinction between human agency and the action of external nature.[17]

Callahan sees that descriptive difference as one having *moral* significance, especially when linked to the customs and legal practices that have sustained society. To legalize physician-assisted suicide or euthanasia, according to Callahan, presents a radical break from general social attitudes concerning the justified taking of human life. In his words,

> . . . we have never allowed killing as a form of contractual relationship between two consenting adults. The killing of another is now justified only in cases of self-defense, capital punishment, and just war. In none of those cases is the killing for the benefit of the person killed, but allowed only to protect the lives or welfare of others, even if that life is our own (as in self-defense). There must, in short, be a public interest at stake in the taking of life. We have otherwise considered it too great

a power to be given to individuals to serve their private ends, even if they be good ends (230).

Other commentators offer lucid speculations regarding the likely consequences—for patients, for physicians, and for society itself—in the wake of legalizing physician-assisted suicide.[18] I will limit myself here to two discussions, one offered by Robert Wennberg, a scholar and commentator, the other a report written by a public body, the New York State Task Force on Life and the Law. In his book, *Terminal Choices,* Wennberg discusses two sorts of arguments relevant to policy judgments about physician-assisted suicide and euthanasia. His first set of considerations, so-called "slippery slope" concerns, include the following: (1) that physician-assisted suicide, once legalized for the *terminally* ill, will be extended to individuals with incurable but *non-terminal* illnesses; (2) that physician-assisted suicide may be extended to those suffering from degenerative diseases; and (3) that physician-assisted suicide may lead to active euthanasia as an extension of substituted judgment for suffering and/or demented patients who cannot speak for themselves, to seriously handicapped children, to terminally ill children, or even to those who suffer from extreme mental illness (194–210).

The second set of concerns Wennberg labels "negative fallout" arguments. These arguments are based on the following contention:

It is claimed that such legalization will have various bad consequences, sufficiently impacting vital societal interests so as to justify retention of the current legal prohibition . . . These bad consequences will occur, it is claimed, whether or not legalizing [physician-assisted suicide] for the terminally ill puts us on a slippery slope that leads to euthanasia for various socially unwanted groups (187).

Negative fallout arguments appeal to two very telling concerns: (1) that physician-assisted suicide, once legalized, will "increasingly lose its voluntary character" (187); and (2) that physician-assisted suicide "might come to be viewed as the [first resort in] tough medical cases" (190).

The New York State Task Force on Life and the Law, in its 1995 report *When Death Is Sought,* discussed the grounds for the consensus reached by its members to maintain the ban on physician-assisted suicide. While Task Force members expressed various opinions concerning the intrinsic morality of suicide and assisted suicide, they unanimously concluded that legalizing physician-assisted suicide would constitute an unacceptable change in public policy. Their arguments appealed to two basic concerns. First, the legalization of physician-assisted suicide poses grave risks to especially vulnerable patients:

> The care of many patients currently fails to meet generally accepted standards of high-quality clinical practice. These failures are most egregious for poor and socially disadvantaged individuals, and for patients in large, overburdened facilities serving the urban and rural poor . . . Many patients will also lack access to psychiatric services. Furthermore, for most patients who are terminally or severely ill, routine psychiatric consultation would be inadequate to diagnose reliably whether the patient is suffering from depression . . . Many patients from all sectors of society cannot rely on a physician-patient relationship marked by good communication, personal concern, and respect. It is unlikely that patients who now face difficulties in obtaining minimally acceptable treatment would receive the excellent care and personal support essential [as prerequisites to legalizing the practice] (143).

The Task Force also presented a second argument, one tied to the interests of society at large. In responding to claims that the legalization of physician-assisted suicide logically extends the right of patients to refuse unwanted medical interventions, the Task Force offers, in effect, an appeal to the common good:

Under current policies, the appropriateness of stopping or withholding treatment for competent patients has been tied to autonomy —to the patient's own values and preferences. This is not just sound public policy, but the only acceptable alternative in a pluralist society. Decisions to accept or to refuse treatment call for choices about the value and nature of human life, tolerance for disability and dependence, and our relationships to family members and to others. As a society, we share no single belief about these profoundly personal questions. Even if held by a majority, one response could not be imposed on those who disagreed.

The decision to commit suicide or to consent to a lethal injection is also tied to personal values and beliefs. But embracing autonomy in the sphere of decisions about life-sustaining treatment does not mandate recognition of a right to assisted suicide and euthanasia. Among individual rights, only the right to believe is absolute. All the others are qualified; they are calibrated depending on the strength of the claim to freedom and the consequences for society as a whole. Our constitutional law as well as our broader structure of civil laws and policies are built on this foundation of social judgments. In the arena of medical choices, as in other spheres of our collective life, autonomy is not all or nothing. Even if the lines are hard to draw, the necessity for doing so is no less compelling (147–148).

## IV. The Relevance of Roman Catholic Arguments to the Debate

In considering the arguments made by Callahan, Wennberg, and the Task Force, it is instructive to note that, quite independent of theological convictions, they appeal to widely shared moral and social values that provide policy warrants for maintaining the ban on physician-assisted suicide. Hence, the fact that Catholic arguments in the prophetic or narrative modes appeal to explicitly theological themes does *not* preclude a "mid-level" of agreement on shared principles and values that can ground consensus conclusions in the ethical or policy modes, on *either* religious or secular grounds.

Indeed, we should hardly be surprised that the appeal to a "common morality" of shared principles and values is available as a warrant for public policy. In their very influential book, *Principles of Biomedical Ethics,* Thomas Beauchamp and James Childress discuss the central function of shared judgments about morality's core principles and assorted rules in making considered judgments, including judgments about appropriate public policy. As Beauchamp and Childress remind us,

If we could be confident that some abstract moral theory was a better source for codes and policies than the common morality, we could work constructively on practical and policy questions by progressive specification of the norms in that theory. But fully analyzed norms in ethical theories [including theologically ground theories] are invariably more contestable than the norms in the common morality. We cannot reasonably expect that a contested moral theory will be better for practical decision making and policy development than the morality that serves as our common denominator. Far more social consensus exists about principles and rules drawn from the common morality . . . than about theories. This is not surprising, given the central role of the common morality and the fact that its principles are, at least in schematic form, usually embraced in some form by all major theories. Theories are rivals over matters of justification, rationality, and method, but they often converge on mid-level principles.[19]

At the same time, independent of such principles and values, which can be justified on religious or secular grounds, we should not minimize the continuing relevance of Roman Catholic moral insights that are specifically theological, and rendered in the prophetic or narrative voice. The tendency to disqualify the latter modes of discourse from debates on public policy confuses the *process* of public discussion and debate, wherein the views of particular communities may exercise legitimate influence, with the *warrants* for and *justification* of policy choices, where parochial appeals cannot serve as the explicit basis for legislation in a pluralistic society. Clearly, then, Catholic arguments offered as ethical or policy discourse are appropriate contributions to both the process of policy formulation and its consensus justification. But Catholic arguments offered as prophetic or narrative discourse also remain vital ingredients in public discussion and debate. For example, Catholic narrative and prophetic discourse, by presenting a markedly different understanding of suffering than the minimal calculus of hedonism, expands and enriches the meaning of human dignity and moral agency. First, it embodies the recognition that human dignity can be maintained, and even fostered, amid circumstances of vulnerability and dependence, thus raising a challenge to the secular equation of autonomy and independence. Second, the Catholic vision enjoins meaningful compassion on all called on to care for suffering patients. The moral logic of compassion requires attention, time, and the hard work of listening, rather than the mute acceptance of proposals to end suffering by ending the sufferer. To be sure, a commitment to effective palliative care, especially the option of hospice, emerges as an obvious implication of the Christian narrative (cf. Bresnahan ). But caregivers are equally called to be present to patients in their suffering, and to help them find meaning in that experience even when it cannot be overcome.

## V. Conclusion

The continuing public debate about legalizing physician-assisted suicide offers an instructive example of the place of Roman Catholic arguments against suicide in that discussion. While one anticipates that explicit theological values will be invoked as focal elements in Catholic prophetic and moral discourse on assisted suicide, Catholic ethical and policy arguments share affinities with arguments that rely on what Beauchamp and Childress label "common morality," those widely shared principles, values, and intuitions that can be justified on either religious or secular grounds. The force of Roman Catholic arguments, then, should not be reduced to either their parochial appeal or to their resonance with broader moral warrants. Rather, the various modes of Roman Catholic moral discourse function to provide a broad basis for both Christian witness and policy consensus. And this, indeed, remains the central drama of being a public church: to witness by persuasion as well as by example, to speak to similarities as well as differences, to discover and celebrate those commonalities of experience and reflection that allow religious values, even if indirectly, to work their leaven on the world.

## Notes

[1]  Derek, Humphry, *Final Exit* (Eugene, OR: Hemlock Society, 1991).
[2]  Howard Brody, "Assisted Death—A Compassionate Response to Medical Failure,"*NEJM* 327, 19 (1992), 1384–1388.
[3]  H. Tristram Engelhardt, *The Foundations of Bioethics*, 2nd edition (New York: Oxford, 1996), 80.
[4]  Willard Gaylin, et al., "Doctors Must Not Kill," *JAMA* 15, 2 (1990), 2139–2140.
[5]  Robert Wennberg, *Terminal Choices* (Grand Rapids: Eerdmans, 1989), 192–210.
[6]  New York State Task Force on Life and the Law, *When Death Is Sought: Assisted Suicide and Euthanasia in the Medical Context* (New York: New York State, 1994), 143–144.
[7]  Daniel Callahan, *The Troubled Dream of Life* (New York: Simon and Schuster, 1990), 107–112.
[8]  Andrew Lustig, "Public Policy on Physician-Assisted Suicide: Reasons for Retaining the Ban," *Bioethics Forum* 10, 2 (1994), 7–10.
[9]  Sidney Hook, "The Ethics of Suicide," in Marvin Kohl, editor, *Beneficent Euthanasia* (Buffalo: Prometheus Books, 1975), 57–69.
[10]  Thomas Aquinas, *Summa Theologica* (Westminister, MD: Christian Classics, 1981).
[11]  Thus, the *Catechism,* in 2273, describes the "inalienable right to life of every inno-

cent human individual" as a *"constitutive element of a civil society and its legislation"* [emphasis in the original]. In specifying the policy implications of the commitment to rights as inalienable, 2263 quotes approvingly from *Donum Vitae:* "The inalienable rights of the person must be recognized and respected by civil society and the political authority. These human rights depend neither on single individuals nor on parents; nor do they represent a concession made by society and the state; they belong to human nature and are inherent in the person by virtue of the creative act from which the person took his origin."

[12] Efforts to legalize physician-assisted suicide or euthanasia may be driven by various motives. Thus *The Gospel of Life Vitae* speaks about the personal and cultural dimensions of the crisis it portrays: "decisions that go against life sometimes arise from difficult or even tragic situations of profound suffering, loneliness, a total lack of economic prospects, depression, and anxiety about the future. Such circumstances can mitigate even to a notable degree subjective responsibility and the consequent culpability of those who make these choices which themselves are evil. But today the problem goes far beyond the necessary recognition of these personal situations. It is a problem which exists at the cultural, social and political level, where it reveals its more sinister and disturbing aspect in the tendency, ever more widely shared, to interpret the above crimes against life as *legitimate expressions of individual freedom, to be acknowledged and protected as actual rights* [emphasis in the original]" (John Paul II, 1995, p. 34).

[13] John Paul's discussion here is worth further elaboration: "Various considerations usually contribute to such a decision, all of which converge in the same terrible outcome. In the sick person the sense of anguish, of severe discomfort, and even of desperation brought on by intense and prolonged suffering can be a decisive factor. Such a situation can threaten the already fragile equilibrium of an individual's personal and family life, with the result that, on the one hand, the sick person, despite the help of increasingly effective medical and social assistance, risks feeling overwhelmed by his or her own frailty; and on the other hand, those close to the sick person can be moved by an understandable even if misplaced compassion. All this is aggravated by a cultural climate which fails to perceive any meaning or value in suffering, but rather considers suffering the epitome of evil, to be eliminated at all costs. *This is especially the case in the absence of a religious outlook wich could help to provide a positive understanding of the mystery of suffering* [emphasis mine]" (John Paul II, 1995, pp. 30–31).

[14] The paragraph elaborates this point further: "What really happens in this case is that the individual is overcome and crushed by a death deprived of any prospect of meaning or hope. We see a tragic expression of all this in the spread of *euthanasia—disguised* and surreptitious, or practiced openly and even legally [emphasis in the original]. As well as for reasons of a misguided pity at the sight of the patient's suffering, euthanasia is sometimes justified by the utilitarian motive of avoiding costs which bring no return and which weigh heavily on society. Thus it is proposed to eliminate the malformed babies, the severely handicapped, the disabled, the elderly, especially when they are not self-sufficient, and the terminally ill" (John Paul II, 1995, p. 31).

[15] James Gustafson, "Moral Discourse About Medicine: A Variety of Forms," *Journal of Medicine and Philosophy* 15, 2 (1990), 125–142.

[16] James Bresnahan, "Observations of the Rejection of Physician-Assisted Suicide: A Roman Catholic Perspective," *Christian Bioethics* 1, 3 (1995), 256–284. Also, Ronald Gula, *What Are They Saying About Euthanasia?* (Mahwah, NJ: Paulist, 1985).

[17] Daniel Callahan, *What Kind of Life* (New York: Simon and Schuster, 1990), 233.

[18] On this subject, David F. Kelly, "Euthanasia, Social Implications of," *New Dictionary of Catholic Social Thought,* 348–353.

[19] Thomas Beauchamp and James Childress, *Principles of Biomedical Ethics,* 4th edition (New York: Oxford, 1994), 108.

# Transforming Culture: Catholic Health Care in the United States

## Gerard Magill

C atholic health care faces an unprecedented challenge to its continuation in the United States. This challenge emerges from a crisis that currently grips our nation. The crisis occurs, at least in part, because of the escalating costs that have characterized the growth of health care over recent years. If costs were our only concern, the crisis would be bad enough. But the crisis also arises because nearly one third of our nation's population has no insurance or is underinsured. It is astounding that approximately seventy million people in this country lack full access to health care. By combining these high costs and lack of universal cover and access, we can grasp the seriousness of the crisis. Health care in the nation requires thorough transformation.

To resolve this crisis, President Clinton attempted unsuccessfully to pass federal reform of health care between 1992 and 1994. In the wake of that failure, market forces began to attend more strenuously to one aspect of the crisis by exploring ways to control the seemingly relentless cost increases. Between 1994 and 1996, there was a dramatic rise in the number of managed care organizations, such as Health Maintenance Organizations, across the United States. Managed care integrates the financing and delivery of health care to control costs.[1] A common example of this sort of integration is the creation of networks among organizations (such as hospitals, physicians, or insurance companies) that previously operated independently. Managed care, which is neither morally good nor bad in itself, has become a common approach to resolving our crisis in health care. And herein lies the challenge to Catholic health care institutions.

Managed care, as the most pervasive market-driven reform of health care today, challenges our Catholic ministry in this way. Previously, Catholic facilities could remain independent of other health care organizations that provided services deemed immoral in Catholic

175

teaching. Increasingly, if Catholic organizations are to continue their presence and ministry in health care, they need to network with other organizations in the new climate. Significant difficulties can arise in these networks. For instance, a network can be so large that it absorbs the Catholic organization to the extent that our religious ministry can be diminished or the Catholic institution can be compromised by practices in the network that are proscribed by Church teaching.

There are many resources from the perspective of health care ethics that can help to deal with the crisis of health care in general. There are resources that explore the principles of health care ethics and relevant virtues that ought to guide us through all sorts of complex situations.[2] And there are resources that deal specifically with Catholic health care ethics that are obviously more suited to the needs of the current challenge to the continuation of the mission and ministry of Catholic health care.[3]

Another valuable resource for dealing with the challenge that Catholic health care faces with regard to its continued ministry is the new *Catechism of the Catholic Church.* The *Catechism* does not discuss health care as such. However, the *Catechism* provides the foundations of Catholic doctrine regarding faith and morality that must direct all of the Church's ministries. These foundations of doctrine, inspired by the Catholic tradition and by the teaching of Vatican II, in particular, provide beacons of light to guide Catholic ministry through *the* current crisis in health care. Moreover, I suggest that the *Catechism* also provides the requirements for transforming culture in the secular arena of health care.

In this essay, I discuss themes in the *Catechism* that can assist the Catholic ministry of health care and can contribute to the transformation of health care in this nation. In particular, the themes I consider address what can be described fairly as three of the major factors of the crisis in the nation's health care today. I have mentioned two factors already: escalating costs and the lack of universal cover and access. There is another factor that arguably undermines the ethos of health care in the nation: the widespread disregard for human life at all stages of development. Discord about the protection of human life, from its beginning to its end, continues to demean health care especially as America grapples with new legislation allowing assisted suicide. To resolve the current crisis in health care in the United States these factors need to be considered together. Because the nation's crisis in health care places the continued ministry of Catholic institutions in jeopardy, a discussion of these three factors can provide guidance for Catholic health care across the nation.

The themes that I select from the *Catechism* deal with the doctrinal foundations of these three factors of the Catholic ministry in health care. And just as the three factors are closely related to one another, the themes in the *Catechism* also are closely interwoven. Hence, as I discuss these themes I consider the divisions of the *Catechism* (the profession of faith, the sacraments, the life of faith, and prayer) in a holistic fashion as an "organic presentation of the Catholic faith in its entirety" (18). And it is the integration of these themes that can contribute to transforming culture in the secular arena of health care.

I combine my discussion of the selected themes from the *Catechism* with an analysis of the revised directives for Catholic health care that the bishops of the United States published in November 1994: *Ethical and Religious Directives for Catholic Health Care Services* (hereafter *Directives*).[4] My analysis follows two steps as I discuss each theme: first I consider the different aspects of the themes that emerge from the doctrinal foundations in the *Catechism;* second, I trace similar aspects in the *Directives* with regard to Catholic health care. Although some repetition results unavoidably, the advantage of this approach is that significant consistencies emerge even though the bishops did not set out to apply the doctrines of the *Catechism* specifically to the needs of Catholic health care in the United States. In other words, by delineating the doctrinal foundations in the *Catechism* for Catholic health care in the *Directives,* the consistencies between the two documents enhance the developing tradition of this specific ministry—in the United States and elsewhere.

The themes I discuss follow this sequence. First, I discuss the meaning of human dignity within the context of social responsibility as the doctrinal foundation of the human right to basic health care for all. This theme addresses the advocacy of the Catholic ministry in health care for universal access and coverage across the United States. Second, I examine the sanctity of life as the doctrinal foundation for protecting human life from its beginning to its end. This theme addresses the stance that Catholic health care must adopt to challenge legislation on abortion and assisted suicide in the United States. Third, I consider the public responsibility of the Church's mission as the doctrinal foundation for prophetic witness in health care. This theme addresses the participation of Catholic health care in a secular environment, and the collaboration of the Catholic ministry with other institutions to have a transformative influence upon the culture of this nation. While this study addresses issues specific to Catholic health care in America, readers will be able to adapt and modify to their own cultures, laws, and current circumstances.

## I. Personal Dignity and Social Responsibility

The foundation stone for Catholic health care is our recognition of the dignity of the human person. But we can understand the meaning of personal dignity only within the context of the human community. Hence, respect for personal dignity necessarily involves social responsibility from a secular perspective and ecclesial accountability from a religious perspective. In the secular arena, to uphold properly the personal dignity of each individual we need to nurture our respect for society as a community of reason. And in the religious arena, we cannot uphold the personal dignity of individuals without also celebrating being together in the community of faith that we call the Church. The very first paragraph of the *Catechism*'s prologue highlights the centrality of "the Church" in our faith in God (1).

While post-modern theologians disagree, the Catholic Church affirms that we can attain "certainty" about the truth of our belief in God based upon what the *Catechism* calls "converging and convincing arguments" (31), including traditional proofs of God's existence. Cardinal John Henry Newman, one of the shaping forces of Vatican II, the *Catechism,* and contemporary Catholic theology, designed a sophisticated theory to justify such an account of belief based on what he referred to as "an *assemblage* of concurring and converging probabilities."[5] The point here is that religious and moral truths in faith are not beyond the grasp of human reason though enlightened by divine revelation. These truths of faith include the revelation that we are created in the image of God (36). However, we must recall that human words and reason necessarily fall short of God's mystery (42). Being created in God's image (Gen 1:27) is the basis of human dignity, both as individuals and as community.

This belief in human dignity as revealed in Scripture is reinforced by the teaching of the Church. God revealed the divine mystery in deeds and words (69) that established the covenant of salvation with humanity (70). However, there is also a living transmission of God's biblical revelation down the ages that occurs through the Holy Spirit. This is the "tradition" that the Church perpetuates and transmits to every generation (78). The authentic interpretation of God's revelation in Scripture and in Tradition is the responsibility of the Magisterium of the Church, which is the teaching office entrusted to the bishops in communion with the pope as the successor of Peter (85). But all the Church's faithful, guided by the Magisterium, share this responsibility for handing on revealed truth (92) and therefore for developing the Church's mission in the world.

The revelation of our inherent dignity as created in the image of God elicits a response from us whereby we submit our intellect and will to God in what is known as "the obedience of faith" (143). This involves giving an assent to God as revealer and to God's revelation. Newman explained that religious assent excludes both reservation and doubt.[6] Similarly, the *Catechism* explains that in the assent of faith our intellect and will cooperate with divine grace (155). Divine grace enables us to understand our faith which defines the task of theology. Hence, St. Anselm explained that in theology "faith seeks understanding" (158). When we assent to God we necessarily assent to human dignity, created in the image of God.

However, divine revelation of our human dignity addresses us as individuals as well as a community. Faith is a personal act within the context of the community with whom God established a religious covenant. So, our profession of faith in the Nicene Creed begins, "We believe" (167). Just as believing is an ecclesial act (181), our assent to human dignity also obtains meaning within the communal context of our covenant with God. Being created in the image of God means that we are called to form a relation with God (299), a relationship that is sustained in divine providence (302), bringing us to our final end when we will see God face to face in the beatific vision (314).

Our dignity is not relegated to only one aspect of the human condition but integrates the spiritual and corporeal dimensions of the human condition. That is, the dignity of the human person entails a corporeal body animated by a spiritual soul, intended to become a temple of the Holy Spirit (364). Only by appreciating both the personal and communal aspects of being created in the image of God can we grasp the proper meaning of human dignity (356). The communal context of human dignity means that personal dignity and social responsibility are inseparable. And it is precisely in this inalienable dignity that we recognize the fundamental equality of gender—God created male and female together, for each other, to be "a community of persons" (372) who are "equal in dignity" (2203). Of course, originally our dignity entailed an original state of holiness before God and justice with one another (375). This original state was seriously damaged, though not destroyed, by the Fall that brought sin into the world (401). Only by the redemptive mission of Christ (421) can we be saved and reconciled with God ( 457).

The redemptive mission of Christ (515) flows from being the Son of God dedicated to his "Father's work" (534). His mission was to proclaim the coming of God's reign, especially in the Paschal mystery of his death and Resurrection (542). In his redeeming act, human dignity is transformed. Everyone is called to enter God's reign (543), especially the poor and lowly (544). In particular, those oppressed by poverty are the object of a preferential love on the part of the Church (2448). The mission of Christ and the Holy Spirit is brought to completion in the Church as the Body of Christ and the Temple of the Holy Spirit. This mission brings the faithful into communion with God to bear much fruit (737).

When we refer to the Church as the Body of Christ we emphasize the Church as communion with Jesus (787). When we refer to the Church as the Temple of the Holy Spirit we emphasize the diverse and complementary charisms in the Church that work together for the common good (801). Both metaphors, then, highlight the communal character of the mission of the Church—to enable all to share in the communion between the Father and the Son in the Holy Spirit (850). The Church shares the mission of the Apostles whose ministry was the continuation of the mission of Jesus (858): "so I send you" (John 17:18). And all members of the Church share in this Apostolic mission (863), serving the poor especially. Charity cannot prevail until the demands of justice are satisfied (2446). Personal dignity culminates in social responsibility.

In the *Catechism,* then, to understand human dignity as being created in God's image necessarily involves the communal context of social responsibility, both in terms of humanity in general and of the Church in particular. As a result of creation, our dignity is aligned to all humanity in God's image. As a result of the revelation of Christ, our dignity is aligned also with the Church as a sacramental sign of salvation, bringing God's saving grace to all humanity. So, our natural dignity is enhanced supernaturally by the mission of Christ and of the Holy Spirit which is continued in the mission of the Church. Therefore, we can ascertain the proper meaning of human dignity when we relate it to the religious mission of the Church. This means nurturing a community that celebrates God's presence, especially by reaching out to serve the poor. Hence, respecting and promoting human dignity in the context of ecclesial community contributes to the fullness of the reign of God. Personal dignity and social responsibility unveil the mystery of God.

This theme of personal dignity and social responsibility in the *Catechism* provides helpful direction for understanding health and health care. Based on human dignity and within the context of the common good, we must respect the health of all. In this regard "the dignity of the human person requires the pursuit of the common good" (1926). We need to safeguard both life and health. "Life and physical health are precious gifts entrusted to us by God. We must take reasonable care of them, taking into account the needs of others and the common good" (2288), as developed in the social doctrine of the Church.[7] Hence, in keeping with our "social nature" the "good of each individual is necessarily related to the common good, which in turn can be defined only in reference to the human person" (1905). This means that "social justice can be obtained only in respecting the transcendent dignity" of each person (1929). But respect for the bodily life is not "an absolute value" (2289). For example, experiments "can contribute to healing the sick and the advancement of public health" ( 2292).[8]

### The *Directives*

The theme of personal dignity and social responsibility in the *Catechism* also provides direction for the development of health care in the United States, especially for Catholic organizations and services. The relation between personal dignity and social responsibility is crucial for the bishops;[9] it is central to the development of their revised directives for Catholic health care. This relation is evident as much in the document's normative principles as in its specific directives (the document is organized around these two categories).

The *Directives* give prominence to the relation between personal dignity and social responsibility. On the one hand, the main purpose of the *Directives* is "to reaffirm the ethical standards of behavior in health care that must flow from the Church's teaching about the dignity of the human person" (*Directives,* Preamble). Our "true dignity" is inseparable from the "vocation of the human person" (*Directives,* Introduction). On the other hand, the bishops also emphasize social responsibility as they explain the distinctive identity of the Church's mission and ministry in health care. They highlight "the ecclesial mission of health care" and affirm "the Church's commitment to health care ministry and the distinctive Catholic identity of the Church's institutional health care services" (*Directives,* Preamble). In other words, the bishops focus upon the communal characteristic of our human dignity. Because we are "created in God's image and likeness, the human family shares in the dominion that Christ manifested in his healing ministry" in service of "the common good" (*Directives,* Introduction). However, the emphasis upon the common good cannot be separated from the ecclesial mission of the Church. The mission of Catholic health care is to continue Christ's mission as we bring healing and compassion to others in what the bishops refer to as the "authentic neighborliness" of Catholic health care institutions and services (*Directives,* Introduction).[10]

The communal context of health care based on human dignity is immediately evident in Part One of the *Directives,* "The Social Responsibility of Catholic Health Care Services." It is within this communal context of human dignity that the bishops identify the right to health care. The *Directives* explain that "Catholic health care ministry is rooted in a commitment to promote and defend human dignity" which entails "a right to the means for the development of life, such as adequate health care" (Part One, Introduction). Human dignity within the context of the common good means that "every person has a right to adequate health care. . . . Health care is more than a commodity; it is a basic human right, an essential safeguard of human life and dignity."[11] And this "commitment to human dignity and the common good" belongs to the "religious mission" of Catholic health care (*Directives,* 9). Insofar as the ministry of Catholic health care "seeks to contribute to the common good," it necessarily advocates for the provision of "adequate health care for the poor" (*Directives,* Part One).[12] Hence, Catholic health care must promote "service to and advocacy for those people whose social condition puts them at the margins of our society" (*Directives,* 3). So for the bishops "every human being has the right to quality health services, regardless of age, income, illness, or condition of life."[13] Health care is essential to human dignity (with its broken condition) and to the character of our communities.[14]

Simply, the integration of personal dignity and social responsibility that is so prominent in the *Catechism* belongs to the religious mission of Catholic health care. Insofar as the bishops align the right to health care with this integration between personal dignity and social responsibility, advocacy for the right to health care is essential for Catholic ministry. In other words, the Church places the defense of human dignity, that reaches especially to the poor, at the heart of Catholic identity.

The celebration of human dignity as central to Catholic mission and ministry is the foundation for proper relations between patients and professionals in health care. The *Directives* explain: "The faith that inspires Catholic health care guides . . . decisions in ways that fully respect the dignity of the person and the relationship with the health care professional" (Part Three, Introduction). Hence the *Directives* emphasize that the "professional-patient relationship is never separated . . . from the Catholic identity of the health care institution" which always represents a "public commitment to the Church's understanding of and witness to the dignity of the human person" (Part Three, Introduction). So the traditional ethical principles that guide health care must be related both to human dignity and to Catholic identity, including: information about rights (*Directives,* 24); free and informed consent (*Directives,* 26, 28); information about treatment and its benefits and risks (*Directives,* nos. 27, 32); and privacy and confidentiality (*Directives,* 34).

The fundamental theme of dignity in the *Catechism* provides guidance for Catholic health care, especially with regard to the recent *Directives* from the bishops of the United States. The *Catechism* delineates a close relation between personal dignity and social responsibility while emphasizing the importance of respecting this relation in the mission of the Church. Likewise, the *Directives* uphold human dignity in Catholic health care, especially with regard to the common good, as indispensable for the mission of the Church. In other words, the doctrinal foundations in the *Catechism* inspire the Catholic ministry of health care in the *Directives* to have a transformative influence upon the culture of the nation.

Catholic health care participates in the royal office of Christ by upholding human dignity in its healing ministry to the poor and suffering. After all, the *Catechism* considers the mission of the Church as participating in the royal office of Christ when the People of God is dedicated in service to the poor and suffering (786). The *Catechism* also explains that the Church participates in the priestly and prophetic offices of Christ insofar as the Spirit bestows many gifts to enable the Church to fulfill its mission (768). I will consider how the Church shares Christ's priestly office when the People of God is consecrated as a spiritual house and holy priesthood (784). This constitutes the basis for pastoral and spiritual care in the arena of health. Also, I will consider how the Church shares Christ's prophetic office when the People of God through its sense of faith becomes Christ's witness in the world (785). This constitutes the basis for the public responsibility of the Church's mission in health care.

However, before considering these themes, I will discuss further the service of Catholic health care to the poor and suffering, in particular to the unborn and to the dying. By upholding the sanctity of life, the Catholic tradition insists upon defending the rights of unborn life and of the dying. The sanctity of life and personal dignity are interwoven with one another. Divine revelation on our personal dignity as being created in the image of God, especially in the context of ecclesial community and social responsibility, allows us to grasp the profound significance of the sanctity of life as a sacred reflection of the mysterious presence of God.

## II. The Sanctity of Human Life

The *Catechism* aligns personal dignity and the sanctity of human life. This connection is crucial for understanding Part Three of the *Catechism* that discusses our "Life in Christ": the Holy Spirit fulfills the human vocation, inspires charity and solidarity, and brings salvation (1699). Human dignity entails sanctity of life because we always stand before God. The dignity of the human person is rooted not only in our "creation in the image and likeness of God" (1700) but also in God always being our sole end: "God alone is the Lord of life from its beginning until its end" (2258). Our dignity and sanctity lies in our moral freedom before God as we fulfill our vocation in commitment to others in salvific grace. The right to the exercise of freedom is "an inalienable requirement of the dignity of the human person" but always "within the limits of the common good" (1738). When we live a moral life in conscience we bear witness in God's grace to the dignity of the human person (1706): "the dignity of the human person implies and requires uprightness of moral conscience" (1780). When we appreciate the inseparable relation between human dignity and the sanctity of life, the right of every person to adequate health care necessarily follows.[15]

Because the meaning of personal dignity can be determined only in its communal context, the human family is a privileged forum for realizing the dignity and sanctity of human life. Insofar as all family members are "persons equal in dignity," the "common good of its members and of society" must be upheld (2203). This means that family members must "learn to care and take responsibility for the young, the old, the handicapped, and the poor," but responsibility can devolve to society "to provide their needs" (2208), including "material and moral support in old age and in times of illness, loneliness, or distress" (2218). Based on human dignity, then, the common good requires justice to be dispensed "by respecting the rights of everyone, especially of families and the disadvantaged" (2237), because the "dignity of persons" and "the good of the community" are inseparable (2238). In other words, the communal significance of human dignity naturally focuses upon the family. This pertains not only on secular grounds such as the common good but also on religious grounds. The "Christian family constitutes a specific revelation and realization of ecclesial communion, and for this reason it can and should be called a *domestic church*" (2204).[16] The metaphor of the "domestic church" underscores that our human dignity places us in the presence of God, according sacredness to every person. Based on this dignity and sanctity, the Catholic tradition upholds "the good of the spouses themselves and the transmission of life" (2363)—the twofold end of marriage—as the indispensable context for discussing the "regulation of births" (2368) and reproductive "techniques" (2376–77).[17]

Also, based on the dignity and sanctity of life, the Catholic tradition insists that "human life must be respected and protected absolutely from the moment of conception" (2270). The sanctity of human life demands respect from its beginning until the end because of its sacred dignity reflecting the holiness of God: "every human life, from the moment of conception until death, is sacred because the human person has been willed for its own sake in the image and likeness of the living and holy God" (2319). This means that abortion, euthanasia, and suicide are morally reprehensible, consistent with the "deposit of Christian moral teaching" (2033) that has been handed on by the bishops as "authentic teachers" constituting the "ordinary and universal Magisterium" (2034).

Abortion is wrong because from the first moment of existence "a human being must be recognized as having the rights of a person—among which is the inviolable right of every innocent being to life" (2270).[18] Pope John Paul II explains that "the sacredness of life gives rise to its *inviolability,*"[19] especially because of being a human person.[20] Both divine law and natural reason exclude the right to the direct killing of an innocent human being, even when that life is only beginning. Hence, direct abortion (that is, willed either as an end or as a means) "is gravely contrary to the moral law" consistent with Church teaching since the first century that abortion at any stage of pregnancy is a moral evil (2271).[21] This means that the embryo "must be treated from conception as a person" (2274). So, unborn life possesses human dignity at all stages of development from syngamy.[22] For example, based on the dignity and sanctity of human life from conception, "it is immoral to produce human embryos intended for exploitation as disposable bio-logical material" (2275).

However, the individual dignity of the embryo has social and ecclesial repercussions. That is why "the inalienable right to life of every innocent human individual is a *constitutive element of a civil society and its legislation*" (2273). Hence, Pope John Paul II explains that "a civil law authorizing abortion or euthanasia ceases by that very fact to be a true, morally binding civil law."[23] His argument is based upon the natural law that the Catholic tradition has adopted (with significant developments) over the centuries.[24] An obvious example of a mistaken civil law is the Supreme Court's 1973 decision on abortion in *Roe* v. *Wade.* The United States bishops condemned this decision as entirely contrary to the fundamental principles of morality and God's law.[25] Also, from the ecclesial perspective of Canon Law, a penalty is attached to those who have an abortion. But this penalty needs to be understood carefully. The text of the *Catechism* is: "The Church attaches the canonical penalty of excommunication to this crime against human life.  A person who procures a completed abortion incurs excommunication *latae sententiae* by the commission of the offense and subject to the conditions provided by Canon Law" (2272).[26] However, in a subsequent encyclical Pope John Paul II carefully explained that excommunication in abortion necessarily requires knowledge of the penalty (and therefore its implications); otherwise the penalty does not pertain.[27]

The *Catechism* also emphasizes that euthanasia and suicide are morally unacceptable because of the dignity and sanctity of life. With regard to euthanasia, any act "which, of itself or by intention, causes death in order to eliminate suffering constitutes a murder gravely contrary to the dignity of the human person and to the respect due to the living God" (2277). Putting an end to the lives of handicapped, sick, or dying persons is wrong. However, this does not mean that we must keep people alive endlessly. There can be procedures that we can forgo morally: "discontinuing medical procedures that are burdensome, dangerous, extraordinary, or disproportionate to the expected outcome can be legitimate" (2278). Hence, using painkillers "to alleviate the suffering of the dying, even at the risk of shortening their days, can be in conformity with human dignity if death is not willed as either an end or a means, but only foreseen and tolerated as inevitable" (2279). This is an example of implementing the traditional principle of double effect: "a bad effect is not imputable if it is not willed either as an end or as a means of an action" (1737). The application of this principle must be consistent with another moral principle: "One may not do evil so that good may result from it" (1756 and 1789).

Suicide is wrong because each person is responsible for life before God: "we are stewards, not owners, of the life God has entrusted to us" (2280).[28] Nonetheless, specific circumstances such as mental suffering "can diminish the responsibility of one committing suicide" (2282). In making this remark the *Catechism* employs the traditional distinction between performing a wrong act (1751) and diminishing the agent's responsibility because of specific circumstances (1754).

### The *Directives*

The *Catechism*'s emphasis upon the relation between human dignity and the sanctity of life provides a solid foundation for the *Directives for Catholic Health Care Services* from the bishops of the United States. The *Directives* explain that we must deal with the whole person whose "innate dignity" and sacredness reflects the divine presence among us: "Christ's redemption and saving grace embrace the whole person, especially in his or her illness, suffering, and earth" (Part Five, Introduction). Moreover, the sanctity of human life relates our human dignity with our eternal destiny. The *Directives* (Part Two, Introduction) explain: the dignity of human life flows from being created in the image of God (Gen 1:26), from redemption by Jesus

Christ (Eph 1:10; 1 Tim 2:4–6), and from our common destiny to share a life with God beyond all corruption (1 Cor 15:42–57).

Just as the *Catechism* relates the dignity and sanctity of life with the flourishing of the human family, the *Directives* make the same connection with family life in the arena of health care. "The Church's commitment to human dignity inspires an abiding concern for the sanctity of human life from its very beginning, and with the dignity of marriage and of the marriage act by which life is transmitted." It is because "the Church has the deepest respect for the family, for the marriage covenant, and for the life that binds a married couple together" that it upholds "the unitive and procreative meaning"[29] of marriage as the context for discussing responsible parenthood and reproductive technologies (Part Four, Introduction).

The *Directives* adopt nuanced language about procedures for reproductive technology, implying that theological discussions remain open on some fertility techniques involving medically assisted conception inside the woman's body.[30] These conditions must be respected. First, a reproductive technique that "does not substitute for the marital act itself" may be used "to help the married couple conceive" (*Directives,* 38). Second, "techniques of assisted conception that respect the unitive and procreative meanings" of marriage must "not involve the destruction of human embryos, or the deliberate generation in such numbers that it is clearly envisaged that all cannot implant" (*Directives,* 39). Third, techniques are forbidden that "achieve extra-corporeal conception" (*Directives,* 41).

Just as occurs in the *Catechism,* the *Directives* for health care apply the Church's respect for the sanctity of life to issues in care for the beginning of life (Part Four) and to issues in caring for the dying (Part Five). "Catholic health care ministry witnesses to the sanctity of life from the moment of conception until death" (Part Four, Introduction). This respect for the sanctity of life in the Catholic tradition includes these distinct but related claims: because of the dignity and equality of human life everyone has the same right to life; because human life is sacred, its value does not depend on medical or developmental conditions. On the basis of the dignity and sanctity of life, the *Directives* condemn abortion and euthanasia.

With regard to abortion, the *Directives* follow the *Catechism* condemning "the directly intended termination of pregnancy before viability" (including "the interval between conception and implantation of the embryo") or "the directly intended destruction of a viable fetus" (*Directives,* 45). Both the *Catechism* and the *Directives* emphasize the condemnation of abortion at any stage of pregnancy by the Catholic tradition from the first century. The scholarly support for this traditional stance is extensive.[31] It is important to notice the Church's proscription applies only to "directly" killing insofar as the principle of double effect can warrant indirect abortion (a justification based on the claim that "the life of the body in its earthly state is not an absolute good").[32] Hence, "operations, treatments, and medications that have as their direct purpose the cure of a proportionately serious pathological condition of a pregnant woman are permitted when they cannot be safely postponed until the unborn child is viable, even if they will result in the death of the unborn child" (*Directives,* 47). However, because of the dignity and sanctity of life from conception, "nontherapeutic experiments on a living embryo or fetus are not permitted" (*Directives,* 51), even though the Church accepts that experiments can contribute legitimately to healing (*Catechism,* 2292). Finally, the dignity and sanctity of life obliges us always to care for those women who choose an abortion, including those whom we consider to be morally culpable. There is a serious obligation for Catholic health care providers "to offer compassionate physical, psychological, moral, and spiritual care to those persons who have suffered from the trauma of abortion" (*Directives,* 46).

With regard to euthanasia, the *Directives* also follow the *Catechism* closely. Understanding euthanasia as any "action or omission that of itself or by intention causes death in order to alleviate suffering," the bishops explain that "Catholic health care institutions may never condone or participate in euthanasia or assisted suicide in any way" (*Directives,* 60). Rather, the *Directives* encourage us to help one another to encounter death in a dignified fashion as a transition to eternal life: "In the face of death . . . the Church witnesses to her belief that God has created each person for eternal life"—understanding that "life is a precious gift from God" means we must account well for our "stewardship over human life" (Part Five, Introduction). Hence, it is imperative to provide dying patients with "appropriate opportunities to prepare for death" (*Directives,* 55).

As emphasized in the *Catechism* (2289), the *Directives* explain that we "do not have absolute power over life"—nor must we preserve life at all costs: "the duty to preserve life is not absolute" (Part Five, Introduction). Also, just as in the *Catechism,* the *Directives* explicitly allow us to "reject life-prolonging procedures that are insufficiently beneficial or excessively burdensome" (Part Five, Introduction). In other words, "a person may forgo extraordinary or disproportionate means of preserving life" when, in the judgment of the patient, they "do not offer a reasonable hope of benefit or entail an excessive burden, or impose excessive expense on the family or the community" (*Directives, 57*). In the *Directives* such judgments about "useless or burdensome technology" that a patient may legitimately forgo are very different from the illegitimate "withdrawal of technology with the intention of causing death" (Part Five, Introduction).

One of the most controversial aspects of the legitimate withdrawal of technology deals with nutrition and hydration. The bishops take a cautious approach that does not exclude the legitimate withdrawal of nutrition and hydration in specific cases. The debate concerns whether nutrition and hydration constitute such basic care for all human life that they can never be withdrawn legitimately. The bishops explain: "There should be a presumption in favor of providing nutrition and hydration to all patients, . . . as long as this is of sufficient benefit to outweigh the burdens to the patient" (*Directives, 58*). This means that in some cases it may be legitimate to withdraw nutrition and hydration. Hence, the *Directives* explain that nutrition and hydration are not morally obligatory "either when they bring no comfort to a person who is imminently dying or when they cannot be assimilated by a person's body" (Part Five, Introduction). This debate remains open-ended in Catholic doctrine and the scholarly literature, especially with regard to patients in a persistent vegetative state (PVS).

The sacredness of life means that all dying patients, perhaps especially those from whom nutrition and hydration are withdrawn, "should be kept as free of pain as possible so that they may die comfortably and with dignity" (*Directives, 61*). This dignity means that they "should not be deprived of consciousness without a compelling reason"; and medicines to alleviate or suppress pain may be administered "even if this therapy may indirectly shorten the person's life so long as the intent is not to hasten death" (*Directives, 61*). The *Directives* emphasize that the "management of pain in all its forms is critical in the appropriate care of the dying" (Part Five, Introduction).

However, when pain cannot be alleviated, the dignity and sanctity of the dying patient leads us to encounter the mystery of Christ's redemption: "Patients experiencing suffering that cannot be alleviated should be helped to appreciate the Christian understanding of redemptive suffering" (*Directives,* 61). With faith we can see "suffering as a participation in the redemptive power of Christ's passion, death, and resurrection" where death is "transformed by the resurrection" (*Directives,* Introduction). This is a sacred opportunity that highlights the spiritual responsibility of health care professionals. In this regard the *Directives* clearly follow the direction offered in the *Catechism:* "the dying should be given attention and care to help them live their last moments in dignity and peace" (2299).

Respect for the sanctity of human life in the mission and ministry of Catholic health care means that we celebrate the mystery of Christ in our daily lives across the spectrum of health care. "The mystery of Christ casts light on every facet of Catholic health care: to see Christian love as the animating principle of health care; to see healing and compassion as a continuation of Christ's mission" (*Directives,* Introduction). The bishops argue forcefully that it is "essential for the Church to continue her ministry of healing and compassion" in the sense of continuing "Jesus' healing mission" including physical, mental, and spiritual healing (*Directives,* Introduction). This is a dramatic statement implying that health care is so intricately related to human dignity that Catholic health care is not an optional ministry but essential to Catholic identity. Pastoral and spiritual responsibility is obviously at the heart of Catholic identity in health care.

The spiritual dimension of human dignity and sanctity is very important for Catholic health care institutions as communities of healing and compassion. The *Directives* insist that, directed to each patient's spiritual needs, "pastoral care is an integral part of Catholic health care" (Part Two, Introduction). Pastoral care personnel must "minister to the religious and spiritual needs" of patients (*Directives,* 10), including ecumenical and interfaith perspectives (*Directives,* 21) as well as the provision of the sacraments (*Directives,* 12), especially the sacrament of penance, Holy Communion, and anointing of the sick (*Directives,* 13–15). Catholic health care services continue "Christ's healing compassion in the world" by seeing their ministry not only as "an effort to restore and preserve health" but also as "a spiritual service" (*Directives,* Conclusion).

The emphasis upon pastoral and spiritual care in the *Directives* implements what is discussed at length in the *Catechism,* especially in Part Two on the "Celebration of the Christian Mystery" and in Part Four on "Christian Prayer" which establish "the context of a moral life bound to and nourished by liturgical life" and the "spirit of prayer" (2041).

In sum, both the *Catechism* and the *Directives* emphasize the centrality of personal dignity and the sanctity of life within the context of the common good of society and the ecclesial life of the Church. This means that to give proper respect to human dignity and sanctity we must do so within the larger context of the public responsibility, especially with regard to the Church's mission to have a religious influence upon the secular domain. In other words, the doctrinal foundations in the *Catechism* inspire the Catholic ministry of health care in the *Directives* to have a transformative influence upon the culture of the nation. Now I consider the third topic of this paper: how human dignity and the sanctity of life necessarily involve the public responsibility of the Church's mission.

### III. The Public Responsibility of the Church's Mission

In the *Catechism* there is an extended explanation of participating in social life and of developing social justice as part of the Church's mission. We develop the virtues, "purified and elevated by divine grace" (1810), in order to "govern our actions, order our passions, and guide our conduct" in personal morality (1804). But this always occurs in the social context of the common good where human dignity enables us to flourish in interpersonal relationships (1807). That is why the virtue of justice and the practice of solidarity (2407) is at the heart of the Church's mission for which "love of neighbor is inseparable from love of God" (1878).

The Church believes that "society is essential to the fulfillment of the human vocation" (1886) because "the dignity of the human person requires the pursuit of the common good" (1926). And by promoting the common good the Church seeks genuine conversion: "the participation of all in realizing the common good calls for a continually renewed *conversion* of the social partners" (1916).

The Church then has a public responsibility to influence the secular realm. As "the universal sacrament of salvation" (776) the Church is "the sacrament of the unity of the human race" (775), sharing the mission of the Apostles to "make disciples of all nations" (Prologue, 2). This understanding of the Church's involvement with society entails an ecclesiology that does not retreat from the world but rather seeks to transform the world. In Vatican II we read: "The Church has a saving and eschatological purpose which can be fully attained only in the next life," and so, as "a visible organization and a spiritual community . . . it is to be a leaven and, as it were, the soul of human society in its renewal by Christ and transformation into the family of God."[33] That is why the Church encourages its members to participate in and to influence society and public policy.

However, arrangements by Catholic institutions to participate in society in order to transform it can lead people astray. There is the danger that Catholic institutions can find themselves cooperating in activities forbidden by the Church. The *Catechism* explains that "we have a responsibility for the sins committed by others when we cooperate in them" (1868). Moreover, when Catholic and secular institutions cooperate legitimately, the danger of scandal should be avoided: "Scandal is an attitude or behavior which leads another to do evil. . . . Scandal is a grave offense if by deed or omission another is deliberately led into a grave offense" (2284). Hence, "formal cooperation in an abortion constitutes a grave offense" (2272). Pope John Paul II has reiterated the Church's condemnation of any sort of formal cooperation in evil in the sense of direct participation in a wrong act. In other words, the prophetic function of the Church invites us to participate actively in society to transform it. But in doing so we can find ourselves cooperating in activities that can be wrong or can cause scandal. I will expand on these concerns regarding cooperation and avoiding scandal when discussing health care.

The bishops of the United States have emphasized this prophetic function of the Church in a secular and pluralistic society. For example, in their pastoral letter on economic justice they emphasized that because "the world is wounded by sin and injustice" it is in "need of conversion and . . . transformation"[34] by enhancing the dignity of the human person in community. The Church is "a community of hope" that can influence the secular arena, though we must always live "under the tension between promise and fulfillment" (53). That is why, as the Church seeks to influence society toward further conversion and transformation, "the quest for economic and social justice will always combine hope and realism" (55). Similarly, in their pastoral letter on health care the bishops explained that Catholic institutions must fulfill the "Church's prophetic role in the health-care field" by developing alternative models of health care.[35]

In the United States the Church's participation in public life means being involved with a democratic and religious pluralism. Democratic pluralism requires the Church to express its moral teaching in the language of the public forum, that is, through reasoned analysis. And religious pluralism requires the Church to draw upon the traditions and insights of all religious communities in an effort to discover the moral wisdom necessary to resolve the major issues facing society, shaping what can be called a public consensus. So, the prophetic function of the Church requires Catholic institutions to engage a public conversation of values in order to have a religious influence upon public policy in the secular arena.[36] The bishops of the United States have been very attentive in providing guidelines for the prophetic function of the Church in health care as Catholic institutions cooperate with secular organizations in a market-driven environment. These guidelines are provided in the recent *Directives for Catholic Health Care Services*.

### The *Directives*

The *Directives* explain clearly that "the ecclesial mission of health care" must engage the "institutional and social factors" that challenge the health care system in the United States because of the "heightened awareness of the Church's social role in the world" and the influence of "the Church's vision of health care" upon "public policy" in society (*Directives*, Preamble).[37] In other words, "Catholic health care institutions have a unique relationship to both the Church and the wider community they serve" (*Directives*, 8). That is why the bishops conclude the *Directives* with a reminder about "the Church's prophetic responsibility" (*Directives*, Appendix).

A crucial part of Catholic leadership, sponsorship, and collaboration in the changing environment of health care today is responsible "stewardship" that has for its "primary purpose the common good" (*Directives*, Introduction).[38] The purpose of responsible stewardship is to continue the ministry of Catholic health care (its relation to the Church) so that there will be a constructive influence upon secular society by Catholic health care (its relation to the wider community). Hence, the *Directives* explain that the "responsible stewardship of health care resources" requires Catholic health care to engage the "economic, technological, social, and moral challenges" in collaborative "dialogue with people from all levels" of our "pluralistic society" (Part One, Introduction). In a society with so many uninsured or underinsured, responsible stewardship especially requires Catholic leadership to provide "service to and advocacy for" those "at the margins of our society" (*Directives*, 3).

By responsible stewardship Catholic health care participates "in the Church's life and mission" providing "leadership in the health care ministry through new forms of sponsorship and governance" (*Directives*, Introduction) as well as providing civic responsibility to enhance the delivery of health care. This involves working closely with the local Church, particularly the diocesan bishop who "fosters the mission of Catholic health care in a way that promotes collaboration among health care leaders, providers, medical professionals, theologians, and other specialists" (*Directives*, Introduction).

An indispensable aspect of responsible stewardship and leadership to enhance the Church's mission will be "collaboration with other health care providers" (*Directives*, 6). This topic is so crucial for the continuation of Catholic health care today that it elicits separate treatment in the *Directives* as Part Six of the document: "Forming New Partnerships with Health Care Organizations and Providers." The point at issue is that for Catholic health care to continue in today's changing environment it needs to establish collaborative arrangements with institutions that do not necessarily share the ethical principles in the Catholic tradition. Some examples of these interwoven arrangements are integrated delivery networks, managed care organizations, or health maintenance organizations.[39]

This scenario presents a double-edge sword for Catholic health care insofar as it needs to protect its Catholic identity while being better situated than previously to influence the secular arena with Catholic values. Hence the *Directives* mention that "new partnerships can be viewed as opportunities for Catholic health care institutions and services to witness to their religious and ethical commitments and so influence the healing profession" (Part Six, Introduction). The *Directives* encourage Catholic health care to nurture new partnerships when these situations occur: when they help Catholic health care to implement the social teaching of the Church; when they enable Catholic health care to realign the local delivery system so that a continuum of care can be provided to the community; when they provide a witness to responsible stewardship of limited resources; and when they offer more equitable access to basic care for poor and vulnerable people (Part Six, Introduction).

Nonetheless, despite these advantages that can accrue when new partnerships are formed, there are also significant disadvantages. The *Directives* identify the most significant disadvantages: the challenge partnerships pose to the viability of the identity of Catholic health care; the constraint that partnerships impose upon the Catholic institution's capacity to follow the ethical principles of the Catholic tradition; the risk of scandal by involving Catholic health care in questionable practices; the threat to the continued existence of other Catholic facilities not involved in the particular partnership and placed in jeopardy by it; the danger of diminishing the autonomy and ministry of the Catholic partner (Part Six, Introduction).

To deal with these dangers the *Directives* delineate basic guidelines to be followed by Catholic health care institutions when they consider entering any new partnership. First, "any partnership that will affect the mission or religious and ethical identity of Catholic health care institutional services must respect Church teaching and discipline" and must collaborate with the appropriate "diocesan bishops and other church authorities" (*Directives,* 68). Second, decisions about partnerships that "entail the high risk of scandal" must be made in consultation with the diocesan bishop or representative (*Directives,* 67); scandal arising from applying the principle of cooperation can prevent the cooperation occurring (*Directives,* 70). Finally, "when a Catholic health care institution is participating in a partnership that may be involved in activities judged morally wrong by the Church, the Catholic institution should limit its involvement in accord with the moral principle governing cooperation" (*Directives,* 69)

There is an *Appendix* to the *Directives* that explains the principle of cooperation as part of the Catholic tradition. To understand this *Appendix* properly it can be helpful to read it in the context of two previous documents from the Sacred Congregation and the bishops of the United States. These documents established guidelines for applying the principle of material cooperation to sterilization in Catholic hospitals.[40]

When applying the principle of cooperation several crucial distinctions need to be made.[41] Before considering them, a simple clarification can shed light on the technical language involved: the phrase "the object of the wrongdoer's activity" refers to an act such as direct sterilization that is forbidden by the Church (*Directives,* 53). First, only material cooperation may be justified; formal cooperation is always wrong:[42] "If the cooperator intends the object of the wrongdoer's activity, then the cooperation is formal and, therefore, morally wrong. . . . If the cooperator does not intend the object of the wrongdoer's activity, the cooperation is material and can be morally licit" (*Directives,* Appendix). This could occur if a Catholic facility joined a network simply to provide in its partner's facilities services that are proscribed by Catholic teaching.

Second, ordinarily only mediate material cooperation can be justified: "When the object of the cooperator's action remains distinguishable from that of the wrongdoer's, material cooperation is mediate and can be morally licit" (*Directives,* Appendix).[43] Ordinarily, there needs to be external duress upon the Catholic facility to employ this principle (Ibid., 2, p.7). For example, mediate material cooperation would occur when a Catholic facility joins a network to remain competitive in order to continue its ministry to a local community ("the object of the cooperator's activity"), even if its partners provide services proscribed by Catholic teaching (the "wrongdoer's" activity). Ordinarily, there should be as much distance as possible between the cooperator's activity and the wrongdoer's activity: the closer the two acts the more serious the justification needs to be. And the justification of applying this principle always requires "a proportionately grave reason" (*Directives,* Appendix).[44] In extraordinary "instances of duress" the bishops accept the possibility of "immediate material cooperation" (*Directives,* Appendix) which could mean providing services proscribed by Catholic teaching in Catholic facilities. This can occur only in extraordinary instances of duress that substantively threaten the continuation of the Catholic facility's ministry. However, despite this teaching, under no circumstances may abortion or euthanasia occur in Catholic facilities: "Catholic health care institutions are not to provide abortion services, even based upon the principle of material cooperation" (*Directives,* 45 and 60).

Third, the decision to apply the principle of cooperation always involves a prudential judgment: "Prudence guides those involved in cooperation" (*Directives,* Appendix).[45] Finally, the danger of scandal must always be assessed when applying this principle: "it is essential that the possibility of scandal should be eliminated" (*Directives,* Appendix). Moreover, scandal is especially significant with regard to abortion: "Catholic health care institutions need to be concerned about the danger of scandal in any association with abortion providers" (*Directives,* 45).

In sum, there is an ecclesial mission of health care that inspires the Church to engage institutional and social factors and to provide transformative leadership for public policy in the secular arena. This heightened awareness of the Church's mission in the world is very important for the Catholic vision of health care. With responsible stewardship and visionary leadership Catholic institutions in health care implement the Church's prophetic responsibility by nurturing the common good. However, this responsibility will require Catholic ministry to establish new forms of sponsorship and governance in health care, perhaps especially through collaboration with other providers. When designed appropriately, opportunities for collaboration can enhance the constructive influence of Catholic health care upon society, transforming the culture of our nation by its religious values.

## Conclusion

I have argued that the doctrinal foundations in the *Catechism* inspire the Catholic ministry of health care in the *Directives* to have a transformative influence upon the culture of the nation. Although the *Catechism* does not discuss health care as such, its doctrinal foundations can guide Catholic ministry through *the* current crisis in health care in the United States.

In this essay I have discussed three themes in the *Catechism* that also recur consistently in the *Directives* of the bishops. These themes can help our Catholic ministry to address the crisis in the nation's health care today. First, the meaning of human dignity within the context of social responsibility is the doctrinal foundation of the human right to basic health care for all. This theme inspires the Catholic ministry in health care to advocate for universal access and coverage across the United States. Second, the sanctity of life is the doctrinal foundation for protecting human life from its beginning to its end. This theme inspires Catholic health care to challenge legislation allowing abortion and assisted suicide in the United States. Third, the public responsibility of the Church's mission is the doctrinal foundation for prophetic witness in Catholic health care. This theme inspires the participation of Catholic health care in a secular environment and collaboration with other institutions. As Catholic health care engages the current challenge to its continued presence, it can have a transformative influence upon the culture of the nation.

# Notes

[1] *New England Journal of Medicine* 331: 17 (October 27, 1994): 1167.

[2] For example: Edmund D. Pellegrino and David C. Thomasma, *The Christian Virtues in Medical Practice* (Washington, DC: Georgetown University Press, 1996); Tom L. Beauchamp and James C. Childress, *Principles of Biomedical Ethics* (New York: Oxford University Press, 1994); H. Tristram Engelhardt, Jr. *Bioethics and Secular Humanism: The Search for a Common Morality* (Valley Forge, PA: Trinity Press, 1994); George J. Annas, *Standard of Care: The Law of American Bioethics* (New York: Oxford University Press, 1993).

[3] For example: Benedict M. Ashley, O.P., and Kevin D. O'Rourke, O.P., *Ethics of Health Care: An Introductory Textbook* (Washington, D.C.: Georgetown University Press, 1994); David F. Kelly, *Critical Care Ethics* (Kansas City: Sheed & Ward, 1991); Richard A. McCormick, *Health and Medicine in the Catholic Tradition* (New York: Crossroad, 1987).

[4] National Conference of Catholic Bishops (NCCB), *Ethical and Religious Directives for Catholic Health Care Services* (Washington, D.C.: United States Catholic Conference [USCC], 1994).

[5] John Henry Newman, *Apologia pro Vita Sua* (1864), edited by M.J. Svaglic (Oxford: Clarendon Press, 1967), 31.

[6] Newman explained in 1870: "Assent is an adhesion without reserve or doubt to the proposition to which it is given." See, John Henry Newman, *An Essay in Aid of a Grammar of Assent*, edited and introduction by I. T. Ker (Oxford: Clarendon Press, 1985), 172.

[7] On the development of social doctrine of the Church, see *Catechism*, no. 2419–25.

[8] "Medical and scientific experimentation on animals, if it remains within reasonable limits, is a morally acceptable practice since it contributes to caring for or saving human lives" (*Catechism*, no. 2417).

[9] Enhancing the dignity of the human person in community is discussed at length in, NCCB, *Economic Justice for All: Pastoral Letter on Catholic Social Teaching and the U.S. Economy* (Washington, D.C.: USCC, 1986), 28. This relation is also very important for non-Catholic Christian ethics. See, for example, Gilbert Meilander's explanation of individuals in community as crucial for Christian vision in, *Bioethics: A Primer for Christians* (Grand Rapids, MI: Eerdmans, 1996), 2.

[10] This constitutes a vision for a "community of concern" that binds everyone together. See, John W. Glaser, *Three Realms of Ethics: Individual, Institutional, Societal* (Kansas City, MO: Sheed & Ward, 1994), 27.

[11] United States' Bishops, "Resolution on Health Care Reform," *Origins* 23: 7 (July 1, 1993): 99.

[12] Also see, Pope John XXIII's encyclical, *Pacem in Terris,* no. 11; the "U.S. Bishops' Pastoral Letter on Health and Health Care," 11:25 (December 3, 1981) *Origins:* 389–402, at 397; and the U.S. Bishops, "Resolution on Health Care Reform," 99.

[13] United States' Bishops, "Resolution on Health Care Reform," 101. Also see, "U.S. Bishops' Pastoral Letter on Health and Health Care," 397–98.

[14] Cardinal Joseph Bernardin, "Making the Case for Not-for-Profit Healthcare," *Origins* 24: 32 (January 26, 1995): 540. Also see, Philip Keane, *Health Care Reform: A Catholic View* (New York: Paulist Press, 1993), especially chapter five "Building Community," 103–21.

[15] "This right flows from the sanctity of human life and the dignity that belongs to all human persons, who are made in the image of God" (United States' Bishops, "Resolution on Health Care Reform," 99).

[16] The phrase "domestic church" was used in Vatican II (*Lumen Gentium*, 11) and in Pope John Paul II's encyclical, *Familiaris consortio,* 21.

[17] These texts develop 1601 of the *Catechism* which Lisa Cahill describes as its "programmatic statement on marriage." See, Lisa Sowle Cahill, "Marriage," in Michael J. Walsh, ed., *Commentary on the Catechism of the Catholic Church* (Collegeville, MN: The Liturgical Press, 1994), 318–29 at 323.

[18] Also see, Sacred Congregation for the Doctrine of the Faith, "Instruction on Respect for Human Life in Its Origin and on the Dignity of Procreation" *(Donum Vitae)* 16:40 *Origins* (March 19, 1987): 697, 699–711; Sacred Congregation for the Doctrine of the Faith, "Declaration on Abortion" (1974), in Odile M. Liebard, *Official Catholic Teachings: Love and Sexuality* (Wilmington, NC: McGrath Publishing, 1978), 408–20; "Humanae Vitae," Encyclical Letter of Pope Paul VI on the Regulation of Birth (1968), in Liebard, *Official Catholic Teachings: Love and Sexuality,* 331–47; Sacred Congregation for the Doctrine of the Faith, "Declaration on Certain Questions Concerning Sexual Ethics" (1975), in Liebard, *Official Catholic Teachings: Love and Sexuality,* 429–44; NCCB, "Documentation on Abortion and the Right to Life, II" (Washington, D.C.: USCC, 1976).

[19] Pope John Paul II, *The Gospel of Life: The Encyclical on Abortion, Euthanasia, and the Death Penalty in Today's World* (New York: Times Books, 1995), no. 40.

[20] *"The human being is to be respected and treated as a person from the moment of conception*; and therefore from [that] same moment his [or her] rights as a person must be recognized, among which in the first place is the inviolable right of every innocent human being to life" (John Paul II, *The Gospel of Life,* no. 60, emphasis original). This text refers to the Congregation of Doctrine of the Faith, "Instruction on the Respect for Human Life in Its Origin," no. I, 1.

[21] Also see the encyclical of Pope John Paul II, *The Gospel of Life,* 61.

[22] In *Donum Vitae* we read: "The inviolability of the innocent human being's right to life 'from the moment of conception until death' is a sign and requirement of the very inviolability of the person to whom the Creator has given the gift of life" ("Instruction on the Respect for Human Life in Its Origin," Introduction, 4).

[23] Pope John Paul II, *The Gospel of Life,* 72.

[24] "This doctrine is based upon the natural law and upon the written Word of God, is transmitted by the Church's Tradition and taught by the ordinary and universal Magisterium," John Paul II, *The Gospel of Life,* 62, 70, and 71. Also see, "Declaration on Abortion," 7, note 11; and John Paul II, *The Gospel of Life,* 72, nn. 96–97. For the thought of Aquinas on natural law that influences the Catholic tradition, see, Thomas Aquinas, *Commentary on the Sentences,* book IV, dist. 31; and *Summa Theologiae,* I–II, q. 93, a. 3, and q. 95, a. 2.

[25] Ad Hoc Committee on Pro-Life Activities of the National Conference of Catholic Bishops, "Pastoral Guidelines for the Catholic Hospital and Catholic Health Care Personnel," NCCB, *Pastoral Letters of the United States Catholic Bishops,* vol. III (Washington, D.C.: 1983), 370–74.

[26] Citing the revised *Code of Canon Law* (1983), commissioned by the Canon Law Society of America, ed. James A. Coriden, Thomas J. Green, Donald E. Heinteschel (New York: Paulist Press, 1985), canons 1398, 1314, 1323–24 in turn.

[27] Pope John Paul II, *Gospel of Life,* 62.

[28] For a development of the religious and the social arguments concerning suicide, see, Margaret Pabst Battin, *Ethical Issues in Suicide* (Englewood Cliffs, New Jersey: Prentice Hall 1995), especially chapters one and two, 26–113.

[29] There has been an extensive literature on this teaching. For a recent theological analysis of whether sex is naturally oriented toward the creation of human life, see, Christine E. Gudorf, *Body, Sex, and Pleasure: Reconstructing Christian Sexual Ethics* (Cleveland, Ohio: The Pilgrim Press, 1994), especially chapter two, "Ending Procreationism," 29–50.

[30] See the opinion of Bartholomew Kiely, a moral theologian who helped to prepare the

Vatican document, *Donum Vitae,* on GIFT (Gamete Intra-Fallopian Transfer) and LTOT (Low Tubal Ovum Transfer). Also, see the supporting opinion of Cardinal Bernardin on these matters. These opinions are documented in the columns beside the Vatican's *Donum Vitae* in *Origins* 16: 40 (March 19, 1987): 699–700 and 701–2 accordingly. For a recent theological argument on new technologies, see, Lisa Sowle Cahill, *Sex, Gender & Christian Ethics* (Cambridge: Cambridge University Press, 1996), especially chapter 7, "The New Birth Technologies and Public Moral Argument," 217–57. Also see, Thomas A. Shannon and Lisa Sowle Cahill, *Religion and Artificial Reproduction* (New York: Crossroad, 1988).

[31] See, for example, John Connery, *Abortion: The Development of the Roman Catholic Perspective* (Chicago, IL: Loyola University Press, 1977), 304–13; John T. Noonan, Jr., "An Almost Absolute Value in History," in John T. Noonan, Jr., ed., *The Morality of Abortion: Legal and Historical Perspectives* (Cambridge, MA: Harvard University Press, 1970), 1–59. Also see, R. Randall Rainey and Gerard Magill, *Abortion & Public Policy: An Interdisciplinary Investigation Within the Catholic Tradition* (Omaha, Nebraska: Creighton University Press, 1996).

[32] John Paul II, *The Gospel of Life,* 47, see also, "Declaration on Abortion," 8. Indirect killing of innocent life can be morally justifiable when double effect pertains. See, David F. Kelly, *The Emergence of Roman Catholic Medical Ethics in North America* (New York: The Edwin Mellen Press, 1979), 275, and Benedict M. Ashley, Kevin D. O'Rourke, *Ethics of Health Care* (Washington, D.C.: Georgetown University Press, 1994), 144.

[33] *Gaudium et Spes,* no. 40.

[34] NCCB, *Economic Justice for All,* 60.

[35] U. S. Bishops' Pastoral Letter on Health and Health Care," 400.

[36] See, Gerard Magill and Marie Hoff, "Public Conversation on Values," in Gerard Magill and Marie Hoff, *Values and Public Life: An Interdisciplinary Study* (Lanham, New York: University of America Press, 1995), 1–25.

[37] See, Richard McCormick, "The Catholic Hospital Today: Mission Impossible?" 24: 39 *Origins* (March 16, 1995): 648–53. See especially his discussion of the importance of "public morality" in health care at the level of policy-making (ibid., 650–51).

[38] For a development of stewardship in the context of the common good, see Gerard Magill, "Planning for Reform," *Health Progress* (January 1994): 78–79, 84.

[39] For example, the Catholic Health Association recommended a design for "Integrated Delivery Networks" to compete based only on quality and service, but not on price (see, *Setting Relations Right: A Proposal for Systematic Healthcare Reform* (St. Louis, MO: The Catholic Health Association, 1993).

[40] "Reply of the Sacred Congregation for the Doctrine of the Faith on Sterilization in Catholic Hospitals," March 13, 1975 (Washington, D.C.: USCC, 1983), and NCCB "Commentary on the Reply of the Sacred Congregation for the Doctrine of the Faith to the National Conference of Catholic Bishops on Sterilization in Catholic Hospitals" (hereafter, *Commentary*) September 15, 1977 (Washington, D.C.: USCC, 1983). These two texts are published together in one document.

[41] See: James F. Keenan and Thomas R. Kopfensteiner, "The Principle of Cooperation," *Health Progress* (April 1995): 23–27; and Jean deBlois, CSJ, and Kevin O'Rourke, OP, *The Revised Ethical and Religious Directives for Catholic Health Care Services: Seeking Understanding in a Changing Environment* (St. Louis, MO: The Catholic Health Association, 1996), reprinted from a series of articles published in *Health Progress.*

[42] For example, "freely approving direct sterilization constitutes formal cooperation in evil" (*Commentary,* Guidelines, 1, p. 6).

[43] "If the cooperation is to remain material, the reason for the cooperation must be something over and above the reason for the sterilization itself" (*Commentary, Guidelines*, 4, p. 7).

[44] For example: "Direct sterilization is a grave evil. The allowance of material cooperation in extraordinary cases is based on the danger of an even more serious evil, e.g. the closing of the hospital could be under certain circumstances a more serious evil" (*Commentary*, p. 7).

[45] "In making judgments about the morality of cooperation each case must be decided on its own merits. Since hospital situations, and even individual cases, differ so much, it would not be prudent to apply automatically a decision made in one hospital, or even in one case, to another" (*Commentary, Guidelines*, no. 5, p. 7).

# INDEX

203